Crime and Criminal Justice in Asia

Crime and Criminal Justice in Asia

Dr. G.S. Rajpurohit

RANDOM PUBLICATIONS
NEW DELHI (INDIA)

Crime and Criminal Justice in Asia

ISBN 978-93-5111-911-1

Published in 2016 in India by

RANDOM PUBLICATIONS

4376-A/4B, Gali Murari Lal, Ansari Road
New Delhi-110 002
Phone : +9111-43580356, 011-23289044, 011-43142548
e-mail: sales@randompublications.com,
info@randompublications.com, randomexports@gmail.com

Reprinted. 2021

Type Setting by : Friends Media, Delhi-110089
Digitally Printed at : Replika Press Pvt. Ltd.

Preface

Crime in India exists in various forms. The statistics of every crime in the country are separately recorded and collected, making it easier to determine the crime rate. Crime is present in various forms in China. Common forms of crime include corruption, drug trafficking, money laundering, fraud, human trafficking, and circulation of fake currencies. China also has a large black market, due in part to government regulations which make certain items difficult to legally obtain, and the mass production of fake goods.

Asian organized crime syndicates are behind a number of serious crimes whose impact is felt on a global level. Criminal activities are not limited to Asia itself but are carried out in countries all over the world. Major activities of these criminal gangs include drug trafficking, human smuggling, money laundering, illegal gambling, extortion and kidnapping.

From a more formalist consideration of international criminal justice, the paper moves out to examine what the 'alternative' global justice paradigms offer China, and vice versa. This is a platform from which to speculate on the opportunities available to China in regional and international governance, through more constructive involvement with international criminal justice. As with China's active role in international commercial arbitration, there is potential for it to influence the development of international criminal justice beyond a formal institutional base. In some respects this perspective allows engagement with themes like adversarial justice and human rights, beyond rather narrow and irredentist normative debates around individuality, and enables some progress from constitutional legality to progressive communitarian practice.

The challenge of crime to society changes with the advance of civilisation, particularly as technology continues to increase. Societal and scientific concepts of crime are related to antisocial behaviour of criminals.

– Author

Contents

1

Crime in Asia

CRIME IN INDIA

Crime in India exists in various forms. The statistics of every crime in the country are separately recorded and collected, making it easier to determine the crime rate.

CRIME OVER TIME

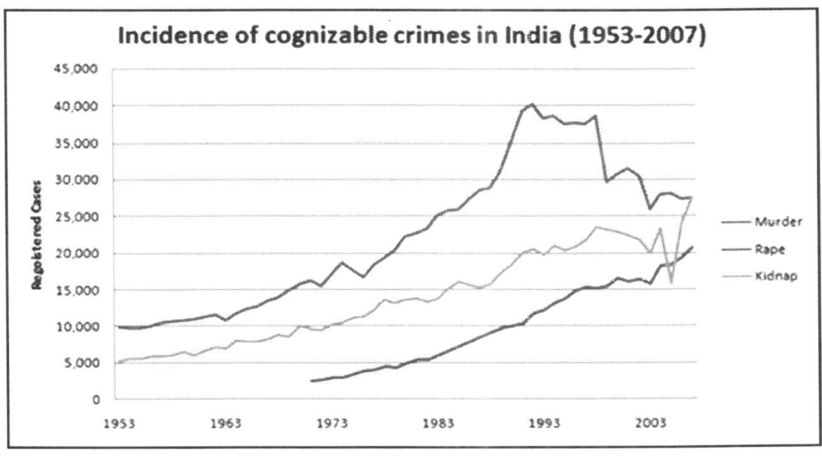

Incidence of cognisable crimes in India 1953–2007.

A report published by the National Crime Records Bureau compared the crime rates of 1953 and 2006. The report noted that burglary (known as house-breaking in India) declined over a period of 53 years by 79.84% (from 147,379, a rate of 39.3/100,000 in 1953 to 91,666, a rate of 7.9/100,000 in 2006), murder has increased by 7.39% (from 9,803, a rate of 2.61 in 1953 to 32,481, a rate of 2.81/100,000 in 2006).

Kidnapping has increased by 47.80% (from 5,261, a rate of 1.40/100,000 in 1953 to 23,991, a rate of 2.07/100,000 in 2006), robbery has declined by 28.85% (from 8,407, rate of 2.24/100,000 in 1953 to 18,456, rate of 18,456 in 2006) and riots have declined by 10.58% (from 20,529, a rate of 5.47/100,000 in 1953 to 56,641, a rate of 4.90/100,000 in 2006).

In 2006, 5,102,460 cognisable crimes were committed including 1,878,293 Indian Penal Code (IPC) crimes and 3,224,167 Special & Local Laws (SLL) crimes, with an increase of 1.5% over 2005 (50,26,337). IPC crime rate in 2006 was 167.7 compared to 165.3 in 2005 showing an increase of 1.5% in 2006 over 2005. SLL crime rate in 2006 was 287.9 compared to 290.5 in 2005 showing a decline of 0.9% in 2006 over 2005.

Year	Total cog. crimes under IPC, per 100,000	Murder per 100,000	Kidnapping per 100,000	Robbery per 100,000	Burglary (known as house-breaking in India) per 100,000	
1953	160.5	2.61	1.40	2.24	39.3	
2006	162.3	2.81	2.07	1.60	7.92	
% Change in 2006 over 1953	1.1	7.39	47.80	-28.85	-79.84	

CRIME BY LOCALE

Location has a significant impact on crime in India. In 2012, Kerala reported the highest cognizable crime rate of 455.8 among States of India, while Nagaland recorded lowest rates (47.7).

The rates were calculated by National Crime Records Bureau as the number of incidents per 1,00,000 of the population.

In 2006, the highest crime rate was reported in Puducherry (447.7%) for crimes under Indian Penal Code which is 2.7 times the national crime rate of 167.7%. Kerala reported the highest crime rate at 312.5% among states. Kolkata (71.0%) and Madurai (206.2%) were the only two mega cities which reported less crime rate than their domain statesWest Bengal (79.0%) and Tamil Nadu (227.6%).

Delhi, Mumbai and Bangalore have accounted for 16.2%, 9.5% and 8.1% respectively of the total IPC crimes reported from 35 mega cities. Indore reported the highest crime rate (769.1%) among the mega cities in India followed by Bhopal (719.5%) and Jaipur (597.1%).

Jammu and Kashmir (33.7%), Manipur (33.0%), Assam (30.4%) and Daman and Diu and Puducherry (29.4%) reported higher violent crime rate compared to 18.4% at national level.

Uttar Pradesh reported the highest incidence of violent crimes accounting for 12.1% of total violent crimes in India (24,851 out of 2,05,656) followed by Bihar with 11.8% (24,271 out of 2,05,6556). Among 35 mega cities, Delhi reported 31.2% (533 out of 1,706) of total rape cases. Madhya Pradesh has reported the highest number of rape cases (2,900) accounting for 15.0% of total such cases reported in the country. Uttar Pradesh reported 10% (5,480 out of 32,481) of total murder cases in the country and 18.4% (4,997 out of 27,230) total attempt to murder cases.

Table. Murder Rate by State in India, per 100,000 persons

State/UT	2011	2012
India		2.8
Bihar	3.3	3.2
Arunachal Pradesh	4.7	5.8
Assam	4.2	4.4
Andhra Pradesh	3.1	3.6
Chhattisgarh	4.3	4.0
Goa	3.3	2.5
Gujarat	1.9	1.9
Haryana	4.2	3.8
Himachal Pradesh	1.9	1.6
Jammu & Kashmir	1.3	1.0
Jharkhand	5.3	5.3
Karnataka	3.0	3.1
Kerala	1.1	1.1
Madhya Pradesh	3.5	3.2
Maharashtra	2.5	2.4
Manipur	2.9	3.3
Meghalaya	2.9	5.1
Mizoram	2.4	2.9
Nagaland	2.3	3.3
Odisha	3.5	3.8
Punjab	3.0	3.0
Rajasthan	2.1	2.1
Sikkim	2.3	1.1
Tamil Nadu	2.6	2.9
Tripura	4.4	3.4
Uttar Pradesh	2.5	2.4
Uttarakhand	1.8	2.1
West Bengal	2.3	2.5
Delhi	3.2	2.7

CRIMES AGAINST WOMEN

Police records show high incidence of crimes against women in India. The National Crime Records Bureau reported in 1998 that the growth rate of crimes against women would be higher than the population growth rate by 2010. Earlier, many cases were not registered with the police due to the social stigma attached to rape and molestation cases. Official statistics show that there has been a dramatic increase in the number of reported crimes against women.

The map shows the comparative rate of violence against women in Indian states and union territories in 2012. Crime rate data per 100,000 women in this map is the broadest definition of crime against women under Indian law. It includes rape, sexual assault, insult to modesty, kidnapping, abduction, cruelty by intimate partner or relatives, trafficking, persecution for dowry, dowry deaths, indecency, and all other crimes listed in Indian Penal Code.

Rape

Rape in India has been described by Radha Kumar as one of India's most common crimes against women. Official sources show that rape cases in India has doubled between 1990 and 2008 In most of the rape cases, the culprit is known to the victim. According to National Crime Records Bureau data of 2012, Gujarat has the lowest rape rate (0.8) while Mizoram had the highest rape rate with a value of 10.1. the National Average was at 2.1. The rates were calculated by National Crime Records Bureau as the number of incidents per 100,000 of the population

Dowry

Dowries are considered a major contributor towards violence against women in India. Some of these offences include physical violence, emotional abuses, and murder of brides and girls. Most dowry deaths occur when the young woman, unable to bear the harassment and torture, commits suicide. Most of these suicides are by hanging, poisoning or by fire. Sometimes the woman is killed by setting herself on fire - this is known as bride burning, and is sometimes disguised as suicide or accident. In dowry deaths, the groom's family is the perpetrator of murder or suicide.

India has by far the highest number of dowry related deaths in the world according to Indian National Crime Record Bureau. In 2012, 8,233 dowry death cases were reported across India. Dowry issues caused 1.4 deaths per year per 100,000 women in India.

Female Infanticides and Sex Selective Abortions

India has a highly masculine sex ratio, the chief reason being that many women die before reaching adulthood. Tribal societies in India have a less masculine sex ratio than all other caste groups. This, in spite of the fact that tribal communities have far lower levels of income, literacy and health facilities. It is therefore suggested by many experts, that the highly masculine sex ratio in India can be attributed to female infanticides and sex-selective abortions.

All medical tests that can be used to determine the sex of the child have been banned in India, due to incidents of these tests being used to get rid of female children before birth. Female infanticide (killing of girl infants) is still prevalent in some rural areas. The abuse of the dowry tradition has been one of the main reasons for sex-selective abortions and female infanticides in India.

Domestic Violence

Domestic violence in India is endemic. Around 70% of women in India are victims of domestic violence, according to Renuka Chowdhury, former Union minister for Women and Child Development. The National Crime Records Bureau reveal that a crime against a woman is committed every three minutes, a woman is raped every 29 minutes, a dowry death occurs every 77 minutes, and one case of cruelty committed by either the husband or relative of the husband occurs every nine minutes. This occurs despite the fact that women in India are legally protected from domestic abuse under the Protection of Women from Domestic Violence Act.

ORGANISED CRIME

Illegal Drug Trade

India is located between two major illicit opium producing centres in Asia – the Golden Crescent comprising Pakistan, Afghanistan and Iran and the Golden Triangle comprisingBurma, Thailand and Laos. Because of such geographical location, India experiences large amount of drug trafficking through the borders. India is the world's largest producer of licit opium for the pharmaceutical trade. But an undetermined quantity of opium is diverted to illicit international drug markets. India is a transshipment point for heroin from Southwest Asian countries like Afghanistan and Pakistan and from Southeast Asian countries like Burma, Laos, and Thailand.Heroin is smuggled from Pakistan and Burma, with some quantities transshipped through Nepal. Most heroin shipped from India are destined for Europe. There have been reports of heroin smuggled from Mumbai to Nigeria for further export.

In Maharashtra, Mumbai is an important centre for distribution of drug. The most commonly used drug in Mumbai is Indian heroin (called desi mal by the local population).Both public transportation (road and rail transportation) and private transportation are used for this drug trade.

Drug trafficking affects the country in many ways.

- *Drug abuse:* Cultivation of illicit narcotic substances and drug trafficking affects the health of the individuals and destroy the economic structure of the family and society.
- *Organized crime:* Drug trafficking results in growth of organised crime which affects social security. Organised crime connects drug trafficking with corruption and money laundering.
- *Political instability:* Drug trafficking also aggravates the political instability in North-West and North-East India.

A survey conducted in 2003–2004 by Narcotics Control Bureau found that India has at least four million drug addicts. The most common drugs used in India are cannabis,hashish, opium and heroin. In 2006 alone, India's law enforcing agencies recovered 230 kg heroin and 203 kg of cocaine. In an annual government report in 2007, the United States named India among 20 major hubs for trafficking of illegal drugs along with Pakistan, Afghanistan and Burma.

However, studies reveal that most of the criminals caught in this crime are either Nigerian or US nationals.

Several measures have been taken by the Government of India to combat drug trafficking in the country. India is a party of the Single Convention on Narcotic Drugs (1961), theConvention on Psychotropic Substances (1971), the Protocol Amending the Single Convention on Narcotic Drugs (1972) and the United Nations Convention Against Illicit Traffic in Narcotic Drugs and Psychotropic Substances (1988). An Indo-Pakistani committee was set up in 1986 to prevent trafficking in narcotic drugs. India signed a convention with the United Arab Emirates in 1994 to control drug trafficking. In 1995, India signed an agreement with Egypt for investigation of drug cases and exchange of information and a Memorandum of Understanding of the Prevention of Illicit Trafficking in Drugs with Iran.

Arms Trafficking

According to a joint report published by Oxfam, Amnesty International and the International Action Network on Small Arms (IANSA) in 2006, there are around 40 million illegal small arms in India out of approximately 75 million in worldwide circulation. Majority of the illegal small arms make its way into the states of Bihar, Chhattisgarh, Uttar Pradesh, Jharkhand, Orissa and Madhya Pradesh. In India, a used AK-47 costs $3,800 in black market. Large amount of illegal small arms are manufactured in various illegal arms factories in Uttar Pradesh and Bihar and sold on the black market for as little as $5.08.

Chinese pistols are in demand in the illegal small arms market in India because they are easily available and cheaper. This trend poses a significant problem for the states of Bihar, Uttar Pradesh, Jharkhand, Chhattisgarh, Orissa, Maharashtra, West Bengal, Karnataka and Andhra Pradesh which have influence of Naxalism. The porous Indo-Nepal border is an entry point for Chinese pistols, AK-47 and M-16 rifles into India as these arms are used by the Naxalites who have ties to Maoists in Nepal.

In North-East India, there is a huge influx of small arms due to the insurgent groups operating there. The small arms in North-East India come from insurgent groups in Burma, black market in South-East Asian countries like Pakistan, Bangladesh, Nepal and Sri Lanka, black market in Cambodia, the People's Republic of China, insurgent groups like the Liberation Tigers of Tamil Eelam, the Communist Party of India (Maoist), the Communist Party of Nepal (Maoist), Indian states like Uttar Pradesh and pilferages from legal gun factories, criminal organisations operating in India and South Asian countries and other international markets like Romania, Germany etc. The small arms found in North-East India are M14 rifle, M16 rifle, AK-47, AK-56, AK-74, light machine guns, Chinese hand grenades, mines, rocket-propelled grenades, submachine guns etc. The Ministry of External Affairs and Ministry of Home Affairs drafted a joint proposal to the United Nations, seeking a global ban on small-arms sales to non-state users.

POACHING AND WILDLIFE TRAFFICKING

Illegal wildlife trade in India has increased. According to a report published by the Environmental Investigation Agency (EIA) in 2004, India is the chief target for the traders of wildlife skin. Between 1994 and 2003, there have been 784 cases where the skins of tiger, leopard or otter have been seized. Leopards, rhinoceros, reptiles, birds, insects, rare species of plants are being smuggled into the countries in Southeast Asia and the People's Republic of China. Between 1994 and 2003, poaching and seizure of 698 otters have been documented in India.

Kathmandu is a key staging point for illegal skins smuggled from India bound for Tibet and PRC. The report by EIA noted there has been a lack of cross-border cooperation between India, Nepal and the People's Republic of China to coordinate enforcement operations and lack of political will to treat wildlife crime effectively. The poaching of theelephants is a significant problem in Southern India and in the North-Eastern states of Nagaland and Mizoram. The majority of tiger poaching happen in Madhya Pradesh, Uttar Pradesh, Orissa, West Bengal, Assam and Arunachal Pradesh. Following is a comparison of reported cases of tiger and leopard poaching from 1998 to 2003:

Year	1998	1999	2000	2001	2002	2003
Reported cases of tiger poaching	14	38	39	35	47	8
Reported cases of leopard poaching	28	80	201	69	87	15

Samir Sinha, head of TRAFFIC India, the wildlife trade monitoring arm of the World Wide Fund for Nature (WWF) and the World Conservation Union (IUCN), told Reuters in an interview "The situation regarding the illegal trade in wildlife parts in India is very grim. It is a vast, a varied trade ranging from smuggling of rare medicinal plants to butterflies to peafowl to tigers and it is difficult to predict how big it is, but the threats and dimensions suggest that the trade is increasing".

Project Tiger, a wildlife conservation project, was initiated in 1972 and was launched by Indira Gandhi on 1 April 1973. With 23 tiger reserves, Project Tiger claimed to have succeeded. But according to critics like conservationist Billy Arjan Singh, temporary increases in tiger population were caused by immigration due to destruction of habitat in Nepal, not because of the widely acclaimed success of wildlife policy in India.

CYBER CRIME

The Information Technology Act 2000 was passed by the Parliament of India in May 2000, aiming to curb cyber crimes and provide a legal framework for e-commercetransactions. However Pavan Duggal, lawyer of Supreme Court of India and cyber law expert, viewed "The IT Act, 2000, is primarily meant to be a legislation to promote e-commerce. It is not very effective in dealing with several emerging cyber crimes like cyber harassment, defamation, stalking and so on".

Although cyber crime cells have been set up in major cities, Duggal noted the problem is that most cases remain unreported due to a lack of awareness. In 2001, India and United States had set up an India-US cyber security forum as part of a counter-terrorism dialogue.

CORRUPTION AND POLICE MISCONDUCT

Corruption is widespread in India. It is prevalent within every section and every level of the society. Corruption has taken the role of a pervasive aspect of Indian politics. In India, corruption takes the form of bribes, evasion of tax and exchange controls, embezzlement, etc. Despite state prohibitions against torture and custodial misconduct by the police, torture is widespread in police custody, which is a major reason behind deaths in custody.The police often torture innocent people until a 'confession' is obtained to save influential and wealthy offenders. G.P. Joshi, the programme coordinator of the Indian branch of the Commonwealth Human Rights Initiative in New Delhi comments that the main issue at hand concerning police violence is a lack of accountability of the police.

In 2006, the Supreme Court of India in a judgment in the Prakash Singh vs. Union of India case, ordered central and state governments with seven directives to begin the process of police reform. The main objectives of this set of directives was twofold, providing tenure to and streamlining the appointment/transfer processes of policemen, and increasing the accountability of the police. In 2006, seven policemen were charge sheeted and eleven were convicted for custodial misconduct. Jan Lokpal Bill is being planned to reduce the corruption.

OTHER CRIMES

Petty Crime

Petty crime, like pickpocketing, theft of valuables from luggage on trains and buses have been reported. Travelers who are not in groups become easy victims of pickpockets and purse snatchers. Purse snatchers work in crowded areas.

Confidence Tricks

Many scams are perpetrated against foreign travellers, especially in Jaipur, the capital of Rajasthan. Scammers usually target younger foreign tourists and suggest to them that money can be made by privately transporting gems or gold, or by taking delivery abroad of expensive carpets, avoiding customs duties. Such incidents occupy the traveller for several days. The traveller is then passed to a new scam artist who offers to show the foreign traveller the sights. Scam artists also offer cheap lodgings and meals to foreign travellers so they can place him or her in the scam artist's physical custody and thus make the foreigner vulnerable to threats and physical coercion. In the process, the foreigner loses his passport.

Taxi Scam

There are also taxi scams present in India, whereby a foreign traveller, who is not aware of the locations around Indian airports, is taken for a ride round the whole airport and charged for full-fare taxi ride while the terminal is only few hundred yards away. Overseas Security Advisory Council in a report mentioned the process about how to avoid taxi-scam. This crime is known in other areas of the world as "long-hauling".

CRIME IN CHINA

Crime is present in various forms in China. Common forms of crime include corruption, drug trafficking, money laundering, fraud, human trafficking, and circulation of fake currencies. China also has a large black market, due in part to government regulations which make certain items difficult to legally obtain, and the mass production of fake goods.

HISTORY

The People's Republic of China was established in 1949 and from 1949 to 1956, underwent the process of transferring the means of production to common ownership. During this time, the new government worked to decrease the influence of criminal gangs and reduce the prevalence of narcotics and gambling. Efforts to crack down on criminal activity by the government led to a decrease in crime. Between 1949 and 1956, larceny, arson, rape, murder and robbery were major nonpolitical offenses. The majority of economic crimes were committed by business people who engaged in tax evasion, theft of public property, and bribery.

Government officials also engaged in illegal economic activity, which included improperly taking public property and accepting bribes. Between 1957 and 1965, rural areas experienced little reported crime. Crime rates increased later. The year 1981 represented a peak in reported crime. This may have been correlated to the economic reform in the late 1970s which allowed some elements of a market economy and gave rise to an increase in economic activity. Below is a comparison of reported cases of crime from 1977 to 1988 (excluding economic crimes):

Year	1977	1978	1979	1980	1981	1982	1983	1984	1985	1986	1987	1988
nber of cases	548,415	535,698	636,222	757,104	890,281	748,476	610,478	514,369	542,005	547,115	570,439	827,706
s of criminal 10,000 people	5.8	5.6	6.6	7.7	8.9	7.4	6.0	5.0	5.2	5.2	5.4	7.5

Crime by youth increased rapidly in the 1980s. Crime by youths consisted 60.2% of total crime in 1983, 63.3% in 1984, 71.4% in 1985, 72.4% in 1986, and 74.3% in 1987. The number of fleeing criminals increased over the years. Economic crimes have increased in recent years. From 1982 to 1988, the total number of economic crimes were 218,000. In 1989, a total of 76,758 cases of economic offenses were registered which included bribery, smuggling and tax evasion. The changes in economic policy had influence in the characteristics of criminality. Since the Third Plenary Session of the Eleventh Central Committee of the Communist Party of China, crime has increased and diversified.

CRIME BY TYPE

Murder

In 2011, the reported murder rate in China was 1.0 per 100,000 people, with 13,410 murders. The murder rate in 2010 was 1.1.

Corruption

The PRC is a one-party state ruled by the Communist Party of China, Corruption is common among government employees. Between 1978 and 2003, an estimated $50 billion was smuggled out of the country by corrupt officials. A legal verdict can be changed from guilt to innocence, death sentence can turn into not-guilty verdict and length of prison terms can be reduced by bribing officials. The armed forces employs naval vessels and airplanes for various smuggling activities. The police stations often open covert gambling houses, or they can provide protection for them. In 2009, 106,000 public officials in China were convicted of corruption.

Coercion

Various types of violent crime have become common in PRC. Restaurants and hotels in the country extort high prices from guests, and those who show resistance are beaten or detained. Threatening of opponents in business operations is common.

Human Trafficking

China is a supply, transit and destination country for women, men, and children trafficked for various purposes. The majority of trafficking in PRC is internal and this domestic trafficking is the most significant human trafficking problem in the country. Approximately 10,000-20,000 victims are trafficked each year. There is also international trafficking of Chinese citizens. Women are lured through false promises of legitimate employment into commercial sexual exploitation in Taiwan, Thailand, Malaysia, and Japan. Chinese men are smuggled to countries throughout the world for exploitative labor. Women and children are trafficked into PRC from Mongolia, Burma, North Korea, Russia, and Vietnam for forced labor and sexual slavery.

Drug Trade

PRC is a major transshipment point for heroin produced in the Golden Triangle. Growing domestic drug abuse is a significant problem in PRC. Available estimates place the domestic spending on illegal drugs to be $17 billion.

Domestic Violence

China has a high rate of domestic violence. In 2004, the All-China Women's Federation compiled survey results to show that thirty percent of the women in China experienceddomestic violence within their homes. The true extent of domestic violence is unclear due to the lack of related law and execution of the law. The Chinese government is in the process of "planning" to pass a "draft of anti-domestic violence law".

CRIME DYNAMICS

Illegal Guns

Criminal organizations have acquired more weapons and vehicles which are often of better quality than that of the police force. In 1995, more than 100,000 illegal small arms were captured nationwide. From January to July 1996, approximately 300,000 illegal small arms were seized from fourteen provinces of the country.

CRIME IN ARMENIA

Crime in Armenia is multi-dimensional. It includes murder, political murder, contract killing, tax evasion,corruption, extortion, money laundering, police brutality, organized crime, and clan or gang violence.

CRIME BY TYPE

Murder

In 2012, Armenia had a murder rate of 1.8 per 100,000 population. There were a total of 54 murders in Armenia in 2012.

Organised Crime

Organized crime permeates the Armenian economy. In Yerevan there are organized, criminal clans known as "akhperutyuns" (Armenian: ambexiuxv–, or brotherhoods). They assert their power through their position and connections. The various factions sometimes battle for rights over their "turf". The origins of akhperutyuns are criminal law and the tradition of Armenian family life (ojakh). Members are guided by the underworld laws brought from Russian prisons.

Domestic Violence

A 2008 study by Amnesty International stated more than a quarter of women in Armenia "have faced physical violence at the hands of husbands or other family members."Since reporting domestic violence is heavily stigmatized in Armenian society, many of these women have no choice but to remain in abusive situations.

Corruption

The United Nations Development Programme in Armenia views corruption in Armenia as "a serious challenge to its development."

BY LOCATION

Yerevan

During the first ten months of 2008, crime in Armenia's capital Yerevan rose nearly 14% from the same period in 2007, while the rate of crime detection went down. 3,857 crimes were registered in Yerevan during this period, up by 462 compared to 2007. The rate of crime detection in the cases under investigation was 56.8%, down from 61.4%.

CRIME IN BHUTAN

Bhutan has a low crime rate. Incidents of petty crime are occasionally reported in the country. Violent crime is very uncommon. Some cases of drug abuse are reported;alcohol abuse is a problem. But in general, drug trafficking is low. The most serious threat to Bhutan's security is terrorism by different terrorist groups from neighboring countries illegally camped in the nation.

BACKGROUND

Serious crimes were very uncommon in Bhutan throughout most of the 20th century. There were reports of increased criminal activity since the 1980s and early 1990s. The main causes of the rise in crime are the influx of foreign laborers, widening economic disparities, and more contact with foreign cultures. In June 1999, television was introduced in the country and Bhutan became the last nation in the world to have television. The introduction of television is often regarded as incompatible with Bhutanese culture and a cause behind the increase in crime. An editorial in Kuensel, the national newspaper of Bhutan, suggested:

We are seeing for the first time broken families, school dropouts and other negative youth crimes. We are beginning to see crime associated with drug users all over the world -shoplifting, burglary and violence." A study conducted by some Bhutanese academics found that cable television has caused strong desire for western products among the people of the country and resulted in the increase in crime rate.

NON-POLITICAL CRIME

Violent crime is extremely low in Bhutan. Levels of theft are low. Petty crime like pickpocketing are occasionally reported in the country. Juvenile crime has relatively increased; the highest rate of juvenile crime was reported in 2003, and 63 youths were convicted across the nation. Rape is not an extensive problem; in 1999 only 10 incidents of rape were reported in Bhutan. Homicide rate is low.

In 1998, homicide rate per 100,000 citizens was 2.78. Bhutan is a source and transit country for human trafficking. Women are trafficked from Bhutan to other countries for commercial sexual exploitation. But Bhutan is not a destination country; women from other nations are not trafficked into Bhutan. In April 2002, Bhutan suffered a wave of crime. Although there were some reports of fraud, violence and few cases of homicide from many towns and villages, Bhutan never experienced serious violation of law before it. The first case of corruption in Bhutan was reported on April 5, 2002, when Parop Tshering, a 42-year-old chief accountant of the State Trading Corporation, was charged with embezzlement. Four cases of white-collar crime and violent crime were reported in April 2003.

In the Corruption Perceptions Index 2012, Bhutan is ranked 33rd out of 174 countries for corruption (least corrupt countries are at the top of the list). Bhutan ranks as the least corrupt nation in South Asia and sixth least corrupt in Asia (after, in order, Singapore, Hong Kong, Japan, Qatar and UAE).

DRUG-RELATED CRIME

Slight drug abuse has appeared in the country. Free trade with neighboring India, presence of porous borders and the refugee population make Bhutan vulnerable to drug trafficking. Bhutan has proximity to certain areas in Nepal and North-East India where intravenous drug use is relatively high. Due to such geographical location, Bhutan also becomes vulnerable to an increase in intravenous drug use. Marijuana, which grows as a shrub in Bhutan, was only used to feed pigs before the introduction of television.But hundreds were arrested in recent years for using marijuana. Use of amphetamines and benzodiazepines smuggled from India is rising in Thimpu and in the Southern Bhutan. However, drug trafficking and production of opium, cannabis and other drugs is not any significant problem in the country.

Alcohol consumption is the most serious addiction related problem in the nation. Alcohol abuse is reported in nearly 80% cases associated with domestic violence.

There are some characteristics of the situation on drug abuse in Bhutan:

- Most of the users of narcotic substances are male and students.
- Majority of the narcotic users are under the age of twenty-five.
- A growing portion of the youth population use multiple drugs.
- Some cases of intravenous drug use are reported in Bhutan, but it is minimal compared to other countries in the region.
- A social stigma is attached to addiction in the country. Because of this, the full nature of the situation becomes difficult to know.

The Government of Bhutan has taken several measures to counter these problems. Bhutan is a party of the United Nations Convention Against Illicit Traffic in Narcotic Drugs and Psychotropic Substances (1988). Many laws have been enacted which include the Civil and Criminal Procedure Code (2000), the Sales Tax, Customs and Excise Act (2000), the Medicines Act (2003), the Penal Code of Bhutan (2004), and the Narcotic Drugs and Psychotropic Substances and Substance Abuse Act (2005). In 2004, selling of tobacco products to Bhutanese citizens was outlawed in the country and thus Bhutan became the first nation in the world to ban tobacco sales. Severe punishment was introduced for selling of tobacco. A fine of $210 was imposed for the culprits and cancellation of business licenses for owners of shops and hotels illegally selling tobacco. Karma Tshering of the Bhutanese Customs said, "If any foreigner is caught selling tobacco products to Bhutanese nationals, he will be charged with smuggling. Tobacco will be treated as contraband." However a black market in tobacco has flourished in the country.

TERRORISM

Many insurgent groups from neighboring countries have set up training camps in the southern part of the country. The United Liberation Front of Asom (ULFA), the National Democratic Front of Bodoland (NDFB) and the Bodo Liberation Tigers Force (BLTF) had bases in Bhutan in 2002. Terrorists were involved in murders, extortion and kidnappings. Under increasing pressure from the Government of India, Bhutan issued an ultimatum to the terrorists for leaving the country by December 2001, and in December 2003, the Royal Bhutan Army, aided by the Special Frontier Force, launched a military campaign. Many terrorist camps were destroyed in the operation. It is suspected that terrorists are trying to make retaliatory attacks against Bhutan. On September 5, 2004, a bomb exploded in Gelephu killing two people and injuring twenty seven. The NDFB was suspected behind the attack.

The Government of Bhutan has taken several legal and military actions for combating terrorism. On September 4, 2004, one hundred and eleven people received various sentences ranging from four years to life imprisonment for helping terrorist organizations camped illegally in Bhutan. The offenders included civil servants, businesspersons, and laborers.

CRIME IN CAMBODIA

Crime is present in various forms in Cambodia.

CRIME BY TYPE

Murder

In 2012, Cambodia had a murder rate of 6.5 per 100,000 population. There were a total of 964 murders in Cambodia in 2012.

Robbery

Petty crime is common, with tourist areas often targeted. This includes snatch theft and pick-pocketing. Perpetrators are usually stricken with poverty, and as a result are driven to steal from foreigners with the knowledge that they bring about a significant amount of money and other valuable items. Owing to the easy accessibility to arms, armed robbery also occurs.

Corruption

The rate of corruption in Cambodia is high; one source goes on to describe the situation as "nothing less than obscene". Corruption is considered a large expense to the Cambodian government. The Cambodian police force is known to inappropriately use violence in certain cases. The misuse of ferocity has raised concerns from the Human Rights Watch.

Prostitution

Prostitution is against the law in Cambodia, but still present and only growing. Le Thi Quy, a professor from the Women's Research Center, interviewed a handful of females in 1993 about prostitution; three quarters of the interviewees found being a prostitute to be a norm and a profession they felt was not shameful having. That same year, the professor estimated that there were some one hundred thousand sex workers in the country.

CRIME IN AFGHANISTAN

Crime in Afghanistan is present in various forms, and includes the following: corruption, contract killings or assassinations, kidnapping, drug trafficking, money laundering, black marketeering, and other ordinary crimes.

Opium poppy cultivation and drug trafficking have important role in the political and economic situation of Afghanistan for last twenty-five years. In the aftermath of the Soviet withdrawal from Afghanistan, opium poppy cultivation increased in the nation. Many mujahideen commanders taxed opium poppy cultivation, even directly participated in illicit drug trade for military financing. Although the Taliban condemned cultivation of narcotic substances, requirements of money encouraged toleration and taxation of drug cultivation. In 1999, Afghanistan produced a peak of over 4,581 metric tons of raw and refined opium. This led to increasing international pressure from states having consumer population of Afghan drugs. In response, the Taliban banned opium poppy cultivation in late 2000, but allowed the opium trade to continue. Under the ban, opium poppy cultivation was reduced to 185 metric tons. This little production of opium continued in areas under the control of the United Islamic Front for the Salvation of Afghanistan.

Since the downfall of the Taliban in 2001, cultivation and trafficking of opium has increased significantly. Throughout the country regional militia commanders, criminal organizations and corrupt government officials have engaged in drug trafficking as a source of revenue. Some anti-government groups make profit from the drug trafficking.

Due to these factors, drug trafficking increases political instability in the nation, and is a threat to the country's weak internal security and embryonic democratic government. Afghanistan is the world's largest producer of opium and in 2001, Afghanistan was the source of 87% of the world's illicit opium. 80-90% of the heroin consumed in Europe comes from opium produced in Afghanistan. According to Antonio Maria Costa "drugs are now a clear and present danger" in Afghanistan. According to a survey in 2007 byUnited Nations Office on Drugs and Crime, 93% of the opiates on the world market originated in Afghanistan.

Unemployment among a large portion of the population and rudimentary basic services are major factors behind crime. Other forms of crime include robbery as well as kidnappings and assault. Many riots have occurred in the country in response to various political and other issues. Since the downfall of the Taliban, crime rate has significantly increased in the capital city Kabul. Armed robberies are regularly reported in the western districts of Kabul.Between March 2002 and January 2003, 48 cases of homicide, 80 cases of theft and 12 cases of kidnappings were reported within Kabul municipal boundaries.

CRIME IN BAHRAIN

There is a low rate of crime in Bahrain. Incidents of petty crime such as pickpocketing and bag snatching are reported especially in the old market areas (souks). Incidents of violent crime is uncommon, but increasing. Much of the crime in the nation is committed by the large South Asian population of guest workers. Though small in size, there is a growing underground drug market in the country. According to Emile Nakhleh, approximately 65% of violent crime and theft are committed by foreign citizens residing inBahrain.

Charisse Tia Maria Coston and Freda Adler in their book Victimizing Vulnerable Groups analyzed the reasons behind the low crime rate in Bahrain. The society of Bahrain follows the teachings of the Qur'an; the Qur'an influences political, economic and social environment. Islam, which is most important in the structure of Bahraini society, teaches wrongdoings will result in downfall of societies and try to uproot crime by exerting influence upon human conscience. This internalization of the religion of Islam is analyzed as a cause behind law-abiding behavior among Bahraini people where violation of law is considered violation of the principles of God.

Bahrain is a destination country for men and women trafficked for the purposes of involuntary servitude and commercial sexual exploitation. Men and women from Africa, South Asia and Southeast Asia migrate voluntarily to Bahrain to work as laborers or domestic servants where some face conditions of involuntary servitude such as unlawful withholding of passports, restrictions on movements, non-payment of wages, threats and physical or sexual abuse. Women from Eastern Europe, Central Asia, Southeast Asian country like Thailand and North African nation like Morocco are trafficked to Bahrain for the purpose of commercial sexual exploitation.

Threat of terrorist attack is a matter of concern. The Department of Foreign Affairs and Trade (DFAT) of the Government of Australia advised travelers "to exercise a high degree of caution in Bahrain" due to high threat of terrorism. According to the DFAT, terrorists can target shopping areas, supermarkets, embassies, hotels, restaurants, clubs, cinemas and theaters, schools, places of worship, outdoor recreation events and tourist areas. In the Corruption Perceptions Index 2007, Bahrain was ranked 46th out of 179 countries for corruption (least corrupt countries are at the top of the list). On a scale of 0 to 10 with 0 the most corrupt and 10 the most transparent, Transparency International rated Bahrain 5.0.

CRIME IN BANGLADESH

Crime in Bangladesh is present in various forms such as Drug Trafficking, Money Laundering, Extortion, Contract killing, Fraud, Human Trafficking, Robbery, Corruption, Black Marketeering, Political Violence, Terrorism and Abduction among others.

Bangladesh is used as a transit route for narcotics produced in neighboring countries. The Annual Report for 2007 from the International Narcotics Control Board (INCB), reports that Bangladesh is now the main transit point for the movement and trafficking of heroin from Southeast Asia into the European market . The report noted that the porous borders between Bangladesh and India contribute to the cross-border trafficking of narcotics.

The known means of trafficking drugs into Bangladesh are couriers from Pakistan, commercial vehicles and trains from India or Burma in addition to shipments from India via theBay of Bengal. It is estimated that 100,000 people are involved in narcotics trafficking in Bangladesh. A total of 10,331 homicides were reported to Bangladesh authorities from 2001 to 2003, showing a significant increase in recent years. For the Asia Pacific region, Bangladesh is ranked as one of the main countries for Software Piracy. It is estimated that the Software Industry loses nearly $102 million (USD) every year as a result.

CRIME IN INDONESIA

Crime is present in various forms in Indonesia.

Crimes Against Foreigners in Indonesia

Petty crime, which includes snatch theft and pick-pocketing, is present in Indonesia, usually taking place in locations with many people. Taxi scams are common in Indonesia, in which fake taxis are passed off as real ones. Foreign travellers often get fooled by this trickery, and end up getting robbed by the conmen operating the fake taxi. Violent crime is another growing issue in the country. Pirated and counterfeit merchandise can be easily found in most parts of Indonesia.

CRIMES AGAINST WOMEN IN INDONESIA

Prostitution

Prostitution, interpreted as a "crime against decency/morality", is illegal in Indonesia. Nevertheless, the practice still is widespread, tolerated and regulated. Prostitution is most visibly manifested in Indonesia's brothel complexes, or lokalisasi, which are found throughout the country. These brothels are managed under local government regulations. During or after raids by the police, the prostitutes are able to bribe the law enforcers and be released from custody; this has led to police raids being called "nothing more than an income source for public order officers".

UNICEF estimates that 30 percent of the female prostitutes in Indonesia are below 18 years of age. The International Labour Organization (ILO) puts the total number of child prostitutes in Jakarta at 5,000; according to the Jakarta city government, this is concentrated in Prumpung (North Jakarta), Grogol (West Jakarta) Tanah Abang (Central Jakarta), Block M (South Jakarta), as well as Jatinegara and Ciracas (both East Jakarta). Child sex tourism is a problem, especially on the resort islands of Bali and Batam.

CORRUPTION AND POLICE MISCONDUCT

Corruption is a known and increasing issue in Indonesia. There are two key areas in the public sector in which corruption in Indonesia can be found. These are the justice and civil service sectors. While hard data on corruption is difficult to collect, corruption in Indonesia is clearly seen through public opinion, collated through surveys as well as observation of how each system runs. Corruption is regarded as a huge expense to the Indonesian government. The Indonesian police force is known to go overboard and there have been reports of assaults against demonstrators in the country. The misuse of ferocity has been panned by the London-based Amnesty International.

OTHER CRIMES

Indonesia has put to death a handful of individuals convicted of the crime of murder. Watching porn is against the law, with effect of March 2008.

PUNISHMENT

Crime is segmented into two broad classifications: "Crimes" and "Offenses". There are a few methods to punish one for crime; this includes imprisonment and fine. Thedeath penalty executed by a firing squad is available and very frequently used, as a deterrent against crime. This has raised concerns from bodies like Amnesty International.

CRIME IN ISRAEL

Crime in Israel is present in various forms which include drug trafficking, arms trafficking, burglary, car theft, human trafficking, etc.

ORGANIZED CRIME

Organised crime has increased dramatically in Israel since the 1990s and is described by the BBC and the Israeli Police as a "booming industry". The Israeli organised crime groups have extended their activities in foreign countries like the United States, South Africa, and the Netherlands. According to a report by the Israel Police, drug trafficking, trafficking of women for the purpose of commercial sexual exploitation, illicit gambling, pirate filling stations and real estate are the major forms of crime in the country.

In 2002, the Israel Police documented 464,854 criminal files and non-prosecution cases while the number was 484,688 in 2003. This was an increase of 4.5% over 2002.

CRIMES IN ISRAEL BY PALESTINIANS

Director of the Latin American Institute of the American Jewish Committee in Washington, D.C. Dina Siegel, criminology professor H. G. van de Bunt, and lecturer in criminology Damián Zaitch showed in their book Global Organized Crime that a significant amount of crime in Israel, especially property crime, is committed by the residents of thePalestinian National Authority (PNA or PA). Motor vehicle theft is a major crime committed by Palestinians. Since the early 1990s, there has been an increase in the rate of robberies in Israel. Between

1994 and 2001, the rate of robberies increased from 14.0 to 30.6 cases per 100,000 population. The reason behind this increase in robberies is analyzed as a result of the establishment of the Palestinian Authority in the West Bank and Gaza Strip which according to the book Global Organized Crime "serves as a safe haven for Palestinian offenders".

However, the organized crime industry associated with motor vehicle theft involves not only Palestinians, but also Israeli citizens, both Jewish and Arab. The parts of the stolen cars are removed in "chop shops" in the Palestinian territories and then these vehicles are sold in the black market in Israel. Media reports suggest some of these vehicles are even handed over to high-ranking Palestinian Authority officials. It was reported that since the beginning of 2010 through the end of February 2010, the Palestinian Authority police have destroyed 910 stolen cars. Although Palestinian criminals are involved in organized crime in the country, Siegel et al. suggested one should not conclude that "organized crime in Israel is dominated by Palestinians. Organized crime committed by Jews or other non-Palestinians has been part of the Israeli crime scene for many years". Arms trafficking is another form of crime and it is directly associated with terrorism. There are many links between Israeli and Palestinian gangsters that facilitate these ventures. In addition to car theft, many cases of rape committed in Israel by West Bank Palestinians, many of them illegally residing in Israel, have been documented, and numerous Palestinians have been arrested for rape in Israel.

DRUGS IN ISRAEL

Heroin abuse has long been a problem in Israel and Cocaine abuse is increasing. The drugs come mainly from neighbouring countries Lebanon and Jordan.

JUVENILE VICTIMS AND PERPETRATORS

Violence against minors is also a problem in Israel. In 1999, approximately 7,000 cases of crimes against minors were documented which included physical assault (54%), molestation (37%) and repeated physical victimization (9%). However, Israeli minors are not solely the victims of crime, they are also sometimes the perpetrators. Teenage violence in schools is a problem in Israel; the first major study on teenage crime in the nation by T. Horowitz and M. Amir in 1981 indicated three major forms of violence in Israeli schools: theft, breaking and entering, and vandalism. Studies have suggested that Israeli Arab youth are more violent than Jews in the country, a fact which academics attribute to cultural, social, and economic differences.

MURDER

In Israel the homicide rate produced by criminal activities is relatively low: 2.4 killed per 100,000 inhabitants in a year (in Switzerland the number is 0.71, in Russia is 14.9, in South Africa is 34, in Venezuela is 49). In 2009, 135 people were murdered in Israel. Two major motivations for homicide in Israel are violence against women (includinghonor killings in Muslim families) and politically motivated violence i.e. Arab terrorism against Israelis.

STREET CRIME

In Israel, street crime is rare. Crime rates are quite evenly spread across the country, albeit with some "bad" neighbourhoods in the larger towns.

FAR-RIGHT AND HATE-CRIMES

Racist incidents, including violence, continue taking place between the Jewish majority and Arab minority. Arab-Jewish race riots have occurred on several occasions. In September 2007, eight white supremacists sporting tattoos including the number 88 (code for Heil Hitler because "H" is the eighth letter of the alphabet) from Petah Tikvawere arrested after a year of being observed desecrating synagogues, giving Nazi salutes in the street, attacking religious Jews, collected weapons explosives and Nazi propaganda and making a video. They were immigrants from Russia, and only one was fully Jewish. The rest had been allowed to immigrate due to some Jewish ancestry, but were not fully Jewish.

CRIME IN JAPAN

Crime in Japan is lower than in all other industrialized countries.

YAKUZA

The yakuza existed in Japan well before the 1800s and followed codes similar to the bushido of the samurai. Their early operations were usually close-knit, and the leader and gang members had father-son relationships. Although this traditional arrangement continues to exist, yakuza activities are increasingly replaced by modern types of gangs that depend on force and money as organizing concepts. Nonetheless, yakuza often picture themselves as saviors of traditional Japanese virtues in a postwar society, sometimes forming ties with right-wing groups espousing the same views and attracting dissatisfied youths to their ranks.

Yakuza groups in 1990 were estimated to number more than 3,300 and together contained more than 88,000 members. Although concentrated in the largest urban prefectures, yakuza operate in most cities and often receive protection from highranking officials. After concerted police pressure in the 1960s, smaller gangs either disappeared or began to consolidate in syndicate-type organizations. In 1990, three large syndicates (Yamaguchi-gumi, Sumiyoshi-kai, Inagawa-kai) dominated organized crime in the nation and controlled more than 1,600 gangs and 42,000 gangsters. Their number have since swelled and shrunk, often coinciding with economic conditions.

The yakuza tradition also spread to the Okinawa Island in the 20th century. The Kyokuryu-kai and the Okinawa Kyokuryu-kai are the two largest known yakuza groups inOkinawa Prefecture and both have been registered as designated boryokudan groups under the Organized Crime Countermeasures Law since 1992.

STATISTICS

In 1990 the police identified over 2.2 million Penal Code violations. Two types of violations — larceny (65.1 percent of total violation) and negligent homicide or injury as a result of accidents (26.2%) — accounted for over 90 percent of criminal offenses. In 1989 Japan experienced 1.3 robberies and 1.1 murders per 100,000 population. Japanese authorities also solve 75.9% of robbery cases and 95.9% of homicide cases. In recent years, the number of crimes in Japan has decreased. In 2002, the number of crimes recorded was 2,853,739. This number halved by 2012 with 1,382,154 crimes being recorded. In 2013, the overall crime rate in Japan fell for the 11th straight year and the number of murders and attempted murders also fell to a postwar low.

LEGAL DETERRENTS

Ownership of handguns is forbidden to the public, hunting rifles and ceremonial swords are registered with the police, and the manufacture and sale of firearms are regulated. The production and sale of live and blank ammunition are also controlled, as are the transportation and importation of all weapons. Crimes are seldom committed with firearms, yet knives remain a problem that the government is looking into, especially after the Akihabara massacre.

CRIMES

Of particular concern to the police are crimes associated with modernization. Increased wealth and technological sophistication has brought new white collar crimes, such as computer and credit card fraud, larceny involving coin dispensers, and insurance fraud. Incidence of drug abuse is minuscule, compared with other industrialized nations and limited mainly to stimulants. Japanese law enforcement authorities endeavor to control this problem by extensive coordination with international investigative organizations and stringent punishment of Japanese and foreign offenders.

Traffic accidents and fatalities consume substantial law enforcement resources. There is also evidence of foreign criminals travelling from overseas to take advantage of Japan's lax security. In his autobiography Undesirables, British criminal Colin Blaney stated that English thieves have targeted the nation due to the low crime rate and because Japanese people are unprepared for crime. Pakistani, Russian, Sri Lankan and Burmese car theft gangs have also been known to target the nation.

CRIME IN NORTH KOREA

Crime is present in various forms in North Korea, officially known as the Democratic People's Republic of Korea (DPRK).

CRIME BY TYPE

Murder

Many people in North Korea are stricken with poverty and as a result, are often forced to take up extreme measures in order to survive. Several defectors have reported hearing rumours that murder and cannibalism is rife in the country; these rumours first arose during the Great Famine of 1994 to 1998.

Political Offences

In North Korea, any perceived criticism of the country's political leaders is seen as a grave offense. Treason is also taken very seriously; traitorous behaviour may include attempting to escape to South Korea, or simply praising any aspect of South Korean culture. Crossing the northern border into China or Russia is also illegal, but this law is less strictly enforced, due to the sheer number of North Koreans driven across the border in search of employment. Criticism or rejection of socialist principles, or idleness in upholding these principles, is another serious political crime. This category of offence includes anything which threatens the socialist system – for example, running a private business, or stealing agricultural goods such as corn, rice or potatoes.

Foreigners Accused of Crimes Against North Korea

A small amount of American citizens have been charged in North Korea for alleged crimes against the nation. This encompasses illegally trespassing into the country or displaying signs of hostility towards the country. Two reporters from the United States were sentenced to penal labour after being found guilty of crimes against the nation. They were freed later the same year, when Bill Clinton visited the then-North Korean leader Kim Jong-il to negotiate their release. In April 2013, American tour operator Kenneth Bae, also known as Pae Jun Ho, was accused of plotting to overthrow the North Korean government. State media reported that there was evidence to substantiate the claim. He has since been released and allowed to return to the United States. According to the law of North Korea, such an act is punishable either by a life sentence in prison, or death.

Prostitution and Child Marriages

Prostitution in North Korea is illegal and, according to the North Korean government, does not exist. However, the government is reported to employ approximately 2,000 women, known as the Kippumjo, to provide sexual services to high-ranking officials. There is also widespread human trafficking within the country; women and girls are often sold abroad, mostly to China, where they are subjected to forced prostitution or forced marriage. Others may willingly migrate to China, only to be kidnapped by traffickers on arrival.

Corruption

Corruption in North Korea is a widespread and growing problem in the country. It is ranked 174 out of 176 countries in Transparency International's 2012 Corruption Perceptions Index, tied with Somalia and Afghanistan, making the country one of the "'most corrupt' nations on Earth". Strict rules and draconian punishments imposed by the regime against, for example, accessing foreign media, are commonly evaded by bribing the police. Informing on colleagues and family members has become less common.

CRIME IN SOUTH KOREA

Crime is present in various forms in South Korea.

OVERVIEW

Violent crimes (such as homicide, assault and arson) and property crimes (such as theft, fraud and vandalism) make up around four-fifths of all Criminal Code Offences Although South Korea has a lower crime rate than other countries of comparable economic status, the crime rate in 2007 was around 2.9 times higher than in 1978, with the total number of crimes committed rising from 513,165 to 1,965,577. On occasion, sudden changes in circumstance have led to cause short-term fluctuations in the crime rate – for example, the crime rate rose by 15% following the 1997 Asian financial crisis, and dropped by 21% during the first ten days of the 2002 FIFA World Cup. There is also a problem in the nation with foreign criminals targeting it due to its relatively affluent status and the perception that it has lax security. 1.4 percent of crimes in the nation are committed by foreigners, which is quite low considering the 3.5% of the population is non-Korean. According to British criminal Colin Blaney in his autobiography 'Undesirables', the country is targeted by English, Canadian, American and German criminals.

HISTORY OF ORGANIZED CRIME

South Korea has undergone dramatic social, economic and political upheaval since the end of the Korean War in 1953. With these changes crime has increased in recent years and has become a major issue in South Korea. Most of the increase has come in the form of violence and illegal activities connected to organized groups (Lee,2006).

Due to the large police and military presence after the Korean War, the expansion of home-grown organized crime was slowed, almost giving South

Korea immunity against international criminal organisations. With no outside conflicts South Korean organized crime has had an advantage to grow, yet because of the location of the Korean peninsula many outside groups from Russia, Japan and China have started to engage in more illegal activities in South Korea (Lee, 2006).

Amid the political confusion of the 1950s, a number of organized gangs emerged and became an influential force in the entertainment districts. Soon these groups began associating with politicians, guarding them from danger and disrupting the political rallies of competing politicians by using organized violence. These particular groups were the so-called "political gangs" or "henchmen" (Lee, 2006)

Organized crime after the War started mainly in the city of Seoul, the capital city of South Korea. Two main gangs formed, the first was known as the "Chong-ro Faction" which was made up of members from southern Korea, and the second was known as the "Myung-dong Faction" whose members where from Pyonyando province. These two gangs claimed dominance over northern Seoul. With the military in control, in the years from 1961 to 1963 13,000 members of these gangs were arrested causing organized gangs to almost completely disappear (Lee, 2006). The 1970s brought an easing of public discipline and control, and opportunities for organized crime emerged again. This saw the emergence of two new groups known as the "Master Sergeant Shin Faction" which was located in the Seoul area and the "Ho-nam Faction" found in the Mugyo-dong area of Seoul. In 1975 there was a violent battle over territories among the two groups which ended with the Ho-nam Faction becoming victorious. The Ho-nam Fraction soon divided into three sub-factions due to internal conflicts. These three factions are now considered the largest organized crime groups in South Korea. They are known as the "Seo-bang Faction," the "Yang-eun Faction" and the "OB Faction" (Lee, 2006).

Traditional South Korean criminal groups fights rarely resulted in deaths as they fought with their hands, feet and heads. Knives and metal bars only began to show up as weapons in the 1970s. In today's South Korean society, a person is not to be in possession of guns, swords or knives which may explain why traditional crime groups did not use weapons (Lee, 2006). Upon the assassination of President Park in 1979 "special measures to uproot social evils" were initiated under the proclaimed martial law which led to a decline in organized criminal violence. But with the a relaxed atmosphere these criminal organizations remerged and flourished yet again (Lee, 2006). With the 1985 Asian Games and the 1988 Seoul Summer Olympics global expansion became a possibility and criminal groups took advantage of this opportunity for rapid economic development. Taking advantage of the Korean government's open-door and globalization policies, these crime groups began to from coalitions with their counterparts in Japan, China, Hong Kong and the United States (Lee,

2006). In 1990 the Korean Government declared a "war on crime" in an effort to crack down on violent and non-violent acts by criminally organized groups. The raids in the fall of 1990 crippled most of the existing criminal groups, but did not destroy them. As one way of better controlling the number of criminal groups, they Korean Government made it illegal to form or join any criminal organization. Statistics from the Supreme Prosecutor's Office showed that in 1999 there were 11,500 members from 404 organized crimes groups ranging from 10 to 88 members in South Korea (Lee, 2006).

With the trend of economic growth and globalization, organized crime groups in South Korea have become larger in scale and broader in their fields of operations. These international linkages have started to include drug trafficking, financial fraud, weapons smuggling, and human trafficking. Organized transnational crime has become a major concern facing not only Korean government, but also the international community (Lee, 2006). It is said that most Korean criminal organizations are much smaller than comparable organizations such as the American Mafia, the Japanese Yakuza, or the Hong Kong Triads. Currently in South Korea there are 3 major Organized crime groups: Seven Star Mob, H.S.S. Mob, and Double Dragon.

But with that said there has been a huge increase in the number of members of organized crime groups who are arrested. In 1995 the number of arrests was 1,660 and in 2005 the number was 3,200 which is a 93% increase in 10 years(Lee, 2006).

DRUGS

The use of drugs in South Korea is a lesser offense; however, there are still drug related offenses in South Korea. Most of the drug related offenses occur in the Gangnam and Yongsan Districts. In 2013, there were 129 drug related crimes reported in the Gangnam area and 48 drug related crimes reported in the Yongsan area. A Gangnam District representative said, "drugs are usually distributed through the club network, in Gangnam, foreign students and club operators tend to be involved in the drug trade, a relatively easy way to make money."

According to the Supreme Prosecutors' Office, there were 7,011 arrests for drug offenses in 2011 which was a 7 percent drop from the previous year. The U.S., by way of comparison, in 2010 made more than 1.6 million drug arrests, more than 36 times Korea's figure, even after differences in population are accounted for. The drug that is most common is Crystalline Methamphetamine also known as Crystal Meth. Crystal Meth remains the most commonly used drug, accounting for most drug related arrests. Other drugs that are well known are club drugs such as XTC. These continue to grow in popularity among college students. However, methamphetamine continues to be the drug of choice for Koreans.

MURDER

In South Korea, murder is an uncommon, but serious, crime. Gangseo District and Yeongdeungpo Districts are the two most well-known areas where murders happen most often. In 2013, there were 21 murder cases in the Gangseo District and 11 murder cases in the Yeongdeungpo District. These two districts are found on the southwest part of the city where it houses many low income citizens and foreign workers.

A Dongguk University Police Administration professor, Kwak Dae-gyung said, "there are many foreign residents that have yet to adapt to Korean society and citizens lower in the economic strata in these areas, there's trouble in terms of economic competition and a lengthy period of cultural assimilation that leads to people committing violent crimes out of frustration and the need for frequent police action.

CORRUPTION

South Korea dropped one notch in an international corruption awareness ranking to 46th place among 177 nations in 2013. According to the 2014 Corruption Perceptions Index (CPI) issued by Transparency International (TI), South Korea scored 55 out of 100. Corruption Perceptions Index . The index shows qualitative assessments of a country's level of corruption in the administrative and public sectors giving a yearly view of the relative degree of corruption by ranking countries from all over the globe. It uses data taken from opinion surveys of experts from each country. The reputation of the country's law enforcement agency has recently been tarnished after a number of ranking government officials, including the head of the state intelligence agency, were indicted for alleged bribery.

Some 86.5 percent of respondents in a Korea Institute of Public Administration survey of small and large companies described corruption among high-ranking public officials as "serious" in 2010, the highest result since the poll began in 2000. Transparency International, a corruption watchdog, gave South Korea a rating of 5.4 in its 2010 corruption perceptions index — midway between highly corrupt and very clean. That ranks South Korea alongside countries and territories such as Botswana, Puerto Rico and Poland but far below many of the developed nations it has sought to emulate.

PROSTITUTION

Prostitution in South Korea is illegal, but according to The Korea Women's Development Institute, the sex trade in the country was estimated to amount to 14 trillion South Korean won ($13 billion) in 2007, roughly 1.6 percent of the nation's gross domestic product. In 2003, the Korean Institute of Criminology announced that 260,000 women, or 1 of 25 of young Korean women, may be engaged in the sex industry. However, the Korean Feminist Association alleged that from 514,000 to 1.2 million Korean women participate in the prostitution industry. In addition, a similar report by the Institute noted that 20% of men in their 20s pay for sex at least four times a month, with 358,000 visiting prostitutes daily.

The sex trade involved some 94 million transactions in 2007, down from 170 million in 2002. The number of prostitutes dropped by 18 percent to 269,000 during the same period. The amount of money traded for prostitution was over 14 trillion won, compared to than 24 trillion won in 2002. Despite legal sanctions and police crackdowns, prostitution continues to flourish in the country, while sex workers continue to actively resist the state's activities.

CRIME IN KUWAIT

There is a low rate of crime in Kuwait. Incidents of violent crime against foreign citizens are extremely uncommon. The country is a destination point for men and women who migrate legally from South and Southeast Asia for domestic or low-skilled labor, but are subjected to conditions of involuntary servitude by employers including physical and sexual abuse, non-payment of wages, confinement to the home, and withholding of passports to restrict their freedom of movement. People from South Asian countries likeBangladesh, India, Pakistan and Sri Lanka and Southeast Asian nation like the Philippines are trafficked into Kuwait. Kuwait along with Qatar, the United Arab Emirates andSaudi Arabia is in Tier 4 rank which has greater wealth, but a worse human trafficking situation.

CRIME BY TYPE

Terrorism

Threat of terrorist attack is a matter of concern. In the early 70's the terrorism threat was mostly against government targets perpetrated by various Palestinian factions. During the Iran - Iraq conflict terrorism was mainly by Iranian agents and supporters, where several bombings took place in public places including a suicide car bomb attempt against the ruler which failed. Also during the military buildup for Gulf War II there was a heightened terrorism threat by extreme Islamist elements with several attacks targeting foreigners. The government cracked down very hard against the budding extremist threat, and several high profile confrontations took place. That along with strong action by the Saudi Arabian regime, seemed to have eliminated or greatly reduced the threat and Kuwait has not had a terrorist incident since 2005. Several Kuwaiti men linked to extremist elements have been know to have gone to Iraq to fight coalition forces, but that seems to have abated as local Iraqi militants seemed eager to use them as "suicide bombers" without the persons knowledge or consent. The Department of Foreign Affairs and Trade (DFAT) of the

Government of Australia reported there is a high threat of terrorist attack in Kuwait. DFAT claimed they received reports that terrorists are masterminding attacks against assets belonging to the Government of Kuwait, hotels, restaurants and Western interests. The United States Department of State reported terrorists in the past attacked hotel chains which they believed belonged to westerners. Western housing complexes were also targeted by terrorist organizations. Terrorism in Kuwait may include bombing, hijacking, hostage taking, kidnapping and assassination. Both military and civilians are the potential targets of terrorist groups. According to the US State Department, terrorists can target oil infrastructure, public transportation, schools, places of worship, clubs, shopping complexes, etc., due to increased security measures in official US facilities. Although these places are potential targets of terrorist organization, DFAT emphasized "that attacks could occur at anytime, anywhere in Kuwait".

Corruption

In the Corruption Perceptions Index 2007, Kuwait was ranked 60th out of 179 countries for corruption (least corrupt countries are at the top of the list). On a scale of 0 to 10 with 0 the most corrupt and 10 the most transparent, Transparency International rated Kuwait 4.3.

CRIME IN MALAYSIA

Crime in Malaysia manifests in various forms, including murder, drug trafficking, money laundering, fraud, corruption, black marketeering, and many others.

HUMAN TRAFFICKING

Malaysia is a destination, supply and transit point for women and children trafficked for commercial sexual exploitation. Women and girls from Burma, Cambodia, China,Indonesia, the Philippines, Thailand, and Vietnam are trafficked to Malaysia. Malaysia is a transit country along with Indonesia, Philippines and Thailand in Chinese human trafficking. Women from Malaysia are trafficked into the People's Republic of China. Migrants from countries in the region work as domestic servants and laborers in the construction and agricultural sectors and face exploitative conditions. Between 2005 to September 2009, more than 36,858 women were arrested for prostitution in Malaysia.

DRUG TRAFFICKING

Drug trafficking is a problem, heroin being the primarily used drug. Drug trafficking is punishable by the death penalty, a measure which was introduced during the 1980s to combat drug offenses, and was highlighted following the 1986 execution of Kevin John Barlow and Brian Geoffrey Chambers.

CRIME AGAINST TOURISTS

Violent crime against foreign tourists is less frequent in Malaysia; however, pickpocketing and burglaries are common criminal activities directed against foreigners. Other types of non-violent crime include credit card fraud and motor vehicle theft; there is a high rate of credit card fraud. Scams are a problem in Kuala Lumpur which involve card games and purchase of gold jewellery.

CORRUPTION

Corruption is a problem, but less common than in many other countries in Southeast Asia. In the 2014 Corruption Perceptions Index by Transparency International Malaysia had a corruption score of 52 out of 100 (high scores are more corrupt); this makes Malaysia the 2nd "cleanest" country in SE Asia, 9th out of 28 in APAC and 50th of the 175 countries assessed worldwide.

Transparency International list Malaysia's key corruption challenges as:

1. *Political and Campaign Financing:* Donations from both corporations and individuals to political parties and candidates are not limited in Malaysia. Political parties are also not legally required to report on what funds are spent during election campaigns. Due in part to this political landscape, Malaysia's ruling party for over 55 years has funds highly disproportionate to other parties. This unfairly impacts campaigns in federal and state elections and can disrupt the overall functioning of a democratic political system.
2. *"Revolving door":* Individuals regularly switch back and forth between working for both the private and public sectors in Malaysia. Such circumstances – known as the 'revolving door' – allow for active government participation in the economy and public-private relations to become elusive. The risk of corruption is high and regulating public-private interactions becomes difficult, also allowing for corruption to take place with impunity. Another factor which highlights the extent of ambiguity between the public sector and private corporate ownership is that Malaysia is also a rare example of a country where political parties are not restricted in possessing corporate enterprises.
3. *Access to information:* As of April 2013, no federal Freedom of Information Act exists in Malaysia. Although, Selangor and Penang are the only Malaysian states out of thirteen to pass freedom of information legislation, the legislation still suffers from limitations. Should a federal freedom of information act be drafted it would conflict with the Official Secrets Act – in which any document can be officially classified as secret, making it exempt from public access and free from judicial review. Additional laws such as the Printing Presses and Publications Act, the Sedition Act 1949 (subsequently replaced with the National Harmony Act), and the Internal Security Act 1969

also ban the dissemination of official information and offenders can face fines or imprisonment.TI). Malaysia suffers from corporate fraud in the form of intellectual property theft. Counterfeit production of several goods including IT products, automobile parts, etc., are prevalent.

In 2013, Malaysia has was identified in a survey by Ernst and Young as one of the most corrupt countries in the region according to the perceptions of foreign business leaders, along with neighboring countries and China. The survey asked whether it was likely that each country would take shortcuts to achieve economic targets.

CRIME IN THE MALDIVES

There is a low rate of crime in the Maldives. Incidents of theft on beaches or in hotels do occur. Although the crime rate in the nation is generally considered to be low, crime rates are increasing. Juvenile delinquency is a growing problem in the Maldives. According to the data available from the Ministry of Defence and National Security, there is an increase in petty crime in the country. In 1992, 169 cases of petty crime were reported while the number was 462 in 1996. The number of sentenced persons under the age of 19 also increased from 391 in 1988 to 512 in 1998. Fraud examiner Peter Lilley in his book Dirty Dealing writes that money laundering is not a significant problem in the Maldives. "Drug abuse in Maldives has reached alarming levels, and, according to several ministries and high ranking officials, is now the most serious problem the country is facing." — Report of the International Narcotics Control Board 2006

Drug abuse is increasing in the country. The Maldives are situated in a location which is not too far from one of two major illicit opium producing centers in Asia - the Golden Triangle comprising Myanmar, Thailand andLaos. Many tourists visit the country from different parts of the world like Europe, the Middle East, South Asiaand East Asia. These factors make the Maldives vulnerable as a point for illegal shipments of drugs meant for other nations. Abuse of illegally produced heroin is a visible problem in the Maldives along with other South Asian countries like Bangladesh, India, Nepal and Sri Lanka. The United Nations Office on Drugs and Crime(UNODC) believes that drug trafficking in the Maldives is a side effect of the nation's increased exposure to the outside world. Drug abuse is also associated with increasing incidents of theft and robbery.

Threat of terrorist attack is a matter of concern. The Department of Foreign Affairs and Trade (DFAT) of the Government of Australia advised travelers "to exercise caution" because of the high threat of terrorism. According to the Foreign and Commonwealth Office (FCO), "Attacks could be indiscriminate, including in places frequented by expatriates".

Rate of criminal homicide and assault in the Maldives declined by 30% between the years 1997-2002. Crime involving bribery and fraud also declined by 33% during this time.In the Corruption Perceptions Index 2007, the Maldives was ranked 84th out of 179 countries for corruption (least corrupt countries are at the top of the list). On a scale of 0 to 10, with 0 being the least and ten being most transparent, Transparency International rated the Maldives 3.3.

CRIME IN MYANMAR

Crime is present in various forms in Myanmar (also known as Burma).

CRIME BY TYPE

Murder

In 2012, Burma had a murder rate of 15.2 per 100,000 population. There were a total of 8,044 murders in Burma in 2012. Factors influencing Burma's high murder rate include communal violence and armed conflict.

Terrorism

Terrorism in Burma primarily consists of anti-government militant activity. Militant separatists in India, such as the United Liberation Front of Assam and the United National Liberation Front, have bases in Burma from which they launch attacks.

Corruption

Burma is one of the world's most corrupt nations. The 2012 Transparency International Corruption Perceptions Index ranked the country at number 171, out of 176 countries in total. The Burmese government has been making an effort to curb corruption in the country.

Crime Against Foreigners in Burma

Crime against foreigners in Burma, although low, is a growing issue; there have been instances of both petty and violent crime in the country.

Opium and Methamphetamine Production

Burma is the world's second largest producer of opium after Afghanistan, producing some 25% of the world's opium, and forms part of the Golden Triangle. The opium industry was a monopoly during colonial times and has since been illegally operated by corrupt officials in the Burmese military and rebel fighters, primarily as the basis for heroin manufacture.

Burma is the largest producer of methamphetamines in the world, with the majority of Ya ba found in Thailand produced in Burma, particularly in the Golden Triangle and Northeastern Shan State, which borders Thailand, Laos and China. Burmese-produced ya ba is typically trafficked to Thailand viaLaos, before being transported through the northeastern Thai region of Isan. In 2010, Burma trafficked 1 billion tablets to neighbouring Thailand. In 2009, Chinese authorities seized over 40 million tablets that had been illegally trafficked from Burma. Ethnic militias and rebel groups (in particular the United Wa State Army) are responsible for much of this production; however, the Burmese military units are believed to be heavily involved in the trafficking of the drugs. The prominence of major drug traffickers have allowed them to penetrate other sectors of the Burmese economy, including the banking, airline, hotel and infrastructure industries. Their investment in infrastructure have allowed them to make more profits, facilitate drug trafficking and money laundering.

Prostitution

Prostitution in Burma is against the law. Prostitution is a major social issue that particularly affects women and children. Burma is a major source of prostitutes (an estimate of 20,000–30,000) in Thailand, with the majority of women trafficked taken to Ranong, a location that borders Burma at its south, and Mae Sai, which is located at the eastern tip of Burma. Burmese sex workers also operate in Yunnan, China, particularly the border town of Ruili. The majority of Burmese prostitutes in Thailand are from ethnic minorities.

60% of Burmese prostitutes are under 18 years of age. Burma is also a source country of sex workers and forced labourers in China, Bangladesh, Taiwan, India, Malaysia,Korea, Macau, and Japan. Internal trafficking of women for the purpose of prostitution occurs from rural villages to urban centres, military camps, border towns, and fishing villages.

Women are often lured into prostitution with the promise of legitimate jobs, substantially higher pay, and because their low educational levels makes it difficult for them to find jobs elsewhere. In many instances, such women come from remote regions. In addition to crimes associated with prostitution, the trafficking of women, largely to china, for Forced marriage remains a problem in Burma. Lack of local brides due to China's long standing One Child Policy is believed to fuel this trade.

War Crimes

The United Nations Human Rights Council has requested an investigation into potential human rights violations, or war crimes, in the country.

CRIME IN OMAN

Crime rate in Oman is low compared to industrialized countries. Incidents of serious crime are rare in the country. Incidents of petty crime including burglary and theft of property of foreign tourists are occasionally reported. The Foreign and Commonwealth Office (FCO) describes the law and order situation in Oman as "generally good".Incidence of street crime is low. Violent crime occurs, but is extremely low compared to the United States. Oman is a destination point for men and women mainly from South Asian nations like Bangladesh, India, Sri Lanka and Pakistan who migrate willingly, but some of whom become victims of trafficking when subjected to conditions of involuntary servitude as domestic workers and laborers. Mistreatment includes non-payment of wages, restrictions on movement and withholding of passports, threats, and physical or sexual abuse. Oman is also a destination point for women trafficked from Asia, Eastern Europe and North Africa for the purpose of commercial sexual exploitation.

The Department of Foreign Affairs and Trade (DFAT) of the Government of Australia and the FCO reported there are incidents where individuals presenting themselves as employees of the Ministry of Health have called private houses offering vaccinations against avian influenza (commonly known as Bird flu). But the Ministry of Health does not provide any service like this. Drugs are given to people as "vaccines" to make them unconscious and then they are robbed.

Threat of terrorist attack is a matter of concern. The DFAT advised travelers "to exercise a high degree of caution in Oman because of the high threat of terrorist attack". TheUnited States Department of State expressed concern over possibility of terrorist attacks against citizens of the United States. According to the FCO, "there is an underlying threat from terrorism in Oman. Attacks, although unlikely, could be indiscriminate, including in places frequented by expatriates and foreign travelers".

Drug trafficking in general is low. However the amount of seized heroin in 1995 was 6.2 kg which was an increase compared to 1 kg in 1994. Oman has established an Inter ministerial committee for the purpose of overseeing drug framework matters. The country has a well-organized Drug Control Unit to deal with drug trafficking. Oman is a party of the Convention on Psychotropic Substances (1971). According to Interpol data, criminal homicide rate in Oman decreased from 0.94 to 0.91 per 100,000 population between 1995 and 2000. It was a decrease of 3.2%. The rate ofrape also decreased by 16.4%. But rate of robbery increased by 108.1%. While the rate of robbery was 1.24 per 100,000 population in 1995, it increased to 2.58 per 100,000 population in 2000. Similarly the rate of aggravated assault, burglary, larceny and motor vehicle theft increased by 10.7%, 57.7%, 317.8% and 112.2% respectively.

CRIME IN PAKISTAN

Crime in Pakistan is present in various forms. Organised crime includes drug trafficking, money laundering, extortion,black marketeering, political violence, terrorism, abduction etc. Pakistan falls under the Golden Crescent, which is one of the two major illicit opium producing centres in Asia. Opium poppy cultivation in Pakistan is estimated to be 800 hectares in 2005 yielding a potential production of 4 metric tons of heroin. Opium is cultivated primarily in the Khyber Pakhtunkhwa province and Pakistan-Afghanistan border. Until the late 1970s, opium production levels were relatively static; it increased after 1979. An estimated $4 billion is generated from drug trafficking in Pakistan. Petty crime like theft is common.

CRIME IN THE PHILIPPINES

Crime is present in various forms in the Philippines.

CRIME BY TYPE

Organized crime

Organized crime in the Philippines can linked to certain families or barkadas (groups) who perpetrate crimes ranging from extortion, sale of illegal narcotics and loan sharking torobbery, kidnapping, and murder-for-hire.

Petty Crime

Petty crime, which includes pick-pocketing, is a problem in the Philippines. It takes place usually in locations with many people, ranging from shopping hubs to churches. Traveling alone to withdraw cash after dark is a risk, especially for foreigners.

Violent Crime

Violent crime is high in the country; foreigners are usually the victims. As many Filipinos are stricken with poverty, one alternative they take is to kidnap others for money.

Prostitution

Prostitution in the Philippines is illegal. It is a serious crime with penalties ranging up to life imprisonment for those involved in trafficking. It is covered by the Anti-Trafficking in Persons Act. prostitution is still sometimes illegally available through brothels (also known as casa), bars, karaoke bars, massage parlors, street walkers and escort services.As of 2009, one source estimates that there are 800,000 women working as prostitutes in the Philippines, with some of them believed to be underage. While victims are largely female, and according to the current Revised Penal Code, there are in fact a small minority of them who are male.

Human Trafficking

Human trafficking and the prostitution of children is a significant issue in the Philippines, often controlled by organized crime syndicates. Human trafficking in the country is a crime against humanity. In an effort to deal with the problem, the Philippines passed Republic Act (R.A.) 9208, the Anti-

Trafficking in Persons Act of 2003, a penal law against human trafficking, sex tourism, sex slavery and child prostitution. Nevertheless, enforcement is reported to be inconsistent.

Corruption and Police Misconduct

Corruption is a great problem in the Philippines. In May 2013, during the country's elections, some 504 political candidates were accused mostly of corruption and some of violent crimes. Police misconduct is a known issue in the country; in April 2013, a short video, titled Like a BOSS, showcasing the assault on an unarmed individual by three police officers went viral online, prompting the Philippine National Police to investigate the matter.

CRIME IN QATAR

Crime in Qatar is relatively low compared to industrialized nations. Petty crime such as pickpocketing and bag snatching does occur, but is extremely uncommon.Although incidents of violence are generally considered to be rare, violence has occurred more frequently due to increase in the population of Doha, the capital and largest city of Qatar, and economic pressures on expatriate workers during the last few years.

Qatar is a destination country for men and women from South and Southeast Asia who migrate willingly, but are subsequently forced into involuntary servitude as domestic workers and laborers, and, to a lesser extent, commercial sexual exploitation.

The most common offense was forcing workers to accept worse contract terms than those under which they were recruited. Other conditions include bonded labor, withholding of pay, restrictions on movement, arbitrary detention, and physical, mental, and sexual abuse. Qatar is in Tier 3 rank; it failed to enforce criminal laws against traffickers, or to provide an effective mechanism to identify and protect victims. The nation detain and deport victims rather than providing them protection. The Government of Qatar made little progress to increase prosecutions for trafficking effectively in 2007.

Threat of terrorist attack is a matter of concern. Al-Qaeda has threatened Western citizens in the region. The Department of Foreign Affairs and Trade (DFAT) of theGovernment of Australia advised travelers "to exercise a high degree of caution in Qatar" due to high threat of terrorism. The DFAT claimed they received reports of terrorist plans to attack a range of targets in the nation. A suicide car bombing at the Doha Players theater on March 19, 2005, which was the first attack of its kind in the nation, killed aBritish citizen and injured twelve other people. The bomber was an Egyptian named Omar Ahmed Abdullah Ali. On March 17, 2005, Saleh al-Oufi, Saudi head of al-Qaeda, urged attacks against what he called "crusader" enemies in Qatar and in other countries like Bahrain, Oman and the United Arab Emirates.

In the Corruption Perceptions Index 2007, Qatar was ranked 32nd out of 179 countries for corruption (least corrupt countries are at the top of the list). On a scale of 0 to 10, with 0 being the most corrupt and 10 the most transparent, Transparency International rated Qatar 6.0.

According to Interpol data, criminal homicide rate in Qatar increased from 1.52 to 2.11 per 100,000 population between 1995 and 1999. It was an increase of 38.8%. The rate for rape decreased by 67.1%, but the rate of robbery increased by 100%. While the rate of robbery was 0.67 per 100,000 population in 1995, it increased to 1.34 per 100,000 population in 1999. Similarly the rate of aggravated assault, larceny and motor vehicle theft increased by 75.1%, 73.1% and 13.5% respectively.

CRIME IN SAUDI ARABIA

The rate of crime in Saudi Arabia is often described as low by foreign ministries and other sources, In 2013, the number of crime cases reported by the Ministry of Justice was 22,113, a 102% increase over 2012.

"Crime in Saudi Arabia is relatively low when compared to some developed nations, but may be increasing due to higher levels of foreign workers and higher levels of unemployment among Saudi residents."

— John Wilson, on the crime situation in Saudi Arabia, in the bookInternational Security and the United States: An Encyclopedia

BACKGROUND

Reporting

According to the US State Department Overseas Security Advisory Council (OSAC) as of 2014, "U.S. citizens and Westerners continue to report incidents of crime, including robberies and attempted robberies." Cases of sexual assault are believed to be underreported "because victims are customarily blamed". (For example in 2009, a 23-year-old woman was sentenced to a year in prison and 100 lashes in 2009 for adultery after being raped by five men. In 2007, a 19-year-old victim of rape by seven men receiving a sentence of six-months in jail and 200 lashes.)

Foreign affairs ministries of other countries have stated that there is a low rate of crime in Saudi Arabia. However according to criminology researcher Dr. Ali Wardak, ranking societies on the basis of official crime rates may be problematic, as in Saudi Arabia criminal complaints are resolved outside formal judicial institutions and as a consequence remain undocumented by the police.

History

While as late as the 1980s the kingdom could and did boast of being "practically crime-free," the crime rate among jobless youth grew by 320% from 1990 to 1996. Convictions for drug possession rose from 4,279 in 1986 to

17,199 in 2001. Credited with rising crime are a "population boom, rapid social change, and massive unemployment" leading to "a breakdown in traditional forms of social control and constraint.

TYPES OF CRIME

Theft

Petty theft is a problem especially in crowded areas. The nation has strict laws prohibiting drug trafficking; drug trafficking is a capital crime. Despite strict laws, however, illicit trafficking takes place in considerable amounts through underground channels especially marijuana, cocaine and homegrown psychedelic drugs. Saudi Arabia is a signatory to all three international conventions on drug control. To curb money laundering, improved anti-money laundering laws have been enacted. The country has implemented all the forty recommendations of the Financial Action Task Force on Money Laundering (FATF) for combating money laundering and all eight recommendations of the FATF regarding terror financing. A Financial Intelligence Unit exists for the purpose of monitoring flows of funds.

The most common crime in 2002 was theft, which accounted for 47% of total reported crime. Saudi Arabia is a destination point for workers from South and Southeast Asiawho are subjected to conditions which include involuntary servitude, non-payment of wages, confinement and withholding of passports as a restriction on their movement.

Domestic workers are particularly vulnerable because some are confined to the house in which they work and are unable to seek help. Saudi Arabia is also a destination country for children trafficked from other Middle Eastern countries like Yemen, African countries like Nigeria, Mali, Somalia, South Sudan, and Sudan and Asian nations like India ,Bangladesh , Pakistan and Afghanistan for the purpose of forced begging and involuntary servitude as street vendors. Some Nigerian women were reportedly trafficked into Saudi Arabia for commercial sexual exploitation.

Terrorism

Threat of Islamic terrorism is a matter of concern. From 2000 to 2004, when a number of expatriate workers were killed in car bombings, questions arose over the seriousness and sincerity of Saudi efforts to prevent or investigate attacks. Before May 2003, the only public statements of any investigation or prosecution of attacks were Saudi accusations against the (mainly British) western expatriates themselves. Saudis arrested and detained several, claiming they were 'alcohol traders' fighting a turf war over the illegal distribution of alcohol. According to author Thomas Hegghammer, "today, few outside Saudi Arabia believe that alcohol traders carried out the bombings", as the suspects were well-paid professionals with no prior record of violent crime, no forensic evidence was provided against them, and attacks of a very similar nature on western nationals continued despite the arrests of the alleged perpetrators.

After 26 foreigners were killed in a May 2004 attack by three car bombs on foreign residential compounds in Riyadh, American intelligence sources quoted by the Daily Telegraph, stated the operation "depended on a significant level of `insider` knowledge of the compounds," and this and other evidence indicates that al-Qaeda has infiltrated even the elite National Guard, which was involved in compound security. Bombers wore uniforms of security forces, in both the May 2003 compound bombing and another in November. In May 2004, militants took dozens of hostages attacking three buildings in the oil-industry town of Khobar over a 25-hour period killing 22 and injuring 25 —mainly foreign workers — killing one victim by tying him to the back of a vehicle and dragged through the street. Despite being surrounded by Saudi security, three of the four gunmen escaped. While attacks by militants have decreased dramatically since late 2004, there are continued reports of terrorist planning. The Department of Foreign Affairs and Trade (DFAT) of the Government of Australia claimed they received reports that terrorists are masterminding attacks against assets belonging to the Government of Saudi Arabia, oil infrastructure, aviation infrastructure, embassies, hotels, shopping malls and many Western interests such as residential housing complexes, gatherings of foreign tourists for recreational or cultural activities etc.

The United States Department of State reported "There is an on-going security threat due to the continued presence of terrorist groups, some affiliated with al Qaida, who may target Western interests, housing compounds, and other facilities where Westerners congregate". Terrorist attacks in the countrytargeted both native people and foreigners. DFAT further stated "Terrorist attacks could occur at any time, anywhere in Saudi Arabia, including in Riyadh, Khobar, and other major cities".

Murder

In 1988, the murder rate in Saudi Arabia was .011 per 100,000 population, sexual offenses were .059 per 100,000 population, and thefts were .005 per 100,000. In 2002, a total of 599 crimes were reported in Saudi Arabia, or .06 crimes for every 100,000 people. By 2006 those numbers had gone down with murder at .010 per 100,000 population, sexual offenses at .046 per 100,000, and thefts offenses at .04 per 100,000.

SHARIA LAW

The Saudi legal system is based on Sharia or Islamic law and thus often prohibits many activities that are not crimes in other nations, such as alcohol or pork consumption, public displays of non-Islamic religious symbols or text, affection between opposite sex, "indecent" artwork or media images, sorcery, homosexuality, cross-dressing, and fornication or adultery. One of the main organizations enforcing traditional Islamic morality in the kingdom is the "Religious Police" or Committee for the Promotion of Virtue and the Prevention of Vice. It is difficult to know, with any certainty, how many people have been charged or punished for violating these laws.

CRIME IN SRI LANKA

Crime is present in various forms in Sri Lanka. Crime is segmented into two broad classifications: grave crimes (those which are indictable) and minor crimes (those which are not). Exceptions can be made for criminal liability on the grounds of duress, insanity, intoxication, necessity, and private defense. Punishment for crime includes several options: community service, fine, forfeiture of property, imprisonment, institutional treatment, probation, suspended sentence, whipping, and death; while the death penalty is available in the country, there have been no executions since 1976. Sri Lanka has a major problem with corruption and war crimes have affected many people in the country.

CRIMES AGAINST WOMEN AND CHILDREN

Sri Lanka is a participant in the prostitution industry, and most consumers of the trade in the country are foreign travellers. Nevertheless, most prostitution-related acts, such asprostitute trafficking and procuring are illegal. Prostitution has not become as severe an issue in Sri Lanka as compared to the situation in some neighbouring countries. Child trafficking is a problem in Sri Lanka.

Most children trafficked are treated unfairly, unwillingly and inhumanely turned into pornographic film actors or sex slaves. Foreigners are not jailed for performing sexual offenses against children.

CORRUPTION

Corruption is prevalent in Sri Lanka. Cited as "one of the most corrupt nations in the world" by Lakshman Indranath Keerthisinghe of the Lanka Standard, there have been instances in which law enforcers take bribes from offenders who wish to have their offences waived. The government has made an effort to curb corruption in the country and a handful of corrupt individuals have been arrested and appropriately charged. Corruption is considered a large expense to the Sri Lankan government. However, corruption does not appear to be significant enough to pose a problem with foreign investment, though it is considered to be a persistent issue with customs clearance and smuggling of some consumer products.

INVESTIGATION

The crime division of the Police Department of Sri Lanka has several branches. Its primary mission is to protect against all types of crimes in the country. It makes appropriate coordination with civil and military agencies, apprehends criminals, and take appropriate legal actions after the commitment of crime. The department also has the Police Human Rights Division which was established in 2002 with a mandate to examine and prevent human rights violations with which their officers may be charged while on duty.

CRIME IN THAILAND

Crime in Thailand is a persistent, growing, complex, internationalized, and under-recognized problem. Since the 2014 coup, crime in Thailand is reported by the Royal Thai Police; however, there is no single agency which acts as a watchdog and publishes statistics. Official corruption is rampant in Thailand. It ranges from bribery to outright police collusion. The interplay of extremely addictive drugs, prostitution, political paralysis, corruption and collusion, a culture of impunity, international tourism and trade, liberal sexual mores, traditional Buddhist tolerance and tendency to ignore problems has led to an increasingly multifaceted and complex crime epidemic in the country. Juvenile delinquency has also been increasing in recent years.

The military coup of May 2014 brought the promise of a crackdown on crime in Thailand. But in November 2015, the New York Times reported that in the fiscal year ending September 2015, the national police have seen a surge in thefts, burglaries, and robberies, more than 75,557 thefts and other property crimes in the fiscal year, 63 percent higher than the previous year. Violent crime was up 17 percent during the same period. These figures have been contested by the police and by Amorn Wanichwiwatana, a criminologist at Chulalongkorn University, who said he was not aware of any significant uptick in crime since the military came to power. "I don't think that's the case. It's not possible," he said of the 60 percent increase reported by the Times. Crime statistics from the Royal Thai Police (RTP) show a statistically negligible increase of 1.9 percent over the same period, with 920 additional crimes reported after an overall decline since 2009.

BY LOCATION

Much of Thailand's crime is in urban areas where tourists congregate as they are easy targets, as well as where rampant prostitution and human trafficking feeds their vices. The prime areas of drug abuse are Bangkok, Phuket, and Pattaya, but not limited to these areas. The prime transit corridor for drugs entering northern Thailand is from theGolden Triangle, as well as from ethnically divided rebel-controlled areas within the fragmented state of Myanmar, especially Shan State. Thailand's international ports, likeLaem

Chabang near Pattaya, and Suvarnabhumi International Airport, have seen a number of African and former Commonwealth of Independent States gangs, as well as other transnational gangs and drug mules involved in the trade.

CRIME BY TYPE

Drugs and Druggings

Thailand has a growing problem of drugs and the violence associated with it. The drugs involved range from the traditional, kratom, to ya baa, opium from Myanmar, and local herbal medicines. Since about 2005, a surge of nightlife-inspired party drugs took hold, with increasingly violent behavior exhibited by users. A previous attempt to control the drug trade by declaring the 2003 War on Drugs, was met with allegations of Thaksin-allied, politically-inspired targeted killings, quotas of dead drug traffickers, and the targeting of innocent victims. In 2012, it was estimated that there were some 1.2 million methamphetamine addicts in Thailand, though this number may have been underestimated. Methampetamines are so widely abused that animals, such as gibbons, slow lorises, and elephants are force-fed the stimulants to make them work longer hours, sedated to allow petting and entertain tourists. In May 2012, it was discovered that nearly 50 million legal pseudoephedrine tablets had been stolen from Thai hospitals. Two billion more tablets were smuggled in from Taiwan and South Korea, with forged documents showing two Thai companies importing some eight billion more. They had reported the drugs to be imports of electronics and automobile parts. Thailand responded by close monitoring of the sale and distribution of pseudoephedrine.

Druggings of tourists and locals alike by sex workers and thieves are a rare, but not uncommon, occurrence in major tourist centers like Pattaya or Phuket. A United Nations report on the situation in Thailand states, "Many of those now incarcerated in Thailand's prisons are likely to be low-level traders and drug users, as they are more easy targets for police, rather than large scale traffickers and organised criminals".

Animal Abuse

Animal abuse in Thailand is widespread, including elephants tortured for tourism, killing elephants for their tusks, smuggling them from Myanmar, exploiting elephants in cities, and trading in animal parts.

Rape

In 2013, some 87 women came forward daily to report sexual abuse or to seek counseling as a result of sexual abuse in Thailand, with most offenders known to the victim. Police refused to accept complaints, giving excuses such as "political unrest". The youngest victim was aged one year and nine months and eldest was 85. The youngest offender was a 10-year-old boy who took part in a gang-rape and the eldest was an 85-year-old man who molested a young girl.

Fraud

Thailand as a major tourist destination is infamous for scams and touts. Among the most famous and lucrative are the gem scam, Thai tailor scam, and fake travel agentsand Thai zig zag scam. The boiler room scam (a fake stock trading scam) is perhaps the most publicized white collar crime in Thailand. Stateless persons are targeted with fake UN working rights cards. Serious passport and identification forgery caught the attention of US authorities after the disappearance of Malaysia Airlines Flight 370. Some 259 stolen visa labels had disappeared from a Thai consulate in Malaysia in August 2013. They were used to cross the Thai border illegally. Thirty-five Iranians, one Cameroonian, 20 Nigerians, four Pakistanis, four Indians, and others from Asia made the crossing.

Human Trafficking and Prostitution

In 2013, the US State Department stated that Thailand faced the lowest rank (e.g. failing) in its Trafficking In Persons Report. The 2013 report stated that Thai police and immigration officials "extorted money or sex" from detainees or "sold Burmese migrants unable to pay labor brokers or sex traffickers,". According to officials from theInternational Labour Organisation (ILO), Thailand was the only government to vote against the United Nations Forced Labour Convention at the ILO's annual ministerial conference in June 2014. In response, Walmart and Costco retail chains in USA have dumped Charoen Pokphand as a supplier of seafood products due to suppliers that "own, operate or buy from fishing boats manned with slaves." The Thai government on 15 June 2014 caved to international pressure and explained its intention to rescind its previous ILO vote.

Domestic Violence

Violence against women has been rising in Thailand, some 27,000 victims have been admitted to hospitals in the years of 2007-2012. In 2006, 13,550 cases of domestic violence against women and children were reported by Thailand's Public Health Ministry.

CRIME DYNAMICS

School Violence and Delinquency

Technical colleges for years have seen rival gang shootings at major intersections in Bangkok and elsewhere, and tends to be an urban phenomenon.

In one famous case, one such shootout began in response to Gangnam style faceoff. One technical school student is quoted as saying, "Guns are like school supplies. On our campus, we might use a gun to protect ourselves from violent, unruly seniors. Outside, we have rival schools..." Juvenile delinquency from 2003 to 2007 exploded, increasing some 70 percent, with both genders reporting large increases, despite the country moving up world economic rankings.

Prison Infrastructure and Corruption

Thailand has woefully inadequate prison infrastructure, as well as a lack of political will to deal with the exploding crime problem. In Rayong Central Prison, which was designed to house 3,000 inmates but holds 6,000, improvised rocket canisters were used to relay goods from the outside world over the top of walls into the prison. Mail sent to prisoners contained items such as mobile phones used to coordinate and organize crime outside of the prison. This situation is not unique to Rayong Prison, and is commonplace throughout Thailand.

Corrupt prison officials add to the issues of dealing with escalating crime. In one case, a prison nurse was caught dealing drugs. In a sting operation some 28 prison wardens were found to be smuggling drugs. Authorities are so corrupt or incompetent that females were found in one male cell feeding five babies. Thai authorities have responded by installing mobile phone jamming equipment, but these jammers has been proven to offer a false sense of security, as a wall crack was used to store phones where the jammers could not penetrate. Other initiatives include x-ray scanners, and installing CCTV equipment. A new super-max prison is in the planning stages.

Buddhist Monks

Crime has infiltrated all components of Thai society, including Buddhist institutions. The monastic life offers a veil of legitimacy to criminal organizations. There have been a number of monks in a string of cases in recent years caught with methamphetamines, selling drugs, prostitutes, pornography, and guns, including senior monks. One case involved two monks attempting to ditch speed pills at a police checkpoint. Another case involved a senior monk who claimed he needed money to "refurbish his temple", yet used the money for drugs and sex. Murder by clergy has been reported increasingly. There was even a case of Thai monks killing each other in the United States.

DEATHS OF FOREIGNERS

A number of high-profile Westerners have died in Bangkok hotels including Hollywood actor David Carradine, The director of Tata Motors, Karl Slym, (British), and American businesswoman Wendy Albano.

David Miller and Hannah Witheridge, a backpacking couple from England, were murdered on the island of Ko Tao in 2014. In December 2015 the suspected killers were found guilty.[1] They face execution by lethal injection. Other British backpackers who have been murdered include Jayne Nixon (found dead in a Bangkok hotel) and in another case Kirsty Jones (tourist) was raped and murdered in Chiang Mai. In 2013 an American expat was chopped to death by his Bangkok cabbie with a sword. Murders are frequent enough that one writer produced a book called How Not To Get Murdered In Thailand The author mentions the case of the murdered American Troy Pilkington and noted the contrasting dangers of both taxi cabs and public transportation.

One of the issues with cabbies is their alleged drug use and abuse at the hands of Chinese organized crime network which often charge them high fee to operate in the city. The cabbies are typically poor farmers trying to earn money for their rural families.Whatever the reasons for their demise, indeed many of the deaths are confusing or have unclear causes, Thailand has remained popular for adventures. One young Brit, Christina Annesley, was found dead on Thai's Ko Tao. Musicians at a Thailand bar stabbed an American businessman to death in front of his son, there to celebrate his birthday with his family. Thai police arrested three of the musicians for the crime.

Foreigners have committed crimes against other foreigners in Thailand; for example in the case of Wendy Albano, the chief suspect was an Indian man who fled Thailand. The Thai government has worked with other countries to manage crime and, for example, has a prisoner exchange agreement with Australia.

CRIME IN TURKEY

Crime in Turkey is combated by the Turkish police and other agencies. Since the 1990s, overall crime in Turkey has been rising. As of 2014, Turkey has seen a 400% rise in drug-related crimes, theft and homicide. In 1994, the number of arrested prisoners was recorded as 38,931; 20 years later, as of the beginning of October 2014, the number of prisoners has reached 152,335. According to the data provided by the Ministry of Justice, the crime rate is growing with each passing day. Turkey's rate of murdered women also has skyrocketed. In 2010, the Ministry of Justice revealed the numbers on murdered women: From 2003 until 2010, there has been a 1,400% increase in the number of murdered women.

CRIME BY TYPE

Murder

Honour Killing

A June 2008 report by the Turkish Prime Ministry's Human Rights Directorate said that in Istanbul alone there was one honor killing every week, and reported over 1,000 during the previous five years. It added that metropolitan cities were the location of many of these, due to growing Kurdish immigration to these cities from the East. In 2009 a Turkish news agency reported that a 2-day-old boy who was born out of wedlock had been killed for honor. The maternal grandmother of the infant, along with six other persons, including a doctor who had reportedly accepted a bribe to not report the birth, were arrested. The grandmother is suspected of fatally suffocating the infant. The child's mother, 25, was also arrested; she stated that her family had made the decision to kill the child.

In 2010 a 16-year-old Kurdish girl was buried alive by relatives for befriending boys in Southeast Turkey; her corpse was found 40 days after she went missing. Ahmet Yildiz, 26, a Turkish physics student who represented his country at an international gay conference in the United States in 2008, was shot dead leaving a cafe in Istanbul. It is believed Yildiz was the victim of the country's first gay honor killing. In Turkey, persons found guilty of this crime are sentenced to life in prison. There are well documented cases, where Turkish courts have sentenced whole families to life imprisonment for an honor killing. The most recent was on January 13, 2009, where a Turkish Court sentenced five members of the same Kurdish family to life imprisonment for the honor killing of Naile Erdas, 16, who got pregnant as a result of rape.

Gang Activity

Over the last ten years, 24391 people have been detained by the police and of those 8602 arrested in 3012 operations against gangs. The gendermarie has likewise detained 10437 people, arrested 6269 in 771 operations. Approximately a third of these arrests took place in 2005-7.

VIOLENCE BY AUTHORITIES

Torture

Since the 1980s this issue has been the subject of studies by Amnesty International, Human Rights Watch and the European Committee for the Prevention of Torture, who in 2004 reported "The legislative and regulatory framework necessary to combat effectively torture and other forms of ill-treatment by law enforcement officials has been put in place; the challenge now is to make sure that all of the provisions concerned are given full effect in practice." and Prime Minister Tayyip Erdoðan has declared that there will be "zero tolerance" of torture in Turkey.

Deaths in Custody

There have been a number of rulings against Turkey in the European Court of Human Rights resulting from deaths in custody in the 1990s, a period when this was raised as an issue by Amnesty International, Human Rights Watch and others. and has been the subject of studies by Ba°ar Çolak of Kocaeli University. In an August 2007 incident, Nigerian footballer Festus Okey was shot by the police while being detained in Beyoðlu police station. According to the police he had tried to wrestle the gun from the officer and was shot in the ensuing struggle. The Interior Minister Be°ir Atalay refused to make a statement, saying "Questions are asked everywhere, they don't all get a reply".

CRIME IN THE UNITED ARAB EMIRATES

The crime rate in the United Arab Emirates is relatively low compared to more highly industrialized nations. Incidents of petty crime such as pickpocketing are low. TheUnited States Department of State states: "Crime generally is not a problem for travelers in the UAE. However, the U.S. Embassy advises U.S. citizens to take normal precautions against theft, such as not leaving a wallet, purse, or credit card unattended. Although vehicle break-ins in the UAE are rare, U.S. citizens are encouraged to ensure that unattended vehicles are locked and that valuables are not left out in plain sight".

Sharia law is a significant part of UAE legislation, therefore flogging and stoning are legal punishments in the UAE. UAE incorporates hudud crimes of Sharia in its Penal Code, thus apostasy is a crime punishable by death in the UAE. Homosexuality is also a crime punishable by death in the UAE, although there have not been any cases of capital punishment being carried out on those convicted of homosexuality.

SHARIA LAW

The UAE's judicial system is derived from the civil law system and Sharia law. The court system consists of civil courts and Sharia courts. According to Human Rights Watch, UAE's civil and criminal courts apply elements of Sharia law, codified into its criminal code and family law, in a way which discriminates against women. Flogging and stoningare legal punishments in the UAE.

Flogging is a punishment for criminal offences such as adultery, premarital sex and alcohol consumption. Due to Sharia courts, flogging is legal with sentences ranging from 80 to 200 lashes. Between 2007 and 2014, many people in the UAE were sentenced to 100 lashes. In Abu Dhabi, people have been sentenced to 80 lashes for kissing in public. Verbal abuse pertaining to a person's sexual honour is illegal and punishable by 80 lashes. In January 2014, an expat in Abu Dhabi was sentenced to 80 lashes and 10 years in prison for alcohol consumption and raping a toddler. Alcohol consumption for Muslims is illegal and punishable by 80 lashes, many Muslims have been sentenced to 80 lashes for alcohol consumption. 80 lashes is the standard amount for anyone sentenced to flogging in some emirates. Sometimes 40 lashes are given. Illicit sex is sometimes penalized by 60 lashes. Sharia courts have penalized domestic workers with floggings.In October 2013, a Filipino housemaid was sentenced to 100 lashes for illegitimate pregnancy. Drunk-driving is strictly illegal and punishable by 80 lashes, many expats have been sentenced to 80 lashes for drunk-driving. Under UAE law, premarital sex is punishable by 100 lashes.

Stoning is a legal punishment in the UAE. In May 2014, an Asian housemaid was sentenced to death by stoning in Abu Dhabi, although a judicial official notes, "Abu Dhabi Criminal Court has previously sentenced defendants in similar cases to death by stoning, but the sentences were never carried out". In 2006, an expatriate was sentenced to death by stoning for committing adultery. Between 2009 and 2013, several people were sentenced to death by stoning. Abortion is illegal and punishable by a maximum penalty of 100 lashes and up to five years in prison.

In recent years, several people have retracted their guilty plea in illicit sex cases after being sentenced to stoning or 100 lashes. The punishment for committing adultery is 100 lashes for unmarried people and stoning to death for married people.

Sharia law dictates the personal status law, which regulate matters such as marriage, divorce and child custody. The Sharia-based personal status law is applied to Muslims and sometimes non-Muslims. Non-Muslim expatriates are liable to Sharia rulings on marriage, divorce and child custody. Sharia courts have exclusive jurisdiction to hear family disputes, including matters involving divorce, inheritances, child custody, child abuse and guardianship of minors. Sharia courts may also hear appeals of certain criminal cases including rape, robbery, driving under the influence of alcohol and related crimes.

Apostasy is a crime punishable by death in the UAE. UAE incorporates hudud crimes of Sharia into its Penal Code - apostasy being one of them. Article 1 and Article 66 of UAE's Penal Code requires hudud crimes to be punished with the death penalty, therefore apostasy is punishable by death in the UAE. Emirati women must receive permission from male guardian to remarry. The requirement is derived from Sharia, and has been federal law since 2005. In all emirates, it is illegal for Muslim women to marry non-Muslims. In the UAE, a marriage union between a Muslim woman and non-Muslim man is punishable by law, since it is considered a form of "fornication".

Homosexuality is illegal: the death penalty is one of the punishments for homosexuality. Article 80 of the Abu Dhabi Penal Code makes sodomy punishable with imprisonment of up to 14 years, while article 177 of the Penal Code of Dubai imposes imprisonment of up to 10 years on consensual sodomy. Kissing in public is strictly illegal and can result in deportation. Expats in Dubai have been deported for kissing in public. More recently in 2010, several expats were deported from Dubai for kissing in public. Article 1 of the Federal Penal Code states that "provisions of the Islamic Law shall apply to the crimes of doctrinal punishment, punitive punishment and blood money." The Federal Penal Code repealed only those provisions within the penal codes of individual emirates which are contradictory to the Federal Penal Code. Hence, both are enforceable simultaneously.

TERRORISM

The threat of a terrorist attack is a matter of concern. The Department of Foreign Affairs and Trade (DFAT) of the Government of Australia advised travelers "to exercise a high degree of caution in the United Arab Emirates (UAE) because of the high threat of terrorist attack". The DFAT claimed they received reports of a terrorist plan to attack Western interests in the nation. The Australian Government has since lowered the warning, telling travellers to now exercise normal safety precautions, as they would do in Australia.

CYBERCRIME

Incidents of cybercrime are increasing. In 2002, there was a 300% rise in computer hacking within six months. According to experts, the United Arab Emirates is among the top ten countries which are most vulnerable to attack by hackers. White-collar crime includes embezzlement of funds, fraud and bribery.

DRUGS

The UAE is a drug transshipment country for traffickers due to its proximity to Southwest Asian drug producing nations. Drug trafficking is a major form of crime in the UAE,and the nation has a zero tolerance policy towards illegal drug use. Possession of the smallest amount of illegal drugs is punishable by a minimum of four years' imprisonment.

MONEY LAUNDERING

The UAE is vulnerable to money laundering due to its position as a major commercial driver in the region. The UAE leadership has taken several measures for combatingorganized crime. A law was enacted in January 2002 for the purpose of curbing money laundering. However, despite government efforts to combat money laundering, regulation of banking is still developing.

MURDER

According to the Global Study on Homicide, United Nations Office on Drugs and Crime (UNODC), the homicide rate in the UAE in 2012 was 2.6 per 100,000. The average global homicide rate for that period was 6.2 per 100,000 population.

HUMAN TRAFFICKING

Human trafficking is a problem which involves involuntary servitude of young boys and women. In 2006, young boys were trafficked into the country for the purpose of being used as camel jockeys. There were many camel jockeys working in the UAE under inhumane conditions but these have now been replaced by robot jockeys. Human trafficking cases in the UAE have been falling over the years. In the first half of 2014, three cases of human trafficking were received by the Dubai Foundation for Women and Children (DFWAC) compared to 12 in the same period of 2013.

PROSTITUTION

Women are trafficked into the country for sexual exploitation. Women from Russia, Azerbaijan, Uzbekistan, Kyrgyzstan, Kazakhstan, Ukraine, Ethiopia, Somalia, Uganda,Morocco, India, Pakistan, the People's Republic of China, the Philippines, Iraq and Iran are reportedly trafficked to the UAE. Porous borders and proximity to war-affected countries like Iraq increase the problem of human trafficking.

CRIME IN VIETNAM

Crime is present in various forms in Vietnam.

CRIMES AGAINST FOREIGNERS IN VIETNAM

Petty crime, which includes pick-pocketing and snatch theft, is a problem in Vietnam. Traveling alone in remote areas after dark is of risk especially to foreigners. Violent crime is a growing issue; most cases of it are reported in the more developed areas of the country, such as Hanoi. Scams are common in the country, and foreign travellers have reported getting raped on fake motorcycle taxis (xe ôm) passed off as real ones. Confidence tricks are a fair sight in the country; often do foreigners receive invitations to somebody else's residence to have a "casual game", which then escalates into a high-stakes match. Counterfeit and pirated merchandise can be easily found in many areas of Vietnam.

CRIMES AGAINST WOMEN IN VIETNAM

Prostitution is against the law in Vietnam. Nevertheless, many women in the country are prostitutes, either willingly or unwillingly. As many females in the country are stricken with poverty, selling their body is deemed as one of, if not the only, option for them. One source estimates the number of prostitutes in Vietnam to be 20,000 to 70,000.

CORRUPTION AND POLICE MISCONDUCT

The Vietnamese government is making an effort to curb corruption in the country. A handful of corrupt individuals, ranging from law enforcers to politicians, have been arrested. The police force in Vietnam is known to go overboard and there have been reports of the police assaulting unarmed individuals. In July 23, while in detainment for a small offense (helmetless driving of motorcycle), 21-year-old Nguyen Van Khuong ultimately lost his life when officers reportedly physically attacked him. The misuse of ferocity has raised concerns from the Human Rights Watch.

CRIME IN YEMEN

Crime is present in various forms in Yemen.

CRIMES AGAINST FOREIGNERS IN YEMEN

There are many instances of crimes against foreigners in Yemen. This includes petty crime and violent crime, both of which usually happen in locations with many people. One serious instance of violent crime against foreigners in Yemen would be the 2008 attack on the American Embassy in Yemen, in Sana'a, Yemen on September 17, 2008, which ultimately resulted in the loss of nineteen lives and 16 injuries. The state of Yemen as it is currently has forced its citizens to commit crimes against one another and foreigners. Fake merchandise can be easily found in Yemen.

CRIMES AGAINST WOMEN IN YEMEN

Prostitution

Prostitution is a significant and growing issue in Yemen. While it is officially illegal, many sex tourists from other gulf states indulge in what are known as "tourist marriages".Prostitutes can also be found in select nightclubs. The punishment for prostitution in the country is 3 years of imprisonment. As many people in Yemen are stricken with poverty, children are often sold off by their parents as prostitutes. Despite the high rate of prostitution in the country, the government has instead chosen to assign its efforts onpart of the War on Terror, and this issue is largely ignored.

Corruption and Police Misconduct

According to the United States Department of State, "[l]ocal police forces are largely unaccountable", and there are known cases of corruption in the Yemeni police force. Law enforcement in the country is said to be lousy, and both the police and the government in Yemen are deemed to be unworthy of trust. Very often do law enforcers in the country abuse their authority to allow others to evade tax or get away with minor or major offences, provided some paper certificates are exchanged for the favour. Corruption in the country burns a big hole in the government's pocket.

2

Organized Crime Groups in Asia

TRIAD (ORGANIZED CRIME)

A triad is one of many branches of Chinese transnational organized crime organizations based in Hong Kong, Macau, Taiwan and also in countries with significant Chinese populations, such as the United States, Canada, Vietnam, Japan, Singapore, Philippines,Indonesia, Malaysia, Thailand, the United Kingdom, Belgium, Netherlands, France, Spain, South Africa, Australia and New Zealand.

ETYMOLOGY

The term "Triad" was assumed to be coined by British authorities in colonial Hong Kong, as a reference to the triads' use of triangular imagery. While never proven, it has been speculated that triad organizations either took after, or were originally part of revolutionary movements such as the White Lotus Society, theTaiping Rebellion, the Boxer Rebellion, and the Heaven and Earth Society.

HISTORY

Origins

18th Century

In the 1760s, the Heaven and Earth Society, a fraternal organization, was founded, and as the society's influence spread throughout China, it branched into several smaller groups with different names, one of which was Three Harmonies Society. These societies adopted the triangle as their emblem, usually accompanied by decorative images of swords or portraits of Guan Yu. Their aim was to overthrow the Qing Dynasty and restore the Ming Dynasty.

19th Century

In Hong Kong as a colony of the Crown, there was a strong intolerance for secret societies. While being unaware of their previous issues the British considered Triads a criminal threat. Triads were charged and imprisoned in Hong Kong which was under British law at that time.

During the 1800s, many such societies were seen as legitimate ways of helping immigrants from China settle into a new country. Secret societies were officially banned by the British government in Singapore during the 1890s and slowly reduced in number by successive colonial governors and leaders over time. Tracing the origins of Singapore gangs, the opium trade, prostitution and brothels were also banned. Immigrants were encouraged to seek help from a local kongsi instead of turning to secret societies, which also contributed to their decline. After World War II, these societies saw a resurgence as gangsters took advantage of the uncertainty and growing anti-British sentiment. Certain Chinese communities, such as some "new villages" of Kuala Lumpur and Bukit Ho Swee in Singapore became notorious for gang violence.

20th Century

When the Chinese Communist Party came to power in 1949 in mainland China, law enforcement became stricter and tough governmental crackdown on criminal organizations forced the triads to migrate to Hong Kong, then a British colony. It was estimated that in the 1950s, there were about 300,000 triad members in Hong Kong. Academics at the University of Hong Kong say that most triad societies were established between 1914 and 1939, and that there were once more than 300 in the territory. Since then the number of such groups has consolidated to around 50, of which 14 are still regularly in the eye of police. There were nine main triads operating in Hong Kong and they had divided the land according to their ethnic groups and geographical locations, with each triad in charge of a region. The nine triads were Wo Hop To, Wo Shing Wo, Rung, Tung, Chuen, Shing, Sun Yee On, 14K and Luen. Each of them had their own headquarters, sub-societies and public fronts. After the 1956 riots, the Hong Kong government introduced stricter law enforcement and the triads became less active.

CRIMINALACTIVITIES

Triads currently engage in a variety of crimes from extortion and money laundering to trafficking and prostitution. They also are involved in smuggling and counterfeiting goodssuch as music, video, and software as well as more tangible goods such as clothes, watches, and money.

Drug Trafficking

Since the 19th century, when the first opium bans started to rise, Chinese criminal gangs have been involved in worldwide illegal drug trade. During the 60s and 70s many triads converted from opium into heroin, which was produced from opium plants in the Golden Triangle and made into heroin in China, and then trafficked to North America and Europe. Nowadays the most important triads active in the international heroin trade are the 14K and the Tai Huen Chai. Recently, the triads have started to smuggle chemicals from Chinese factories to North America, for the production of methamphetamine, and to Europe for the production of ecstasy.

Counterfeiting

Triads have been engaging in counterfeiting since the 1880s. Between the 1960s and 1970s, triads were involved in counterfeiting currency, often of the Hong Kong 50-cent piece. In the same decade, the gangs were also involved in copying books, usually expensive ones, and selling them in the black market. With the advent of new technology and the improvement of the average person's standard of living, triads have progressed to producing counterfeit goods such as watches, film VCDs / DVDs and designer apparel such as clothing and handbags. Since the 1970s, triad turf control was weakened and some triads shifted their revenue streams to underground as well as legitimate businesses.

Health Care Fraud

In 2012 in Japan, four triad members were found conducting operations regarding health care fraud and arrested.

STRUCTURE AND COMPOSITION

Triads use numeric codes to distinguish between ranks and positions within the gang; the numbers are inspired by Chinese numerology based on the I Ching."489" refers to the "Mountain" or "Dragon" Master (or 'Dragon Head'), while 438 is used for the "Deputy Mountain Master", a "438" indicates "Grass Slipper" rankand the Mountain Master's proxy, "Incense Master", who oversees inductions into the Triad, and "Vanguard", who assists the Incense Master.

"426" refers to a "military commander", also known as a "Red Pole", overseeing defensive and offensive operations, while "49" denotes the position of "soldier" or rank-and-file member. The "White Paper Fan" (415) provides financial and business advice, and the "Straw Sandal" (432) functions as a liaison between different units. "25" refers to an undercover law enforcement agent or spy from another triad, and has become popularly used in Hong Kong as a slang for "snitch", i.e. informant. "Blue Lanterns" are uninitiated members, equivalent to Mafia associates and, as such, do not have a number designation.

RITUALS AND CODES OF CONDUCT

Initiation

Similar to the Italian mafia or the Japanese yakuza, Triad members tend to be subject to initiation ceremonies. A typical ceremony takes place at an altar dedicated to Guan Yu, with incense and an animal sacrifice, usually a chicken, pig or goat. After drinking a mixture of wine and blood of the animal or the candidate, the member will pass beneath an arch of swords while reciting the triad's oaths. The paper on which the oaths are written will be burnt on the altar to confirm the member's obligation to perform his duties to the gods. Three fingers on the left hand will be raised as a binding gesture.

36 Oaths

The Triad initiate is required to adhere to "the 36 oaths."

After having entered the Hung gates I must treat the parents and relatives of my sworn brothers as my own kin. I shall suffer death by five thunderbolts if I do not keep this oath.

I shall assist my sworn brothers to bury their parents and brothers by offering financial or physical assistance. I shall be killed by five thunderbolts if I pretend to have no knowledge of their troubles.

When Hung brothers visit my house, I shall provide them with board and lodging. I shall be killed by myriads of knives if I treat them as strangers.

I will always acknowledge my Hung brothers when they identify themselves. If I ignore them I will be killed by myriads of swords.

I shall not disclose the secrets of the Hung family, not even to my parents, brothers, or wife. I shall never disclose the secrets for money. I will be killed by myriads of swords if I do so.

I shall never betray my sworn brothers. If, through a misunderstanding, I have caused the arrest of one of my brothers I must release him immediately. If I break this oath I will be killed by five thunderbolts.

I will offer financial assistance to sworn brothers who are in trouble in order that they may pay their passage fee, etc. If I break this oath I will be killed by five thunderbolts.

I must never cause harm or bring trouble to my sworn brothers or Incense Master. If I do so I will be killed by myriads of swords.

I must never commit any indecent assaults on the wives, sisters, or daughters, of my sworn brothers. I shall be killed by five thunderbolts if I break this oath.

I shall never embezzle cash or property from my sworn brothers. If I break this oath I will be killed by myriads of swords.

I will take good care of the wives or children of sworn brothers entrusted to my keeping. If I do not I will be killed by five thunderbolts.

If I have supplied false particulars about myself for the purpose of joining the Hung family I shall be killed by five thunderbolts.

If I should change my mind and deny my membership of the Hung family I will be killed by myriads of swords.

If I rob a sworn brother or assist an outsider to do so I will be killed by five thunderbolts. If I should take advantage of a sworn brother or force unfair business deals upon him I will be killed by myriads of swords.

If I knowingly convert my sworn brother's cash or property to my own use I shall be killed by five thunderbolts.

If I have wrongly taken a sworn brother's cash or property during a robbery I must return them to him. If I do not I will be killed by five thunderbolts.

If I am arrested after committing an offence I must accept my punishment and not try to place blame on my sworn brothers. If I do so I will be killed by five thunderbolts. If any of my sworn brothers are killed, or arrested, or have departed to some other place, I will assist their wives and children who may be in need. If I pretend to have no knowledge of their difficulties I will be killed by five thunderbolts.

When any of my sworn brothers have been assaulted or blamed by others, I must come forward and help him if he is in the right or advise him to desist if he is wrong. If he has been repeatedly insulted by others I shall inform our other brothers and arrange to help him physically or financially. If I do not keep this oath I will be killed by five thunderbolts.

If it comes to my knowledge that the Government is seeking any of my sworn brothers who has come from other provinces or from overseas, I shall immediately inform him in order that he may make his escape. If I break this oath I will be killed by five thunderbolts.

I must not conspire with outsiders to cheat my sworn brothers at gambling. If I do so I will be killed by myriads of swords.

I shall not cause discord amongst my sworn brothers by spreading false reports about any of them. If I do so I will be killed by myriads of swords.

I shall not appoint myself as Incense Master without authority. After entering the Hung gates for three years the loyal and faithful ones may be promoted by the Incense Master with the support of his sworn brothers. I shall be killed by five thunderbolts if I make any unauthorized promotions myself.

If my natural brothers are involved in a dispute or lawsuit with my sworn brothers I must not help either party against the other but must attempt to have the matter settled amicably. If I break this oath I will be killed by five thunderbolts. After entering the Hung gates I must forget any previous grudges I may have borne against my sworn brothers. If I do not do so I will be killed by five thunderbolts.

I must not trespass upon the territory occupied by my sworn brothers. I shall be killed by five thunderbolts if I pretend to have no knowledge of my brothers' rights in such matters.

I must not covet or seek to share any property or cash obtained by my sworn brothers. If I have such ideas I will be killed.

I must not disclose any address where my sworn brothers keep their wealth nor must I conspire to make wrong use of such knowledge. If I do so I will be killed by myriads of swords. I must not give support to outsiders if so doing is against the interests of any of my sworn brothers. If I do not keep this oath I will be killed by myriads of swords. I must not take advantage of the Hung brotherhood in order to oppress or take violent or unreasonable advantage of others. I must be content and honest. If I break this oath I will be killed by five thunderbolts.

I shall be killed by five thunderbolts if I behave indecently towards small children of my sworn brothers' families.

If any of my sworn brothers has committed a big offence I must not inform upon them to the Government for the purposes of obtaining a reward. I shall be killed by five thunderbolts if I break this oath.

I must not take to myself the wives and concubines of my sworn brothers nor commit adultery with them. If I do so I will be killed by myriads of swords.

I must never reveal Hung secrets or signs when speaking to outsiders. If I do so I will be killed by myriads of swords.

After entering the Hung gates I shall be loyal and faithful and shall endeavour to overthrow Ch'ing and restore Ming by co-ordinating my efforts with those of my sworn brethren even though my brethren and I may not be in the same professions. Our common aim is to avenge our Five Ancestors.

CURRENT CLANS

Triads Based in Hong Kong

These are the triad organizations with the most power, money and influence, also worldwide. There are almost fifty triads based in Hong Kong. *The following are the most powerful:*

- 14K
- Sun Yee On
- Tai Huen Chai
- Wo Shing Wo
- Shui Fong
- Wo Hop To
- Luen Group
- Rung Group
- Tung Group
- Chuen Group
- Shing Group

Triads Based Elsewhere

Because of immigration many criminal organizations were founded in Taiwan, ROC as well as Chinese communities internationally:

- Bamboo Union, Taiwan
- Four Seas Gang, Taiwan
- Lo Fu-chu, Taiwan

- Sio Sam Ong, Malaysia
- Ang Soon Tong, Singapore
- Wah Kee, Singapore
- Salakau,Singapore
- Ghee Hin Kongsi, Singapore
- Wah Ching, San Francisco
- Black Dragons, Los Angeles
- Flying Dragons, New York City
- Born to Kill, New York City
- Ah Kong, Amsterdam
- Black Jade, Texas

Tongs

Tongs are similar to triads except that they originated among early immigrant Chinatown communities independently, rather than as extensions of modern triads. The word literally means "social club," and Tongs are not specifically underground organizations. The first Tongs formed in the second half of the 19th century among the more marginalized members of early immigrant Chinese American communities for mutual support and protection from nativists.

These Tongs modeled themselves on triads, but they were established without clear political motives, yet they become involved in criminal activities such as extortion, illegal gambling, drug trafficking, human trafficking, murder and prostitution. In recent years, some Tongs have reformed to eliminate their criminal elements and have become civic-minded organizations.

Southeast

Triad activities were also present in Chinese communities around Southeast Asia. When Malaysia and Singapore, which have the region's largest population of ethnic Chinese, first became Crown Colonies, secret societies and triads were much more common and controlled the local communities similar to the way the Sicilian Mafia did through extortion of "protection money" and illegal money lending. Many conducted blood rituals such as drinking one another's blood as a sign of brotherhood, while others engaged in running opium dens and brothels.

Remnants of these former gangs and societies still exist. Due to the efforts of the government in both countries to reduce crime, such societies have largely faded away from the public eye, especially in Singapore.

Triads were also common in Vietnamese cities with large Chinese (in particular Cantonese and Teochew) communities. Especially during Vietnam's French colonial period, many businesses and wealthy residents in Saigon (especially in the Chinatown district) and Haiphong were under the tutelage and control of various protection racket gangs. Failure to provide such payments often result in various reprisals from the triad, ranging from assault, kidnapping for ransom, destruction of property, robbery and even murder of the client or a family member.

However, with the arrival of Vietnamese independence in 1945 (in the North) and 1955 (in the South), organized crime activity, including protection rackets, was drastically reduced as both the Northern and Southern governments purged criminal activity in their halves of the country. President Ngô Đình Di-m in the South ordered the military to eliminate, disarm, and imprison organized crime groups in the Saigon-Gia Đ-nh-Biên Hòa- Vi´ng Tàu region and in cities like M Tho and C n Thõ in the Mekong Delta. Diem also banned brothels, massage parlours, casinos and gambling houses, opium dens, bars, drug houses and nightclubs (which are all establishments triads frequented). In the North under Ho Chi Minh, law enforcement was even stricter with stringent control and monitoring in the activities of its citizens. The Northern communist government purged and imprisoned organized criminals, including triads, in the Haiphong and Hanoi areas, along with shutting down businesses which it viewed as "capitalist", "Western" or "decadent" while collectivizing and nationalizing all other private businesses and properties.

International Activities

Triads are also active in other regions with significant overseas Chinese populations: Macau, Taiwan, Hong Kong Triads and countries such as the United States, Canada, Japan, Australia, the United Kingdom, Germany, France, Italy, Brazil, Peru and Argentina. They are often involved in helping immigrants enter countries illegally. Shanty & Mishra (2007) estimate that annual profits from narcotics is $200 billion; revenues from human trafficking into Europe and the United States are believed to amount to $3.5 billion per year.

TRIAD COUNTERMEASURES

Law Enforcement Means

The Organized Crime and Triad Bureau (OCTB) is a division within the Hong Kong Police Force that is responsible for triad countermeasures. The OCTB and Criminal Intelligence Bureau work together with the Narcotics Bureau and Commercial Crime Bureau to process data and information collected by their operation units to counter triad leaders. Other departments involved in countering triad activities include Customs and Excise Department, Immigration Department and ICAC. They cooperate with the police to impede triads' expansions and other organized gangs. Police actions regularly target organised crime, including raids on entertaining establishments under control of triads, and the placing of operatives deep undercover – this was the central theme to the Infernal Affairs trilogy.

Canada

The Guns and Gangs Unit of the Toronto Police Service is a specialized command detective unit that is responsible for handling triads. Formerly the Asian Gang Unit of the Metro Toronto Police was responsible for dealing with triad related matters, but a larger unit was created to deal with the broader array of ethnic gangs in the city. At the national (and in some cases provincial) level, the Royal Canadian Mounted Police's Organized Crime Branch is responsible for investigating all gang related activities including triads. The Canada Border Services Agency Organized Crime units works with the RCMP to detain and remove non-Canadian triad members. Asian organized gangs are found in many cities, primarily in Toronto, Vancouver, Calgary, and Edmonton.

The Organized Crime and Law Enforcement Act was created to deal with organized crime and gives a tool for police forces in Canada to handle organized criminal activities. This Act enhances the general role of the Criminal Code (with amendments to deal with organized crime) in dealing with triad criminal activities. Asian organized crime groups were ranked the fourth most organized crime problems in Canada next to Outlaw motorcycle clubs, Aboriginal crime groups, and Indo Canadian crime groups. As of 2011, it was estimated that criminal gangs associated with triads controlled 90% of the heroin trade in Vancouver. Due to its geographic as well as demographic characteristics, Vancouver is the point of entry into North America for much of the heroin produced in Southeast Asia, much of the trade being controlled by international organized crime groups associated with the triads. From 2006 to 2014 both Asians (Southeast Asians/East Asians) and South Asians constituted for 21% of gang deaths in British Columbia only behind Caucasians who represented 46.3% of gang deaths.

Legislative measures

Primary laws in addressing the triad problem are the Societies Ordinance and the Organized & Serious Crimes Ordinance. The former was enacted in 1949 to outlaw triads in Hong Kong. It stipulates that any person convicted of professing or claiming to be an office bearer or managing or assisting in the management of a triad can be fined up to HK$1 million and a prison term of up to 15 years.

Since the 1970s, the power of triads has further diminished due to the establishment of the Independent Commission Against Corruption in 1974. The agency targeted brazen corruption within police ranks linked with triads. Being a member of a triad is already an offence punishable by fines ranging from HK$100,000 to HK$250,000 and three to seven years imprisonment under an ordinance enacted in Hong Kong in 1994, and aims to provide the police with special investigative powers, to provide heavier penalties for organized crime activities and to authorize the courts to confiscate the proceeds of such crimes.

ORGANISED CRIME IN INDIA

Organised crime in India is a reference to organised crime elements originating in India and active in many parts of the world. The mafia is involved in many criminal activities based in India and international as well. The Mafia may also refers to those powerful families that have criminal aspects to them.

D-COMPANY

D-Company is the name given to the organised crime group controlled by Dawood Ibrahim. It has been argued that the D-Company is not a stereotypical organised crime cartel in the strict sense of the word, but rather a collusion of sole criminal and terrorist groups based around Dawood Ibrahim's personal.

PUNJABI MAFIA

Punjabi mafia originates in Punjab, India. They operate in Germany, Canada, New York, New Jersey, Virginia and the UK. A major form of Indian organised crime are the foreign-based, Indian-Canadian criminal organisations, the vast majority of them being of Punjabi origin from the Jat Sikhcommunity, whose exploits have led to over 100 gang deaths of young men of Punjabi descent in the Canada since the 1990s. Indo-Canadian gangs are one of Canada's major organised crime problems, ranked third behind motorcycle clubs and Aboriginal criminal groups. These criminal organisations are mainly active in the provinces of British Columbia.

PATHAN MAFIA

The Pathan mafia, a term coined by Mumbai law enforcement because of the majority of the crime syndicate's members were ethnic Pashtuns that immigrated from theAfghanistan's Kunar province, dominated organised crime in Mumbai from the 1940s till the 1980s. In the beginning they were led by Karim Lala, who's often called the founder of the Mumbai mafia, and operated in the Mumbai docks. They were especially involved in hashish trafficking, protection rackets, extortion, illegal gambling, gold smuggling andcontract killing and held a firm stranglehold over Mumbai's underworld.

The Pathan mafia's reign ended when the elderly Karim Lala was replaced by his nephew and a myriad of younger gang members. The monopoly of the Pathans was challenged by a crime syndicate composed of local Indian gangsters led by ambitious Dawood Ibrahim, the later founder of the D-Company. This led to vicious gang wars in the 1980s with casualties on both sides, but which eventually ended the complete control over the Mumbai underworld of the Pathan mafia. The crime syndicate however is till active and still has a certain degree of influence in the city, albeit on a much smaller scale it used to have. They allegedly also have stakes in real estate which still occasionally brings them into conflict with the Indian gangs in the city.

Unrelated to the historical mafia in Mumbai, Pathan criminal organisations have also appeared in Europe. Cities such as Birmingham in the UK and Hamburg in Germany are the most notable ones. Especially in Hamburg, Afghan criminal organisations are active in hashish trafficking, protection rackets and Extortion and have directly rivalled the traditional underworld dominance of Albanian and Turkish-Kurdish gangs in the city.

ACTIVITIES

India is a major transit point for heroin from the Golden Triangle and Golden Crescent en route to Europe. India is also the world's largest legal grower of opium, and experts estimate that 5–10% of the legal opium is converted into illegal heroin and 8–10% is consumed in high quantities as concentrated liquid. The pharmaceutical industry is also responsible for a lot of illegal production of mandrax, much of which is smuggled into South Africa. Diamond smuggling via South Africa is also a major criminal activity, and diamonds are also sometimes used to disguise shipments of heroin. Finally, a lot of money laundering takes place in the country, mostly through the use of the traditional hawalasystem, although India has criminalised money laundering as of 2003.

ISRAELI MAFIA

The Israeli mafia is the general term for organized crime groups operating in Israel and also internationally. Allegedly there are 16 crime families operating in Israel, five major groups active on the national level, and 11 smaller organizations.

There are reputed to be six Maghrebi Jewish crime families active and three Arab crime families. Many heads and members of the crime groups have either been killed or are in prison.

ORGANIZED CRIME IN ISRAEL

The major crime groups are the Abergils, the Abutbuls, the Alperons, the Dumranis, the Shirazis, the Amir Molnar and Zeev Rosenstein syndicates. *The illegal activities they are engaged in include:*

- Operating casinos and other forms of gambling inside and outside Israel
- Car theft and smuggling
- Prostitution
- Drug trafficking
- Human trafficking
- Money Laundering
- Protection and extortion rackets
- Loan sharking
- Drugs and arms dealing

- Fencing stolen goods
- Diamond smuggling

According to Israel's former Police Commissioner David Cohen, Israeli crime organizations had penetrated the formal economic sector and local governments, and "equipped themselves with large quantities of combat means explosives and arms." In a mob war starting in the early 2000s between the crime families, several crime bosses were killed. It also cost the life of innocent bystanders. The Iakhbal is the Israeli Special Police Unit that fights organized crime.

Ex-Soviet Organized Crime

Ex-Soviet organized crime in Israel began with the mass immigration of Russian Jews to Israel in 1989. The Russian mafia saw Israel as an ideal place to launder money, as Israel's banking system was designed to encourage aliyah, the immigration of Jews, and the accompanying capital. Following the trend of global financial deregulation, Israel had also implemented legislation aimed at easing the movement of capital.

Combined with the lack of anti-money laundering legislation, "Russian" organised crime found it an easy place to transfer ill-gotten gains. In 2005, police estimated that Russian organised crime had laundered between $5 and 10 billion in the fifteen years since the end of the Soviet Union. Even non-Jewish criminals such as Sergei Mikhailov sought to get Israeli passports, using fake Jewish documentation.

Russian and Ukrainian Jewish criminals have also been able to set up networks in the USA, following the large migration of Russian Jews to New York and Miami, but also in European cities such as Berlin and Antwerp. Many of these Russian gangsters have Israeli passports as well. Infamous Russian-Jewish mobsters include Marat Balagula,Evsei Agron and their respective criminal gangs in the USA.

In Europe Semyon Mogilevich and Boris Nayfeld are well-known crime bosses, among others. Soviet-Jewish criminal groups in the USA are involved in racketeering, prostitution, drug trafficking, extortion, and gasoline fraud as well as murder.

Georgian-Jewish Organized Crime

Outside of said criminal organizations consisting of Russian and Ukrainian Jews, family-based organized crime groups were formed among Georgian Jewish immigrants as well. Georgian-Jewish crime families have been able to expand their operations to Western European cities such as Antwerp. They are involved in counterfeiting, fraud, money laundering, drug trafficking, weapon trafficking, prostitution and armed robbery. Such was the case with the Georgian-Jewish Melikhov clan in Antwerp.

North-African Crime Families

The immigration of Egyptian and Moroccan Jews to Israel and their settlement in the more impoverished neighborhoods led to the creation of crime families among Maghrebi Jews as well. This is evident in the fact that a large number of Israeli organized criminals have fled to Morocco in recent years. Israeli crime families of Moroccan Jewishdescent expanded their operations to Europe and the USA, especially with their involvement in drug trafficking. Some of Israel's more well-known crime families are of North African Jewish descent: the Abergil crime family as well as the Abutbul and Domrani clans are originally from Morocco, the Alperon clan came from Egypt, and the Shirazi clan from Iran.

Palestinian Organized Crime

Apart from the largely ex-Soviet and North African Jewish crime families, Palestinian organized crime groups (a fair amount are in fact of Bedouin descent) were formed as well. It is alleged that several Palestinian villages are home to local crime families, the most famous of them being the Doghmush clan. Palestinian crime families are involved in extortion, drug and weapon trafficking, fraud as well as money laundering, often in cooperation with their Jewish counterparts. Palestinian criminals are internationally active as well. An example was the criminal gang around Moussa Aliyan in New York whose main business was the importation of heroin.

IN THE UNITED STATES

In the 1980s Israelis set up a crime syndicate headed by Johnny Attias in New York, dubbed the "Israeli mafia". It pulled off the biggest gold heist in the history of Manhattan's jewelry district, getting away with over $4 million in gold jewelry. Attias was murdered in January 1990, and New York's Israeli mafia fell apart soon after. Several members among them Ron Gonen had turned informant and the authorities arrested the rest of the gang in September of that year.

Israeli crime organizations such as the Abergil crime family and Zeev Rosenstein are heavily involved in ecstasy trafficking in the United States. In a statement before Congress in 2000, officials with the U.S. Customs Service noted that "Israeli organized-crime elements appear to be in control" of the multibillion-dollar U.S. ecstasy trade, "from production through the international smuggling phase". The main drug supplier of former Gambino crime family underboss Sammy Gravano in his Arizona drug ring allegedly was New York based Israeli mobster Ilan Zarger, who allegedly distributed more than one million ecstasy pills from May 1999 to May 2000 with a wholesale value of $7 million. He pleaded guilty to charges of running a drug gang that flooded Arizona and New York with almost four million ecstasy pills over three years. Another

Israeli, Oded Tuito, said to head one of the largest ecstasy-smuggling organization, which imported millions of ecstasy pills from Paris, Brussels and Frankfurt into New York, Miami and Los Angeles, was arrested in May 2001.

In 2006 Zeev Rosenstein was extradited to the U.S., after being arrested in Israel. He pleaded guilty before a federal court in Florida to charges that he distributed ecstasy pills and was sentenced to 12 years in prison which he serves in Israel. In January 2011, Itzhak (Itzik) Abergil and Meir Abergil and three other suspects were extradited to the U.S. They are facing a 77-page, 32-count federal indictment that alleges murder, massive embezzlement, money laundering, racketeering and running a large Los Angeles-based ecstasy ring. The trial is set for November 8, 2011 in the Los Angeles Federal District Court.

YAKUZA

Yakuza , also known as gokudô, are members of transnational organized crime syndicates originating inJapan. The Japanese police, and media by request of the police, call them bôryokudan, while the yakuza call themselves "ninkyô dantai". The yakuza are notorious for their strict codes of conduct and organized nature. They have a large presence in the Japanese media and operate internationally with an estimated 102,000 members.

DIVISIONS OF ORIGIN

Despite uncertainty about the single origin of yakuza organizations, most modern yakuza derive from two classifications which emerged in the mid-Edo Period (1603–1868):tekiya, those who primarily peddled illicit, stolen or shoddy goods; and bakuto, those who were involved in or participated in gambling. "Tekiya" (peddlers) were considered one of the lowest social groups in Edo. As they began to form organizations of their own, they took over some administrative duties relating to commerce, such as stall allocation and protection of their commercial activities. During Shinto festivals, these peddlers opened stalls and some members were hired to act as security. Each peddler paid rent in exchange for a stall assignment and protection during the fair.

The Edo government eventually formally recognized such tekiya organizations and granted the oyabun (leaders) of tekiya a surname as well as permission to carry a sword—the wakizashi, or short samurai sword (the right to carry the katana, or full-sized samurai swords, remained the exclusive right of the nobility and samurai castes). This was a major step forward for the traders, as formerly only samurai and noblemen were allowed to carry swords. Bakuto (gamblers) had a much lower social standing even than traders, as gambling was illegal. Many small gambling houses cropped up in abandoned temples or shrines at the edge of towns and villages all over Japan. Most of these gambling houses ran loan sharking businesses for clients, and they usually maintained their own security personnel. The places themselves, as well as the bakuto, were regarded with disdain by society at large, and much of the undesirable image of the yakuza originates from bakuto; this includes the name yakuza itself (ya-ku-za, or 8-9-3, is a losing hand in Oicho-Kabu, a form of blackjack).

Because of the economic situation during the mid-period and the predominance of the merchant class, developing yakuza groups were composed of misfits and delinquents that had joined or formed yakuza groups to extort customers in local markets by selling fake or shoddy goods. The roots of the yakuza can still be seen today in initiation ceremonies, which incorporate tekiya or bakuto rituals. Although the modern yakuza has diversified, some gangs still identify with one group or the other; for example, a gang whose primary source of income is illegal gambling may refer to themselves as bakuto.

ORGANIZATION AND ACTIVITIES

Structure

The oyabun-kobun relationship is formalized by ceremonial sharing of sake from a single cup. This ritual is not exclusive to the yakuza—it is also commonly performed in traditional Japanese Shinto weddings, and may have been a part of sworn brotherhood relationships. During the World War II period in Japan, the more traditional tekiya/bakuto form of organization declined as the entire population was mobilised to participate in the war effort and society came under strict military government. However, after the war, the yakuza adapted again.

Prospective yakuza come from all walks of life. The most romantic tales tell how yakuza accept sons who have been abandoned or exiled by their parents. Many yakuza start out in junior high school or high school as common street thugs or members of bôsôzoku gangs. Perhaps because of its lower socio-economic status, numerous yakuza members come from Burakumin and ethnic Korean backgrounds. Yakuza groups are headed by an oyabun or kumichô who gives orders to his subordinates, the kobun. In this respect, the organization is a variation of the traditional Japanese senpai-kôhai (senior-junior) model. Members of yakuza gangs cut their family ties and transfer their loyalty to the gang boss. They refer to each other as family members - fathers and elder and younger brothers. The yakuza is populated almost entirely by men, and there are very few women involved who are called ane-san. When the 3rd Yamaguchi-gumi boss (Kazuo Taoka) died in the early 1980s, his wife (Fumiko) took over as boss of Yamaguchi-gumi, albeit for a short time.

Yakuza have a complex organizational structure. There is an overall boss of the syndicate, the kumicho, and directly beneath him are the saiko komon (senior advisor) and so-honbucho (headquarters chief). The second in the chain of command is the wakagashira, who governs several gangs in a region with the help of a fuku-honbucho who is himself responsible for several gangs. The regional gangs themselves are governed by their local boss, the shateigashira.

Each member's connection is ranked by the hierarchy of sakazuki (sake sharing). Kumicho are at the top, and control various saikô-komon. The saikô-komon control their own turfs in different areas or cities. They have their own underlings, including other underbosses, advisors, accountants and enforcers.

Those who have received sake from oyabun are part of the immediate family and ranked in terms of elder or younger brothers. However, each kobun, in turn, can offer sakazuki as oyabun to his underling to form an affiliated organisation, which might in turn form lower ranked organizations. In the Yamaguchi-gumi, which controls some 2,500 businesses and 500 yakuza groups, there are fifth rank subsidiary organizations.

Rituals

Yubitsume, or the cutting off of one's finger, is a form of penance or apology. Upon a first offense, the transgressor must cut off the tip of his left little finger and give the severed portion to his boss. Sometimes an underboss may do this in penance to the oyabun if he wants to spare a member of his own gang from further retaliation. Its origin stems from the traditional way of holding a Japanese sword. The bottom three fingers of each hand are used to grip the sword tightly, with the thumb and index fingers slightly loose. The removal of digits starting with the little finger moving up the hand to the index finger progressively weakens a person's sword grip. The idea is that a person with a weak sword grip then has to rely more on the group for protection—reducing individual action. In recent years, prosthetic fingertips have been developed to disguise this distinctive appearance. Many yakuza have full-body tattoos (including their genitalia). These tattoos, known as irezumi in Japan, are still often "hand-poked", that is, the ink is inserted beneath the skin using non-electrical, hand-made and handheld tools with needles of sharpened bamboo or steel. The procedure is expensive, painful, and can take years to complete.

When yakuza members play Oicho-Kabu cards with each other, they often remove their shirts or open them up and drape them around their waists. This enables them to display their full-body tattoos to each other. This is one of the few times that yakuza members display their tattoos to others, as they normally keep them concealed in public with long-sleeved and high-necked shirts. When new members join, they are often required to remove their trousers as well and reveal any lower body tattoos.

SYNDICATES

Three Largest Syndicates

Although yakuza membership has declined following an anti-gang law aimed specifically at yakuza and passed by the Japanese government in 1992, there are thought to be more than 58,000 active yakuza members in Japan today.

Although there are many different yakuza groups, together they form the largest organized crime group in the world.

Designated Boryokudan

A designated boryokudan is a "particularly harmful" yakuza group registered by the Prefectural Public Safety Commissions under the Organized Crime Countermeasures Law enacted in 1991. Under the Organized Crime Countermeasures Law, the Prefectural Public Safety Commissions have registered 22 syndicates as the designated boryokudan groups. Fukuoka Prefecture has the largest number of designated boryokudan groups among all of the prefectures, at 5; the Kudo-kai, the Taishu-kai, the Fukuhaku-kai, the Dojin-kai and theKyushu Seido-kai.

Designated boryokudan groups are usually large, old-established organizations (mostly formed before World War II, some even formed before the Meiji Revolution of the 19th century), however there are some exceptions such as the Kyushu Seido-kai which, with its blatant armed conflicts with the Dojin-kai, was registered only two years after its formation. The numbers which follow the names of boryokudan groups refer to the group's leadership. For example, Yoshinori Watanabe headed the Yamaguchi-gumi fifth; on his retirement, Shinobu Tsukasa became head of the Yamaguchi-gumi sixth, and "Yamaguchi-gumi VI" is the group's formal name.

Name	Headquarters	Reg. in
Yamaguchi-gumi VI	Hyogo, Kobe	1992
Sumiyoshi-kai	Minato, Tokyo	1992
Inagawa-kai	MinatoTokyo	1992
Kudō-kai V	Kitakyushu, Fukuoka	1992
Taishū-kai	Tagawa, Fukuoka, Fukuoka	1993
Kyokuryū-kai	Okinawa, Okinawa	1992
Aizu-Kotetsu-kai VI	Kyoto, Kyoto	1992
Kyōsei-kai V	Hiroshima, Hiroshima	1992
Gōda-ikka VII	Shimonoseki, Yamaguchi	1992
Kozakura-ikka IV	Kagoshima, Kagoshima	1992
Asano-gumi V	Kasaoka, Okayama	1992
Dōjin-kai	Kurume, Fukuoka	1992
Shinwa-kai II	Takamatsu, Kagawa	1992
Sōai-kai	Ichihara, Chiba	1992
Kyōdō-kai III	Onomichi, Hiroshima	1993
Sakaume-gumi IX	Osaka, Osaka	1993
Kyokutō-kai	Toshima, Tokyo	1993
Azuma-gumi II	Osaka, Osaka	1993
Matsuba-kai	Taito, Tokyo	1994
Fukuhaku-kai III	Fukuoka, Fukuoka	2000
Namikawa-kai	Omuta, Fukuoka	2008

CURRENT ACTIVITIES

Japan

Yakuza are regarded as semi-legitimate organizations. For example, immediately after the Kobe earthquake, the Yamaguchi-gumi, whose headquarters are in Kobe, mobilized itself to provide disaster relief services (including the use of a helicopter), and this was widely reported by the media as a contrast to the much slower response by the Japanese government. The yakuza repeated their aid after the 2011 Tôhoku earthquake and tsunami, with groups opening their offices to refugees and sending dozens of trucks with supplies to affected areas. For this reason, many yakuza regard their income and hustle (shinogi) as a collection of a feudal tax.

...The yakuza tend to be gentler than their Italian cousins. In general, they are not involved in theft, burglary, armed robbery, or other street crimes. — Jake Adelstein Many yakuza syndicates, notably the Yamaguchi-gumi, officially forbid their members from engaging in drug trafficking, while some yakuza syndicates, notably the Dojin-kai, are heavily involved in it.

Some yakuza groups are known to deal extensively in human trafficking. The Philippines, for instance, is a source of young women. Yakuza trick girls from impoverished villages into coming to Japan, where they are promised respectable jobs with good wages. Instead, they are forced into becoming prostitutes and strippers. Yakuza frequently engage in a unique form of Japanese extortion known as, sôkaiya. In essence, this is a specialized form of protection racket. Instead of harassing small businesses, the yakuza harasses a stockholders' meeting of a larger corporation. They simply scare the ordinary stockholder with the presence of yakuza operatives, who obtain the right to attend the meeting by making a small purchase of stock.

Yakuza also have ties to the Japanese realty market and banking, through jiageya. Jiageya specialize in inducing holders of small real estate to sell their property so that estate companies can carry out much larger development plans. Japan's bubble economy of the 1980s is often blamed on real estate speculation by banking subsidiaries. After the collapse of the Japanese property bubble, a manager of a major bank in Nagoya was assassinated, and much speculation ensued about the banking industry's indirect connection to the Japanese underworld.

Yakuza have been known to make large investments in legitimate, mainstream companies. In 1989, Susumu Ishii, the Oyabun of theInagawa-kai (a well known yakuza group) bought US$255 million worth of Tokyo Kyuko Electric Railway's stock. Japan's Securities and Exchange Surveillance Commission has knowledge of more than 50 listed companies with ties to organized crime, and in March 2008, the Osaka Securities Exchange decided to review all listed companies and expel those with yakuza ties.

As a matter of principle, theft is not recognised as a legitimate activity of yakuza. This is in line with the idea that their activities are semi-open; theft by definition would be a covert activity. More importantly, such an act would be considered a trespass by the community.

Also, yakuza usually do not conduct the actual business operation by themselves. Core business activities such as merchandising, loan sharking or management of gambling houses are typically managed by non-yakuza members who pay protection fees for their activities.

There is much evidence of yakuza involvement in international crime. There are many tattooed yakuza members imprisoned in various Asian prisons for such crimes as drug trafficking and arms smuggling. In 1997, one verified yakuza member was caught smuggling 4 kilograms (8.82 pounds) of heroin into Canada. In 1999, Italian-American mafia Bonanno family member Mickey Zaffarano was overheard talking about the profits of the pornography trade that both families could profit from. Another yakuza racket is bringing women of other ethnicities/races, especially East European and Asian, to Japan under the lure of a glamorous position, then forcing the women into prostitution.

Because of their history as a legitimate feudal organization and their connection to the Japanese political system through the uyoku(extreme right-wing political groups), yakuza are somewhat a part of the Japanese establishment, with six fan magazines reporting on their activities. One study found that 1 in 10 adults under the age of 40 believed that the yakuza should be allowed to exist. In the 1980s in Fukuoka, a yakuza war spiraled out of control and civilians were hurt. It was a large conflict between the Yamaguchi-gumi andDojin-kai, called the Yama-Michi War. The police stepped in and forced the yakuza bosses on both sides to declare a truce in public.

At various times, people in Japanese cities have launched anti-yakuza campaigns with mixed and varied success. In March 1995, the Japanese government passed the Act for Prevention of Unlawful Activities by Criminal Gang Members, which made traditional racketeering much more difficult. Beginning in 2009, led by agency chief Takaharu Ando, Japanese police began to crack down on the gangs. Kodo-kai chief Kiyoshi Takayama was arrested in late 2010.

In December 2010, police arrested Yamaguchi-gumi's alleged number three leader, Tadashi Irie. According to the media, encouraged by tougher anti-yakuza laws and legislation, local governments and construction companies have begun to shun or ban yakuza activities or involvement in their communities or construction projects. The police are handicapped, however, by Japan's lack of an equivalent to plea bargaining, witness protection, or the United States' Racketeer Influenced and Corrupt Organizations Act. Laws were enacted in Osaka and Tokyo in 2010 and 2011 to try to combat Yakuza influence by making it illegal for any business to do business with the Yakuza.

Yakuza's Aid in Tohoku Catastrophe

Following the Tôhoku earthquake and tsunami on 11 March 2011, the yakuza sent hundreds of trucks filled with food, water, blankets, and sanitary accessories to aid the people in the affected areas of the natural disaster. CNN México said that although the yakuza operates through extortion and other violent methods, they "[moved] swiftly and quietly to provide aid to those most in need." Such actions by the yakuza are a result of their knowing of what it is like to "fend for yourself," without any government aid or community support, because they are also considered "outcast" and "dropouts from society". In addition, the yakuza's code of honor (ninkyo) reportedly values justice and duty above anything else, and forbids allowing others to suffer.

United States

Yakuza activity in the United States is mostly relegated to Hawaii, but they have made their presence known in other parts of the country, especially in Los Angeles and the Bay Area, as well as Los Angeles, San Francisco, Seattle, Las Vegas, Arizona, Virginia, Chicago, and New York City. The Yakuza are said to use Hawaii as a midway station between Japan and mainland America, smuggling methamphetamine into the country and smuggling firearms back to Japan. They easily fit into the local population, since many tourists from Japan and other Asian countries visit the islands on a regular basis, and there is a large population of residents who are of full or partial Japanese descent. They also work with local gangs, funneling Japanese tourists to gambling parlors and brothels.

In California, the Yakuza have made alliances with local Vietnamese and Korean gangs as well as Chinese triads, with Vietnamese as the most common alliance. The alliances with Vietnamese gangs dated back in the late 1980s, and most Vietnamese gangsters were used as muscle, as they had potential to become extremely violent as needed. (Yakuza saw the potential following the constant Vietnamese cafe shoot outs, and home invasion burglaries throughout the 1980s and early 1990s). In New York City, they appear to collect finders fees from Russian, Irish and Italian mafiosos and businessmen for guiding Japanese tourists to gambling establishments, both legal and illegal.

Handguns manufactured in the US account for a large share (33%) of handguns seized in Japan, followed by China (16%), and the Philippines (10%). In 1990, a Smith & Wesson .38 caliber revolver that cost $275 in the US could sell for up to $4,000 in Tokyo. By 1997 it would sell for only $500, due to the proliferation of guns in Japan during the 1990s. The FBI suspects that the Yakuza use various operations to launder money in the U.S. In 2001, the FBI's representative in Tokyo arranged for Tadamasa Goto, the head of the group Goto-gumi, to receive a liver transplant at the UCLA Medical Center in the United States, in return for information of Yamaguchi-gumi operations in the

US. This was done without prior consultation of the NPA. The journalist who uncovered the deal received threats by Goto and was given police protection in the US and in Japan.

North Korea

In 2009, a yakuza member Yoshiaki Sawada was released in North Korea after spending 5 years in the country for attempting to bribe a North Korean official and smuggle drugs.

CONSTITUENT MEMBERS

According to a 2006 speech by Mitsuhiro Suganuma, a former officer of the Public Security Intelligence Agency, around 60 percent of Yakuza members come from burakumin, the descendants of a feudal outcast class and approximately 30 percent of them are Japanese-born Koreans, and only 10 percent are from non-burakumin Japanese and Chinese ethnic groups.

Burakumin

The Burakumin are a group that is socially discriminated against in Japanese society, whose recorded history goes back to the Heian Period in the 11th century. The burakumin are descendants of outcast communities of the pre-modern, especially the feudal era, mainly those with occupations considered tainted with death or ritual impurity, such as butchers, executioners, undertakers, or leather workers. They traditionally lived in their own secluded hamlets. According to David E. Kaplan and Alec Dubro, burakumin account for about 70% of the members of Yamaguchi-gumi, the largest yakuza syndicate in Japan.

Ethnic Koreans

While ethnic Koreans make up only 0.5% of the Japanese population, they are a prominent part of yakuza, perhaps because they suffer severe discrimination in Japanese society alongside the burakumin. In the early 1990s, 18 of 90 top bosses of Inagawa-kai were ethnic Koreans. The Japanese National Police Agency suggested Koreans composed 10% of the yakuza proper and 70% of burakumin in the Yamaguchi-gumi. Some of the representatives of the designated Bôryokudan are also. The Korean significance had been an untouchable taboo in Japan and one of the reasons that the Japanese version of Kaplan and Dubro's Yakuza (1986) had not been published until 1991 with the deletion of Korean-related descriptions of the Yamaguchi-gumi.

Japanese-born people of Korean ancestry are considered resident aliens because of their nationality and are often shunned in legitimate trades, and are therefore embraced by the yakuza precisely because they fit the group's "outsider" image. Notable yakuza members of Korean ancestry include Hisayuki Machii, the founder of the Tosei-kai,Tokutaro Takayama, the president of the

4th-generation Aizukotetsu-kai, Jiro Kiyota, the president of the 5th-generation Inagawa-kai, Hirofumi Hashimoto, the head of the Kyokushinrengo-kai, and the bosses of the 6th / 7th Sakaume-gumi.

INDIRECT ENFORCEMENT

Since 2011 regulations making business with members illegal and enactments of yakuza exclusion ordinances which led to the group's membership declining from its 21st century peak. Methods include that which brought down Al Capone, checking the organizations finance. The Financial Services Agency ordered Mizuho Financial Group Inc. to improve compliance and that its top executives report by 28 October 2013 what they knew and when about a consumer-credit affiliate found making loans to crime groups. This adds pressure to the group from the U.S. as well where an executive order in 2011 required financial institutions to freeze yakuza assets. As of 2013, the U.S. Treasury Department has frozen about US$55,000 of yakuza holdings including two Japan-issued American Express cards.

LEBANESE MAFIA

Lebanese mafia is a colloquial term for organized crime groups of Lebanese origin. Lebanese organized crime is active in the country of Lebanon itself, as well as in countries and areas with a large Lebanese community, most notably Australia, Germany and the in the Triple Frontier in South America.

BEQAA VALLEY

The Beqaa Valley, a fertile valley in east Lebanon and one of the country's most important farming regions, is also known for being one of the most important cannabiscultivating regions in the Middle East. In certain parts of the region, life is structured around extended clan families, a number of whom are active in criminal activities such as narcotics trafficking, kidnapping for ransom and car theft. Due to the vast international Lebanese diaspora and along with a certain amount of organized criminals active in their respective communities, the Beqaa Valley has become one of the most infamous marijuana and hashish exporting regions in the world.

LEBANESE ORGANIZED CRIME IN AUSTRALIA

Lebanese organized crime was introduced in Australia after the mass immigration of Lebanese people after the Lebanese Civil War in the 1970s to the end of the 1980s. The first community of Lebanese in Australia were Maronite Christians, quickly followed by a large Muslim community. The main center of Lebanese organized crime is Sydney, with a significant community of 120,000, followed by Melbourne. Criminal organizations are mostly based around extended crime families with a large number of associates from their community. The main activities of Lebanese gangs in Australia are narcotics and weapons trafficking, extortion, prostitution, car theft and money laundering. Often different rival criminal families are interlocked in feuds, resulting in a fair amount of violence. Criminal organizations however often transcend religious and cultural barriers, with members of the Sunni, Christian, Shia and Mhallami (mostly counted as part of the Sunni population) communities all involved in the same criminal organizations.

LEBANESE ORGANIZED CRIME IN GERMANY

In analogy with Australia, Lebanese organized crime also came to Germany following the Lebanese Civil War. A large number of former Lebanese citizens immigrated to several major German cities under political asylum and refugee status. Compared to the Lebanese population in Australia, a much larger number of Lebanese in Germany are originally from the Mhallami community. The Mhallami, a cultural community with origins in the Mardin Province of Southeastern Turkey, have traditionally settled in large numbers in Lebanese regions such as Tripoli, the Beqaa Valley and Beirut where they have become an integral part of the country's Sunni community.

Under a large number of refugees, there were also several extended clans that already in Lebanon were deeply entrenched in organized crime. In Germany these clans mostly settled in Berlin and Bremen where they became involved in narcotics trafficking, weapons trafficking, extortion, prostitution, illegal gambling, car theft, money laundering and armed robbery. Some of the more notorious Lebanese crime families include the Al-Zein Clan and the infamous Miri-Clan from Bremen. These criminal organizations are mostly based around extended criminal Mhallami clans, but also include members from other Lebanese cultures.

ORGANIZED CRIME IN THE TRI-BORDER AREA

The Triple Frontier, a tri-border area along the junction of Paraguay, Argentina, and Brazil, is often used by Lebanese groups connected to political parties but also by Lebanese "mafia" groups as a haven for smuggling and money laundering.

ORGANISED CRIME IN PAKISTAN

Organized crime in Pakistan refers to the activities of groups of organized crime in Pakistan, The Pakistani Mafia is spread in many countries and are also politically supported and politicized. Pakistani Mafia groups are mostly ethnically-based and have influence over government. The Pakistani Mafia is involved in drug trafficking, assassination, land grabbing, arms smuggling and various other illegal activities. The world's third most wanted fugitive and Indian underworld don, Dawood Ibrahim, is probably hiding in Karachi, according to an article written by an Indian writer(Nathan Vardi) on Forbes. Other known gangsters from Pakistan are Rehman Dakait of the Peoples' Aman Committee. Pakistan is also known to large drug cartels which export heroin created in Afghanistan. Afghanistan is known to be the largest producer of heroin on earth (see Opium production in Afghanistan), but due no existing connections to the International waters, most heroin is exported through Pakistan to various regions on earth, such as Middle east, Europe, and Australia.

Political parties such as MQM or the Peoples' Aman Committee, accused of being behind crime in cities like Karachi, are however not as such organized crime groups. Pakistani gangs active in the United Kingdom, as well as several Scandinavian countries to a lesser extent, are a much closer and traditional example of organized crime. Great Britain-based Pakistani organized crime groups mostly come from Mirpuri and Pathan backgrounds and are mostly known for drug trafficking (mainly heroin), arms dealing, as well as other criminal activities. Research published in 2014 by the Punjab University indicated a sizable and growing number of Pakistani Mafia members are actively involved in pedophilia, having themselves been abused as children.

ARMENIAN POWER

Armenian Power, also known as West Side AP XIII, AP, the Armenian Mob, or Armenian Mafia is an Armenian American criminal organization and street gang located in Los Angeles County, California. They are involved in drug trafficking, murder, assault, fraud, identity theft, illegal gambling, kidnapping, racketeering, robbery and extortion. They are believed to have over 150 documented members and hundreds of associates, according to the U.S. attorney's office.

HISTORY

Armenian Power has strong ties to Russian organized crime, as organized crime in the Soviet Union was multi-ethnic and continues to be multi-ethnic in today's Russia. The gang also has some Hispanic members. In the summer of 1988, two dozen gang members took over the parking lot of a mini-mall in East Hollywood and turned it into their headquarters. They intimidated patrons of the mall's restaurants and clothing stores, forcing the shop owners to hire some off-duty LAPD officers for security.

By mid-1997 the Armenian Power gang was believed to be responsible for a dozen driveby murders. The Armenian Power gang is composed of about 200 members, making it relatively small compared to many other ethnic gangs in the United States. In United States, Caucasian gangs in general composed only 14% of the total percentage of gangs versus other racial/ethnic groups. Gang activity has never been reported in East Coast, Midwestern, Northern or Southern Armenian-American communities primarily composed of Van (central) Armenians, Syrian-Armenians and Iraqi-Armenians. The unique ethnic composition of the Los Angeles area, which had a strong presence of many different gangs, played a major role in the creation of the Armenian Power gang.

Though on the street-level Armenian Power may seem to be merely a loosely organized youth street gang, the street gang component is merely one aspect of the organization, with younger street gang members often serving as the enforcement arm or "soldiers" for a more organized Armenian-American criminal organization consisting of higher-up members.

Armenian Power's status as a highly organized crime group rather than simply a street gang became apparent when Armenian-American gangsters were found to be involved in the 2010 Medicaid fraud case and the 2011 FBI-led Operation Power Outage. According to the official FBI website: "The Southern California crime ring called Armenian Power may look like a traditional street gang—members identify themselves with tattoos and gang clothing—but the group is really an international organized crime enterprise whose illegal activities allegedly range from bank fraud and identity theft to violent extortion and kidnapping."

Latino-Armenian Conflict

Armenian Power has had a history of conflict with Latino gang members in the past but it is thought to have simmered down in recent years. Armen "Silent" Petrosyan, a founder of Armenian Power, was shot to death on May 22, 2000 by Jose Argueta, a member of the Latino gang White Fence. On May 24, 2000, Latino gang members shot an Armenian person outside a restaurant in Hollywood, California. It was recorded as the third clash involving Armenian and Latino gang members in that month. In 2000, a killing of a 17-year-old Latino outside of Hoover High School by Armenian gang youth sparked dialogue to find ways to help stop violence between these groups.

OPERATION POWER OUTAGE

On February 16, 2011 during Operation Power Outage over 800 federal and local law enforcement authorities arrested nearly 100 people allegedly involved in Armenian organized crime in the Los Angeles area. Much of the crime was white collar in nature, including identity theft crimes such as credit card skimming. The range of crimes included kidnapping, fraud, extortion, identity theft, loansharking, robbery, witness intimidation, drug trafficking, drug charges including marijuana cultivation and bringing narcotics into prison, gun-related offenses, and murder.

INVOLVEMENT IN THE SYRIAN CIVIL WAR

In 2014, two Los Angeles gang members, one belonging to Armenian Power and the other a Sureño, were videotaped in Syria fighting on the side of the Assad government.

AZERBAIJANI MAFIA

The Azerbaijani mafia is a general term for organized criminal gangs, mostly based in Moscow and other major Russian cities, that consist of ethnic Azeris. Outside of Russia they are active in most former Soviet states such as Ukraine, Baltic States such asEstonia and Latvia as well as in Central Asian countries such as Kazakhstan and Uzbekistan.

HISTORY

The Azerbajani mafia is one of the oldest crime groups in Russia. Outside of a large ethnic Azerbaijani community in Dagestan, Russian cities have always been known destinations for Azerbaijani immigrants. Following the formation of important and powerful organized crime groups among Russians, Chechens, Armenians and Georgians in Moscow, Azerbaijani criminal gangs quickly developed in the early 1980s. In the 1990s the Azerbaijani groups quickly began their rise to power following the conflicts between the Russian and the Chechen groups. Large-scale immigration of Azerbaijanis to Moscow followed. As well as refugees, ex-guerilla fighters and warlords illegally immigrated to the major Russian cities. Since the position of the Chechen mafia groups was at the time greatly weakened, the newly formed Azerbaijani criminal groups were able to take over a large chunk of the heroin trade. At the time a lot of the trafficking funded military and guerilla operations in the region of Nagorno-Karabakh. After the war ended, younger generation of impoverished Azerbaijanis living in Moscow and other Russian cities learned their trade, which quickly led to the further formation of Azeri criminal outfits in the former Soviet Union.

ACTIVITIES

While the most important activity of Azerbaijani gangs was drug trafficking (mostly heroin), they've quickly expanded their operations to other areas of organized crime such asarms trafficking, fraud, money laundering, car theft, extortion, illegal gambling, counterfeiting, prostitution and contract killing. Azerbaijani crime groups have been known to invest in real estate by means of money laundering.

Rivalry with Armenian Mafia

Like the situation between Armenia and Azerbaijan, the Azerbaijani mafia doesn't like the Armenian mafia. Most of the clashes between the Armenian and Azeri mafias happened outside of Moscow in other cities of Russia, alongside Ukraine, Kazakhstan, and Uzbekistan. Major fighting between the two rival mafias have caused bloodshed resulting from deadly violence. However, for a few years, the Armenian mafia and Azeri mafia clashed outside of Russia and CIS nations. Most of the mass killings happened in Italy, the USA, Mexico and Colombia,from both the hands of the Armenian and Azeri mafias.

RUSSIAN MAFIA

The Russian Mafia (Russian: ðóññêàÿ ìàôèÿ; russkaya mafiya) or Bratva (brothers, brotherhood), is a term used to refer to thecollective of various organized crime elements originating in the former Soviet Union. Although not a singular criminal organization, most of the individual groups share similar goals and organizational structures that define them as part of the loose overall association.

Organized crime in Russia began in the imperial period of the Tsars, but it was not until the Soviet era that vory v zakone ("thieves-in-law") emerged as leaders of prison groups in gulags (Soviet prison labor camps), and their honor code became more defined. After World War II, the death of Joseph Stalin, and the fall of the Soviet Union, more gangs emerged in a flourishing black market, exploiting the unstable governments of the former Republics, and at its highest point, even controlling as much as two-thirds of the Russian economy. Louis Freeh, former director of the FBI, once said that the Russian mafia posed the greatest threat to U.S. national security in the mid-1990s.

In modern times, there are as many as 6,000 different groups, with more than 200 of them having a global reach. Criminals of these various groups are either former prison members, corrupt Communist officials and business leaders, people with ethnic ties, or people from the same region with shared criminal experiences and leaders.However, the existence of such groups has been debated. In December 2009, Timur Lakhonin, the head of the Russian National Central Bureau of Interpol, stated "Certainly, there is crime involving our former compatriots abroad, but there is no data suggesting that an organized structure of criminal groups comprising former Russians exists abroad", while in August 2010, Alain Bauer, a French criminologist, said that it "is one of the best structured criminal organizations in Europe, with a quasi-military operation."

HISTORY

Origins

The Russian mafia can be traced back to Russia's imperial period, which began in the 1700s, in the form of banditry and thievery. Most of the population were peasants in poverty at the time, and criminals who stole from government entities and divided profits among the people earned Robin Hood-like status, being viewed as protectors of the poor and becoming folk heroes. In time, the Vorovskoy Mir (Thieves' World) emerged as these criminals grouped and started their own code of conduct that was based on strict loyalty with one another and opposition against the government. When the Bolshevik Revolution came around in 1917, the Thieves' World was alive and active. Vladimir Leninattempted to wipe them out after being robbed by a gang of highwaymen (who also performed an attempted rape), but failed, and the criminals survived intoJoseph Stalin's reign.

1917–1991: Soviet Era

During Stalin's reign as ruler, millions of criminals were sent to gulags (Soviet labor camps), where powerful criminals worked their way up to become vory v zakone ("thieves-in-law"). These criminal elite often conveyed their status through complicated tattoos, symbols still used by Russian mobsters.

After Hitler's invasion of the Soviet Union during World War II, Stalin was desperate for more men to fight for the nation, offering prisoners freedom if they joined the army. Many flocked to help out in the war, but this act betrayed codes of the Thieves' World that one must not ally with the government. When the war was over, however, Stalin sent them back to prison. Those who refused to fight in the war referred to the traitors as suka ("bitch"), and the latter landed at the bottom of the "hierarchy". Outcast, the sukiseparated from the others and formed their own groups and power bases by collaborating with prison officials, eventually gaining the luxury of comfortable positions. Bitterness between the groups erupted into a series of Bitch Wars from 1945 to 1953 with many killed every day. The prison officials encouraged the violence, seeing it as a way to rid the prisons of criminals.

After the death of Stalin, around eight million inmates were released from gulags. Those that survived the imprisonment and Bitch Wars became a new breed of criminal, no longer bound to the laws of the old Thieves' World. They adopted an "every-man-for-himself" attitude that meant cooperating with the government if necessary. As corruption spread throughout the Soviet government, the criminal underworld began to flourish. This corruption was common during the Brezhnev era, and the nomenklatura(the power elite of the country, usually corrupt officials) ran the country along with criminal bosses. In the 1970s, small illegal businesses sprang up throughout the country, with the government ignoring them, and the black market thrived. Then, in the 1980s, Mikhail Gorbachev loosened up restrictions on private businesses, allowing them to grow legally, but by then, the Soviet Union was already beginning to collapse.

Also during the 1970s and 1980s, the United States expanded its immigration policies, allowing Soviet Jews, with most settling in a southern Brooklyn area known as Brighton Beach (sometimes nicknamed as "Little Odessa"). Here is where Russian organized crime began in the US. The earliest known case of Russian crime in the area was in the mid-1970s by the "Potato Bag Gang," a group of con artists disguised as merchants that told customers that they were selling antique gold rubles for cheap, but in fact, gave them bags of potatoes when bought in thousands. By 1983, the head of Russian organized crime in Brighton Beach was Evsei Agron.

Pauol Mirzoyan was a prime target among other mobsters including rival Boris Goldberg and his organization, and in May 1985 Agron was assassinated. Boris "Biba" Nayfeld, his bodyguard, moved on to employ under Marat Balagula, who was believed to have succeeded Agron's authority. In the following year, Balagula fled the country after he was convicted in a fraud scheme of Merrill Lynch customers, and was found in Frankfurt, West Germany in 1989, where he was extradited back to the US and sentenced to eight years in prison.

Balagula would later be convicted on a separate $360,000 credit card fraud in 1992. Nayfield took Balagula's place, partnering with the "Polish Al Capone", Ricardo Fanchiniin, in an import-export business and setting up a heroin business. In 1990, his former friend, Monya Elson, back from a six-year prison sentence in Israel, returned to America and set up a rival heroin business, culminating in a Mafia turf war.

1992–2000: Growth and Internationalization

When the USSR collapsed and a free market economy emerged, organized criminal groups began to take over Russia's economy, with many ex-KGB soldiers and veterans of the Afghan war offering their skills to the crime bosses. Gangster summit meetings had taken place in hotels and restaurants shortly before the Soviet's dissolution, so that topvory v zakone could agree on who would rule what, and set plans on how to take over the post-Communist state. It was agreed upon that Vyacheslav "Yaponchik" Ivankov would be sent to Brighton Beach in 1992, allegedly because he was killing too many people in Russia and also to take control of Russian organized crime in North America. Within a year, he built an international operation that included, but was not limited to, narcotics, money laundering, and prostitution and made ties with the American Mafia and Colombiandrug cartels, eventually extending to Miami, Los Angeles, and Boston. Those who went against him were usually killed.

Prior to Ivankov's arrival, Balagula's downfall left an empty void for America's next vory v zakone. Monya Elson, leader of Monya's Brigada (a gang that similarly operated from Russia to Los Angeles to New York), was in a feud with Boris Nayfeld, with bodies dropping on both sides. Ivankov's arrival virtually ended the feud, although Elson would later challenge his power as well, and a number of attempts were made to end the former's life. Nayfield and Elson would eventually be arrested in January 1994 (released in 1998) and in Italy in 1995, respectively.

Ivankov's reign, too, ended in June 1995 when a $3.5 million extortion attempt on two Russian businessmen, Alexander Volkov and Vladimir Voloshin, ended in an FBI arrest that resulted in a ten-year maximum security prison sentence. Before his arrest and besides his operations in America, Ivankov regularly flew around Europe and Asia to maintain ties with his fellow mobsters (like members of the Solntsevskaya Bratva), as well as reinforce ties with others.

This did not stop other people from denying him growing power. In one instance, Ivankov attempted to buy out Georgian boss Valeri "Globus" Glugech's drug importation business. When the latter refused the offer, he and his top associates were shot dead. A summit held in May 1994 in Vienna rewarded him with what was left of Glugech's business. Two months later, Ivankov got into another altercation with drug kingpin and head of the Orekhovskaya gang, Segei "Sylvester" Timofeyev, ending with the latter murdered a month later.

Back in Eastern Europe in May 1995, crime boss Semion Mogilevich held a different summit meeting of Russian mafia bosses in his U Holubu restaurant in Andìl, a neighborhood of Prague. The excuse to bring them together was that it was a birthday party for Victor Averin, the second-in-command of the Solntsevskaya Bratva. However, Major Tomas Machacek of the Czech police got wind of an anonymous tip-off that claimed that the Solntsevskaya were planning to assassinate Mogilevich at the location (it was rumored that Mogilevich and Solntsevskaya leader Sergei Mikhailov had a dispute over $5 million), and the police successfully raided the meeting. 200 guests were arrested, but no charges were put against them; only key Russian mafia members were banned from the country, most of whom moved to Hungary.

One person that wasn't there, though, was Mogilevich himself. He claimed that "[b]y the time I arrived at U Holubu, everything was already in full swing, so I went into a neighboring hotel and sat in the bar there until about five or six in the morning." Mikhailov would later be arrested in Switzerland in October 1996 on numerous charges,including that he was the head of a powerful Russian mafia group, but was exonerated and released two years later after evidence was not enough to prove much.

The worldwide extent of Russian organized crime wasn't realized until Ludwig "Tarzan" Fainberg was arrested in January 1997, primarily because of global arms dealing. In 1990, Fainberg moved from Brighton Beach to Miami and opened up a strip club called Porky's, which soon became a popular hangout for underworld criminals.

Fainberg himself gained a reputation as an ambassador among international crime groups, becoming especially close to Juan Almeida, a Colombian cocaine dealer. Planning to expand his cocaine business, Fainberg acted as an intermediary between Almeida and the corrupt Russian military. He helped him get six Russian military helicopters in 1993, and in the following year, helped arrange to buy a submarine for cocaine smuggling. Unfortunately for the two of them, federal agents had been keeping a close eye on Fainberg for months. Alexander Yasevich, an associate of the Russian military contact and an undercover DEA agent, was sent to verify the illegal dealing, and in 1997, Fainberg was finally arrested in Miami. Facing the possibility of life imprisonment, the latter agreed for his testimony against Almeida in exchange for a shorter sentence, which ended up being 33 months.

2001–Present

As the 21st century dawned, the Russian mafia remained alive and well. New Mafia bosses sprung up, while imprisoned ones were released. Among the released were Johanithan Pochival Slokavich, Marat Balagula and Vyacheslav Ivankov, all three in 2004.

The latter was extradited to Russia, but was jailed once more for his alleged murders of two Turks in a Moscow restaurant in 1992; he was cleared of all charges and released in 2005. Four years later, he was assassinated by a shot in the stomach from a sniper. Meanwhile, Monya Elson, along with Leonid Roytman, were arrested in March 2006 for an unsuccessful murder plot against two Kiev-based businessmen.

In 2009, FBI agents in Moscow targeted two suspected Mafia leaders and two other corrupt businessmen. One of the leaders is Yevgeny Dvoskin, a criminal who had been in prison with Ivankov in 1995 and was deported in 2001 for breaking immigration regulations; the other is Konstantin "Gizya" Ginzburg, who is reportedly the current "big boss" of Russian organized crime in America, it being suspected that Ivankov handed over control to him. Some facts state that Sheaib was present in Eastern Europe right before the death of Vyacheslav Ivankov as well as Aslan Usoyan.

In the same year, Semion Mogilevich was placed on the FBI Ten Most Wanted Fugitives list for his involvement in a complex multimillion-dollar scheme that defrauded investors in the stock of his company YBM Magnex International, swindling them out of $150 million. He was indicted in 2003 and arrested in 2008 in Russia on account of tax fraud charges, but because the US does not have an extradition treaty with Russia, he was released on bail. Monya Elson stated that "e's the most powerful mobster in the world" in 1998.

Around the world, Russian mafia groups have popped up as dominating particular areas: Alec Simchuk and his group ripped off and robbed unsuspecting tourists and businessmen in South Florida, leading to Rick Brodsky of the FBI to say that "Eurasian organised crime is our no. 1 priority"; Russian organized crime has a rather large strong hold in the city of Atlanta where members are distinguished by their tattoos. Russian organized crime was reported to have a stronger grip in the French Riviera region and Spain in 2010; and Russia was branded as a virtual "mafia state" according to the WikiLeaks cables. The Jewish branch of the Russian mafia has created tremendous problems for the Israeli government. There has been a large increase in criminal activity in Israel due to the large influx of Russian-Jews. The Israeli police and intelligence services have focused their resources on the Palestinians and have not paid adequate attention to this growing problem. The Russian Jewish mafia has cooperated with Israeli mafiosi.

As of 2009, Russian mafia groups have been said to reach over 50 countries and, as of 2010, have up to 300,000 members.

STRUCTURE AND COMPOSITION

Bratva Structure

Note that all these positions are not always official titles, but rather are understood names for roles that the individual performs.

- Pakhan – is the Boss or Krestnii Otets "Godfather" and controls everything. The Pakhan controls four criminal cells in the working unit through an intermediary called a "Brigadier."
- Sovietnik – ("Councilor"), is the advisor and most close trusted individual to the Pakhan, similar to the Consigliere in Italian-American Mafia crime families and Sicilian Mafia clans.
- Kassir or Kaznachey – the bookmaker, collects all money from Brigadiers and bribes the government to Obshchak (money mafia intended for use in the interests of the group), similar to the underboss position in Italian-American Mafia crime families.
- Brigadier – or Avtoritet ("Authority"), is like a captain in charge of a small group of men, similar to Caporegime in Italian-American Mafia crime families and Sicilian Mafia clans. He gives out jobs to Boeviks ("warriors") and pays tribute to Pakhan. He runs a crew which is called a Brigade (Bratva). A Brigade is made up of 5–6 Boyeviks and Shestyorkas. There are four Brigadiers running criminal activity in the Russian Bratva.
- Boevik – literally "warrior" works for a Brigadier having a special criminal activity to run, similar to soldiers in Italian-American Mafia crime families and Sicilian Mafia clans. A Boevik is in charge of finding new guys and paying tribute up to his Brigadier. Boevik is also the main strike force of a brigade (bratva).
- Krysha – literally "roofs", "covers". Those are an extremely violent "enforcers" as well as cunning individuals. Such enforcer is often employed to protect a business from other criminal organizations.
- Torpedo – "Contract killer"
- Byki – bodyguards (literally: bulls)
- Shestyorka – is an "associate" to the organization also called the "six", similar to associates in Italian-American Mafia crime families and Sicilian Mafia clans. Is an errand boy for the organization and is the lowest rank in the Russian Mafia. The sixes are assigned to some Avtorityets for support.
- They also provide an intelligence for the upcoming "dielo" or on a certain target. They usually stay out of the main actions, although there might be exceptions, depending on circumstances. During a "delo" Shestyorkas perform security functions standing on the look out (Shukher – literally: danger). It is a temporary position and an

individual either making it into the Vor-world or being cast aside. As they are earning their respect and trust in Bratva they may be performing roles of the regular Boyeviks or Byki depending on the necessities and patronage of their Brigadier or Avtorityet. Etymology of 'shestyorka' word comes from the lowest rank of 36 playing card deck – sixes.

In the Russian Mafia to become a "Vor" (plural: Vory) (a Thief) is an honorary title denoting a made man. The honor of becoming a Vor is only given when the recruit shows considerable leadership skills, personal ability, intellect and charisma. A Pakhan or another high-ranking member of an organization can decide if the recruit will receive such title. When you become a member amongst the Vor-world you have to accept the code Vor v Zakone or Thief inside the Law (compare to outlaws).

Although most Russian criminal groups vary in their structure, there have been attempts at trying to figure out a model in how they work. One such model, which could be possibly out-dated structure, as it is based on the old style of Soviet criminal enterprises, works out like the following:

1. Elite group – led by a Pakhan who is involved in management, organization and ideology. This is the highest group controls both support group and security group.
2. Security group – is led by one of his spies. His job is to make sure the organization keeps running and also keeps the peace between the organizations and other criminal groups and also paying off the right people. This group works with the Elite group and is equal in power with the Support groups. Is in charge of security and in intelligence.
3. Support group – is led by one of his spies. His job is to watch over the working unit collecting the money while supervising their criminal activities. This group works with the elite group and is equal in power with the Security group. They plan a specific crime for a specialized group or choose who carries out the operation.
4. Working Unit – There are four Brigadiers running a criminal activity in the working unit. Each Brigade is controlled by a Brigadier. This is the lowest group working with only the Support group. The group is involved in burglars, thieves, prostitution, extortion, street gangs and other crimes.

Strongest Ethnic Criminal Groups

Russian criminal gangs are rarely formed along ethnic lines. Within the post-Soviet criminal world there exist a multitude of strong ethnic criminal gangs who often cooperate with each other regardless of ethnic origin. The strongest, most well-represented groups are the following:

Russian Criminal Groups

These mostly consist of both Slavic as well as Jewish criminals. The most well-known of these gangs is the Solntsevskaya Bratva. It is alleged the leader of this faction is Boris "Brandon" Fuchs suspected of multiple murders.

Chechen Criminal Groups

The Chechen mafia has long held an important place in the Russian criminal underworld.

Armenian Criminal Groups

Armenian criminals have establish many prominent Vors in Mocscow, Rostov, and Yerevan that have influenced the Vory world.

Georgian Criminal Groups

Organized crime operating out of Georgia is regarded to be the strongest in the former Soviet Union. Georgian criminals are mainly based out of the ethnic Georgian Kutaisiregion, the Svaneti and Mingrelian community and the Georgia-based Yazidi community (such as Aslan Usoyan). Georgian criminal groups are active throughout the former Soviet Union and Western Europe.

NOTABLE INDIVIDUAL GROUPS

Groups based in and around the City of Moscow:

- *Solntsevskaya Bratva:* Led by Sergei "Mikhas" Mikhailov, it is Russia's largest criminal group with about 5,000 members, and is named after the Solntsevo District.
- *The Brothers' Circle:* Headed by Temuri Mirzoyev, this multi-ethnic transnational group is "composed of leaders and senior members of several Eurasian criminal groups largely based in countries of the former Soviet Union but operating in Europe, the Middle East, Africa, and Latin America." In 2011, US President Barack Obama and his administration named it one of four transnational organized crime groups that posed the greatest threat to US national security, and sanctioned certain key members and froze their assets. A year later, he extended the national emergency against them for another year.
- *The Odessa Mafia:* The most prominent and dominant Russian criminal group operating in the US; its headquarters is in Brighton Beach.
- *Lyuberetskaya Bratva (Russian:):* or Lyubery (Russian:) One of the largest criminal groups in late 1980 early-mid-1990s in the USSR. Based in (and originating from) Lyubertsy district of Moscow.
- *The Dolgoprudnenskaya gang:* Russia's second largest criminal group. Originally from the City of Dolgoprudny.

- *The Izmaylovskaya gang:* One of Russia's oldest modern gangs, it was started in the mid- to late-1980s by Oleg Ivanov; it has around 200–500 members in Moscow alone, and is named after the Izmaylovo District.
- *The Orekhovskaya gang:* Founded by Sergei "Sylvester" Timofeyev, this group reached its height in Moscow in the 1990s. When Timofeyev died, Sergei Butorin took his place. However, he was sentenced to jail for life in 2011.
- The Slonovskaya gang was one of the strongest criminal groups in CIS in 1990s. It was based in Ryazan. It had a long-term war with other criminal groups of the city (Ayrapetovskaya, Kochetkovskie, etc.)
- *The Grekov Gang:* Named after Grecoff Bradlik, this group has been known to dominate Saint Petersburg and has sects in Montreal, Canada; the man most associated with them is Vladimir Kumarin.
- *The Semion Mogilevich organization:* Based in Budapest, Hungary and headed by the crime boss of the same name, this group numbered approximately 250 members as of 1996. Its business is often tied with that of the Solntsevskaya Bratva and the Vyacheslav Ivankov Organization. Aleksey Anatolyevich Lugovcov is the second-in-command, and Vitaly Borisovich Savalovsky is the "underboss" to Mogilevich.
- The Uralmash gang of Yekaterinburg.
- The Mkhedrioni was a paramilitary group involved in organised crime led by a Thief in law Jaba Ioseliani in Georgia in 1990s.
- Armenian Power, or AP-13, is a California-based crime syndicate tied to Russian and Armenian organised crime.
- The city of Kazan was known for its gang culture, which later progressed into more organised, mafia-esque groups. This was known as the Kazan phenomeon.
- *Order of Ronova:* An organization with ties to Russian and Italian organized crime, based throughout Salt Lake City, Utah, Carson City, Nevada, Tacoma, Washington, and Phoenix, Arizona. It has an estimate of 100 made members, and 400 associates.

UKRAINIAN MAFIA

Ukrainian mafia is a type of criminal organization with origins in Ukraine. Such organizations are regarded as one of the most influential types of organized crime coming out of the former USSR next to the established Russian mafia, Georgian mafia, Chechen mafia, Armenian mafia and Azerbaijani mafia. Ukrainian criminal organizations are involved in a vast amount of illegitimate enterprises. Although Ukrainian criminal organizations are for the most part independently operating enterprises they are most closely connected with Russian mafia organizations, as is the case with Semyon Mogilevich.

HISTORY

Following the collapse of the former Soviet Union, there were large stockpiles of arms left in the Ukraine. The first prominence of theUkrainian mafia came through their participation in the illicit international trafficking in these arms. Between 1992 and 1998, some $32 billion in military material disappeared from military depots in the Ukraine and ended up primarily in West Africa and Central Asia. Allegedly, Ukrainian criminal organizations were also behind trafficking weapons to war-torn places such as Afghanistan at the time.

From trafficking in arms, Ukrainian crime syndicates entered into the international trade in illegal drugs, becoming a major player in the narcotics traffic from Central Asia to Central Europe. The reach of Ukrainian gangs has become extended, having been reported from Central European countries such as the Czech Republic and Hungary, where they're involved in prostitution, to North American countries and Israel, where they founded a significant power base following the mass immigration of Ukrainian Jews which among the many law-abiding people had also criminal elements profiting from the open borders.

ODESSA MAFIA

The most infamous form of Ukrainian organized crime, and the one which became the most famous, is the so-called Odessa Mafia named after the Black Sea port city of Odessa. Odessa is an infamous smugglers' haven and a key hub in post-Soviet global trafficking networks, not least moving Europe-bound Afghan heroin arriving from the Caucasus. Even in Ukraine's west, gangs are often closely involved in the lucrative trafficking of heroin, people, and counterfeit cigarettes into Europe, often in cooperation withRussian mafia gangs.

Odessa traditionally had an ancient culture of banditry, dating back to the large and impoverished Jewish population. Famous writers such as Isaac Babel often wrote about the infamous exploits of Jewish gangsters, thieves and crime lords in the port city. 20th century thuggery made way for sophisticated organized crime when local crime lords began to use the city's sprawling port to their advantage.

The at first locally active Odessa Mafia, sometimes also called the Malina, became well known when it branched out toNew York City at first and later on Israel, when both countries gave the opportunity to Soviet Jews to immigrate. Many people from Odessa's Jewish population migrated abroad, among them a large part of the city's most infamous career criminals. Although the gang was born in the city of Odessa, it has since established most of its headquarters in cities such as New York City, Tel Aviv, Antwerp and Budapest with brigades composed of former Odessan or Odessa-connected criminals active in a large amount of other cities. In the United States the Odessa mafia is based in the Brighton Beach district of Brooklyn, New York. It is regarded as the most powerful post-Soviet criminal organization in the USA and has since expanded its operations to Los Angeles, where it has established connections with locally based Armenian and Israeli crime figures, and the San Francisco Bay. It's known for being a very secretive organization, being involved in protection rackets, loan-sharking, murder-for-hire, as well as the infamous fuel tax fraud rackets and narcotics trafficking.

Nonetheless a large amount of Odessa Mafia-connected gangsters have become part of the US' criminal folklore, examples being Marat Balagula, Evsei Agron and Boris Nayfeld. Feuds, often resulting in extreme violence, happened in the 1980s and 1990s between Odessa gangsters such as the internal war between Balagula and Agron at first, and later on between the Nayfeld brothers and Monya Elson.

KKANGPAE

A Kkangpae , also known as Ggangpae, Gangpae, or Gangpaeh, is the name of literally either the South Koreanmafia or street gang. The Korean mafia operates primarily in Seoul, Mokpo, and Gwangju, although it is known to operate in Tokyo, Japan; New York City, New York; and Los Angeles, California. The South Korean mafia is well known for its ruthless extortion and loan sharking tactics. Since the early 2000s, the South Korean entertainment industry has regularly popularized the South Korean mafia, through films and television.

ETYMOLOGY

Kkangpae literally translates to "Thug" in the Korean language, and usually refers to unorganized street gangs. The South Korean mafia is referred to in South Korea as the Geondal, or Jopok which usually refers to mafiosos and organized crime.

HISTORY

Historians believe that the rise of the Korean mafia started back in the 19th century, in the fading days of the Joseon Dynasty. With the rise of commerce and the emergence of investment from European colonial powers, pre-existing street gangs, often consisting of lower class muscle and operated by wealthy merchants, gained influence. The modern history of Korean criminal organizations divides into four periods—the "Romantic Period" during the Colonial era, political mobs of the late 1950s and early 1960s underSyngman Rhee, the "Civil War period" under the military rule of Park Chung Hee and Chun Doo Hwan, and the present.

Colonial Era

During the 35 years of Korea under Imperial Japanese rule, some Koreans were subjected to forced labor and sex slavery. This intensified during World War II when the Empire of Japan spread its empire throughout Manchuria, and parts of China. Koreans fled to mainland Japan and formed mobs to overcome discrimination and crime. The most infamous "mobster" during this period was Kim Doo Han, the son of a famous Korean independence fighter and insurgent leader Kim Jwa-jin, a freedom fighter against Colonial rule. After his father and mother were killed, he grew up as a beggar and hung out with a local gang, named Jumok (fist). He rose through the ranks and became infamous for fighting groups against the yakuza.

The colonial branch of the Imperial Japanese Yakuza was then under the control of Hayashi, an ethnic Korean who defected to the Japanese and joined the Yakuza. The rival mob to Hayashi's Yakuza was controlled by Koo Majok, but the Korean mafia was always short of money and many local mob bosses were disloyal to Koo and formed separated mobs, notably Shin Majok and Ssang Kal (twin knives).

Koo Majok finally tried to solidify his control over the Korean mobs by knocking out Ssang Kal and taking over his territory but it caused a backlash. Kim Doo Han, originally a member of Ssang Kal, rebelled against Koo Majok. Kim killed both Shin Majok and Koo Majok and unified all the Korean mobs under his command at the age of 18. After solidifying his rule by beating the revolting groups, Kim made his move against the Yakuza, starting the famous trial war between Jumok and Yakuza, which became symbolic of the resistance by Koreans against Japanese. Kim Doo Han was a major figure of the movement against the colonial rule. To this date, many Korean mobs are still at war with Japanese mobs, or yakuza.

ORGANIZED CRIME IN SOUTH KOREA

Organized crime was widespread in South Korea during the 1960s, 1970s and 1980s. The criminal syndicates controlled large parts of the South Korean entertainment scene, as well politics, and the media. The common modus operandi of the South Korean mafia included racketeering, prostitution, loan sharking, money laundering, such as through construction, and gambling. However, in 1990, the South Korean government announced a war against organized crime, which resulted in the incarceration of thousands of South Korean mafiosos and mob bosses. However South Korean gangs transformed themselves into business corporations, and started expansion in 1997 as South Korea fell victim to the East Asian Financial Crisis.

Current activities of the South Korean mafia include extortion, prostitution, illegal goods (drugs, guns), money laundering (e.g. through construction or fisheries), loan sharking, kidnappings, and night club management. The South

Korean mafia has a larger presence in smaller towns and cities, where the government and police influence is less common.

South Korean mafiosos often have tattoos of the pa (English: mob) they are in. When confronted by other mobs, they show their tattoos to help identify themselves. The tattoo can also be used as a warning to the general public. As a result, tattoos are often considered taboo in South Korean society.

The stereotypical image of the quintessential South Korean mafioso is one with a gakdoogi hairstyle, which consists of the sides of the head shaved, with hair remaining on top, a big build, dark, black clothing, tacky suits, black-painted luxury cars, prominent tattoos, and regional accents or dialects (Korean: Saturi). Contrary to popular belief, Seoul is not a known hotbed of South Korean mob presence.

The most prominent organizations of the South Korean mafia operate in the Jeolla region, in cities such as Gwangju andMokpo, with other South Korean mafiosos known to be operating in Busan and Incheon.

Prominent South Korean Gangs

There are many named local gangs and organized crime affiliates in South Korea. They often operate small, local businesses to earn extra money, however, their usual source of income comes from protection fees, in which they take over a certain neighborhood designated as their "territory", demanding that all businesses in the neighborhood make a monthly payment to the gang leaders in exchange for not damaging their business.

Currently, there are three major South Korean crime syndicates, which compete amongst each other regularly. They are the Seven Star Mob, the Double Dragon, and the H.S.S. Mob.

Seven Star Mob

The Seven Star Mob is a major South Korean gang. The name apparently originates from the gang's seven founders (of which three are imprisoned, and two are dead). Functioning much like Japan's yakuza, it has gained notoriety in the South Korean criminal underground.

However, as their criminal activities are very secretive, the South Korean police cannot act against them, although they have suspicions regarding their illegal deeds. Chil-Sung-Pa is headquartered in Busan and are considered to be the most powerful gang in South Korea. Their gang tattoo is a pattern of seven stars on their chest.

H.S.S. Mob

cn, Song, and Sung are the third letters in their Korean names. However, this theory is in doubt as the gang was originally called Hwan-Song Pa, meaning that the previous explanation would mean that the gang had a new founder added as recently as the summer of 2009. Hwan-Song-Sung-Pa is usually referred to as "H.S.S. Mob" and has maintained a rather quiet presence in South Korea since 2008. Despite this, their criminal activities with international gangs have grown tremendously.

The gang maintains active treaties with American, Mexican, Japanese, Chinese, Russian and Brazilian gangs, putting the gang on the international organized crime stage.

The gang has been reported to operate in Suwon and Gunsan; their signature gang tattoo is the Hanja character of "Son" the founders' family name, on any part of their body. Where the tattoo is positioned signifies the bearer's rank inside the gang. Underage gang members are not required to get these tattoos until they turn 18. It is also theorized that this gang originated out of the Book-Moon-Pa, a prominent South Korean gang from Suwon.

Double Dragon

The Double Dragon is a South Korean gang that is believed to have largely vanished from South Korean society. The origin of the gang's name is unknown and remains a mystery.

The oldest out of South Korea's top three gangs, Ssang-Yong-Pa mafiosos were known to be very violent and brutal during the late 1980s through the late 1990s. Although their presence has decreased since the late 1990s, in 2005, the Ssang-Yong-Pa resurfaced by raiding several night clubs and businesses. However, since the mid-2000s, the Ssang-Yong-Pa went underground yet again. The gang's main turf is Gwangju, the sixth largest city in South Korea. Their gang tattoo is of two dragons curling over each other; it is worn on the bearer's upper arm.

TURKISH MAFIA

Turkish mafia is the general term for criminal organizations based in Turkey and/or composed of (former) Turkish citizens. Crime groups with origins in Turkey are active throughout Western Europe, where a strong Turkish immigrant community exists and theMiddle East. Turkish criminal groups participate in a wide range of criminal activities, internationally the most important being drug trafficking, especially heroin. In the trafficking of heroin they cooperate with Bulgarian mafia groups who transport the heroin further to countries such as Italy. Criminal activities such as the trafficking of other types of drugs, illegal gambling, human trafficking,prostitution or extortion are committed in Turkey itself as well as European countries with a sizeable Turkish community such asGermany, United Kingdom, Netherlands and Belgium.

Turkish crime groups are not solely gangs composed of ethnic Turks. Individuals of ethnic groups other than Turks but originating in the country are also involved in organized crime. Major Turkish crime syndicates mostly have their origin in two main regions: the Trabzon province on the Black Sea coast of northeastern Turkey and the mostly Kurdish-populated regions of East and Southeast Anatolia in the south of the country.

TURKISH CRIME GROUPS

Criminal groups composed of ethnic Turks are active throughout the country and in communities with a large ethnically Turkish population. Certain Turkish criminal groups have strong links with corrupt politicians and corrupt members of the local law enforcement. They are active in different sections of organized crime and can often be linked to politically motivated groups, such as the Grey Wolves. This can especially be the case with criminals in immigrant Turkish communities. Powerful and important Turkish criminal organizations mostly have their origin in the Trabzon Province and incorporate members of both the ethnic Turkish and the Turkish Laz populations.

Laz Crime Groups

Even though crime groups composed of ethnic Turks come from all over the country, a relatively high amount of them have origins in the Black Sea region of Turkey. These groups consisting of Turkified Laz people and Turks are especially strong in the country itself. Black Sea crime bosses such as Alaattin Cakici are known from having links to or being members of the politically motivated group Grey Wolves.

Turkish Cypriot Crime Groups

Following the substantial immigration of Turkish Cypriots to London criminal gangs composed of Turkish Cypriots were formed in working-class neighborhoods. Mainly involved in drug trafficking, armed robbery, money laundering these crime clans have more in common with the traditional White British crime firms than with the Turkish mafia. Turkish Cypriot crime groups are native to the United Kingdom, as is the case with the Arif crime family.

KURDISH CRIME GROUPS

The ethnically Kurdish crime groups have their origin in the Southeast Anatolia part of Turkey. These groups are largely clan based and their main source of income is the trafficking of heroin and weapons. Kurdish crime bosses such as Huseyin Baybasin have been active in Western European countries, especially Great Britain. Links to the PKKexist. Kurdish organized crime groups incorporate members of both the Kurmanji as well as the Zaza speaking populations.

Zaza Kurdish Crime Families in the United Kingdom

While ethnically Zaza Kurdish groups are not noteworthy in Turkey itself, large Alevi Zaza immigrant communities have formed in Great Britain and

Germany. Criminal gangs from these communities have links with other Kurdish crime bosses and are involved in drug trafficking and contract killing. An example in London is the brutal turf war between Turkish gangs of mostly Kurdish and Zaza Kurdish origin, such as the so-called Tottenham Boys and the Hackney Turks.

3

Violence Against Women in Asia

TALIBAN TREATMENT OF WOMEN

While in power in Afghanistan, the Taliban became notorious internationally mostly for their apparent, sexism and misogyny. With regards to claims of sexism and misogyny made by various quarters; the stated aim of the Taliban, in respect to their contentious and non-contentious treatment of women, was to create a "secure environment where the chastity and dignity of women may once again be sacrosanct," reportedly based on Pashtunwali beliefs about living in purdah.

Afghan women were forced to wear the burqa at all times in public, because, according to one Taliban spokesman, "the face of a woman is a source of corruption" for men not related to them. In a systematic segregation sometimes referred to as gender apartheid, women were not allowed to work, they were not allowed to be educated after the age of eight, and until then were permitted only to study the Qur'an.

Women seeking an education were forced to attend underground schools, where they and their teachers risked execution if caught. They were not allowed to be treated by male doctors unless accompanied by a male chaperone, which led to illnesses remaining untreated. They faced public flogging and execution for violations of the Taliban's laws. The Taliban allowed and in some cases encouraged marriage for girls under the age of 16. Amnesty International reported that 80% of Afghan marriages wereforced.

GENDER POLICIES

From the age of eight, females were not allowed to be in direct contact with males other than a close "blood relative", husband, or in-law (seemahram).

Other restrictions were:

- Women should not appear in the streets without a blood relative or without wearing a burqa
- Women should not wear high-heeled shoes as no man should hear a woman's footsteps lest it excite him

- Women must not speak loudly in public as no stranger should hear a woman's voice
- All ground and first floor residential windows should be painted over or screened to prevent women being visible from the street
- Photographing or filming of women was banned as was displaying pictures of females in newspapers, books, shops or the home
- The modification of any place names that included the word "women". For example, "women's garden" was renamed "spring garden".
- Women were forbidden to appear on the balconies of their apartments or houses
- Ban on women's presence on radio, television or at public gatherings of any kind

Mobility

The Taliban rulings regarding public conduct placed severe restrictions on a woman's freedom of movement and created difficulties for those who could not afford a burqa or didn't have any mahram. These women faced virtual house arrest. A woman who was badly beaten by the Taliban for walking the streets alone stated "my father was killed in battle...I have no husband, no brother, no son. How am I to live if I can't go out alone?" A field worker for the NGO Terre des hommes witnessed the impact on female mobility at Kabul's largest state-run orphanage, Taskia Maskan. After the female staff was relieved of their duties, the approximately 400 girls living at the institution were locked inside for a year without being allowed outside for recreation.

Decrees that affected women's mobility were:

- Ban on women riding bicycles or motorcycles, even with their mahrams.
- Women were forbidden to ride in a taxi without a mahram.
- Segregated bus services introduced to prevent males and females traveling on the same bus.

The lives of rural women were less dramatically affected as they generally lived and worked within secure kin environments. A relative level of freedom was necessary for them to continue with their chores or labor. If these women traveled to a nearby town, the same urban restrictions would have applied to them.

Employment

The Taliban disagreed with past Afghan statutes that allowed the employment of women in a mixed sex workplace. They claimed this was a breach of purdah and sharia law.On September 30, 1996, the Taliban decreed that all women should be banned from employment. It is estimated that 25 percent of government employees were female, and when compounded by losses in other sectors, many thousands of women were affected. This had a devastating impact on household incomes, especially on vulnerable or widow-headed households, which were common in Afghanistan.

Another loss was for those whom the employed women served. Elementary education of children, not just girls, was shut down in Kabul, where virtually all of the elementary school teachers were women. Thousands of educated families fled Kabul for Pakistan after the Taliban took the city in 1996. Among those who remained in Afghanistan, there was an increase in mother and child destitution as the loss of vital income reduced many families to the margin of survival.

Taliban Supreme Leader Mohammed Omar assured female civil servants and teachers they would still receive wages of around US$5 per month, although this was a short term offering. A Taliban representative stated: "The Taliban's act of giving monthly salaries to 30,000 job-free women, now sitting comfortably at home, is a whiplash in the face of those who are defaming Taliban with reference to the rights of women. These people through baseless propaganda are trying to incite the women of Kabul against the Taliban".

The Taliban promoted the use of the extended family, or zakat system of charity to ensure women should not need to work. However, years of conflict meant that nuclear families often struggled to support themselves let alone aid additional relatives.

Qualification for legislation often rested on men, such as food aid which had to be collected by a male relative. The possibility that a woman may not possess any male relatives was dismissed by Mullah Ghaus, the acting foreign minister, who said he was surprised at the degree of international attention and concern for such a small percentage of the Afghan population. For rural women there was generally little change in their circumstance, as their lives were dominated by the unpaid domestic, agricultural and reproductive labour necessary for subsistence.

Female health professionals were exempted from the employment ban, yet they operated in much-reduced circumstances. The ordeal of physically getting to work due to the segregated bus system and widespread harassment meant some women left their jobs by choice. Of those who remained, many lived in fear of the regime and chose to reside at the hospital during the working week to minimise exposure to Taliban forces. These women were vital to ensuring the continuance of gynaecological, ante-natal and midwifery services, be it on a much compromised level. Under the Rabbani regime, there had been around 200 female staff working in Kabul's Mullalai Hospital, yet barely 50 remained under the Taliban. NGOs operating in Afghanistan after the fall of the Taliban in 2001 found the shortage of female health professionals to be a significant obstacle to their work.

The other exception to the employment ban allowed a reduced number of humanitarian workers to remain in service. The Taliban segregation codes meant women were invaluable for gaining access to vulnerable women or conducting outreach research. This exception was not sanctioned by the entire Taliban movement, so instances of female participation, or lack thereof, varied with each circumstance. The city of Herat was particularly affected by Taliban adjustments to the treatment of women, as it had been one of the more cosmopolitan and outward-looking areas of Afghanistan prior to 1995. Women had previously been allowed to work in a limited range of jobs, but this was stopped by Taliban authorities. The new governor of Herat, Mullah Razzaq, issued orders for women to be forbidden to pass his office for fear of their distracting nature.

Education

The Taliban claimed to recognize their Islamic duty to offer education to both boys and girls, yet a decree was passed that banned girls above the age of 8 from receiving education. Maulvi Kalamadin insisted it was only a temporary suspension and that females would return to school and work once facilities and street security were adapted to prevent cross-gender contact. The Taliban wished to have total control of Afghanistan before calling upon an Ulema body to determine the content of a new curriculum to replace the Islamic yet unacceptable Mujahadin version.

The female employment ban was felt greatly in the education system. Within Kabul alone the ruling affected 106,256 girls, 148,223 male students and 8,000 female university undergraduates. 7,793 female teachers were dismissed, a move that crippled the provision of education and caused 63 schools to close due to a sudden lack of educators.Some women ran clandestine schools within their homes for local children, or for other women under the guise of sewing classes, such as the Golden Needle Sewing School. The learners, parents and educators were aware of the consequences should the Taliban discover their activities, but for those who felt trapped under the strict Taliban rule, such actions allowed them a sense of self-determination and hope.

Health Care

Prior to the Taliban taking power in Afghanistan male doctors had been allowed to treat women in hospitals, but the decree that no male doctor should be allowed to touch the body of a woman under the pretext of consultation was soon introduced. With fewer female health professionals in employment, the distances many women had to travel for attention increased while provision of ante-natal clinics declined.

In Kabul, some women established informal clinics in their homes to service family and neighbors, yet as medical supplies were hard to obtain their effectiveness was limited. Many women endured prolonged suffering or a premature death due to the lack of treatment. For those families that had the means, inclination, and mahram support, medical attention could be sought in Pakistan. In October 1996, women were barred from accessing the traditional hammam, public baths, as the opportunities for socialising were ruled un-Islamic. This affordable hot-water right had been enjoyed by women and was an important facility in a nation where few possessed running water. It gave cause for the UN to predict a rise in scabies and vaginal infections among women denied methods of hygiene as well as access to health care. Nasrine Gross, an Afghan-American author, stated in 2001 that it has been four years since many Afghan women had been able to pray to their God as "Islam prohibits women from praying without a bath after their periods". In June 1998, the Taliban banned women from attending general hospitals in the capital, whereas before they had been able to attend a women-only ward of general hospitals. This left only one hospital in Kabul at which they could seek treatment.

Forced Confinement

Family harmony was badly affected by mental stress, isolation and depression that often accompanied the forced confinement of women. A survey of 160 women concluded that 97 percent showed signs of serious depression and 71 percent reported a decline in their physical well being. Latifa, a Kabul resident and author, wrote:

The apartment resembles a prison or a hospital. Silence weighs heavily on all of us. As none of us do much, we haven't got much to tell each other. Incapable of sharing our emotions, we each enclose ourselves in our own fear and distress. Since everyone is in the same black pit, there isn't much point in repeating time and again that we can't see clearly. The Taliban closed the country's beauty salons. Cosmetics such as nail varnish and make-up were prohibited. Taliban restrictions on the cultural presence of women covered several areas. Place names including the word "women" were modified so that the word was not used. Women were forbidden to laugh loudly as it was considered improper for a stranger to hear a woman's voice. Women were prohibited from participating in sports or entering a sports club. The Revolutionary Association of the Women of Afghanistan (RAWA) dealt specifically with these issues. It was founded by Meena Keshwar Kamal, a woman who amongst other things established a bi-lingual magazine called Women's Message in 1981. She was assassinated in 1987 at the age of 30, but is revered as a heroine among Afghan women.

PUNISHMENTS

Punishments were often carried out publicly, either as formal spectacles held in sports stadiums or town squares or spontaneous street beatings. Civilians lived in fear of harsh penalties as there was little mercy; women caught breaking decrees were often treated with force.

Examples:

- In October 1996, a woman had the tip of her thumb cut off for wearing nail varnish.
- In December 1996, Radio Shari'a announced that 225 Kabul women had been seized and punished for violating the sharia code of dress. The sentence was handed down by a tribunal and the women were lashed on their legs and backs for their misdemeanor.
- In May 1997, five female CARE International employees with authorisation from the Ministry of the Interior to conduct research for an emergency feeding programme were forced from their vehicle by members of the religious police. The guards used a public address system to insult and harass the women before striking them with a metal and leather whip over 1.5 meters (almost 5 feet) in length.
- In 1999, a mother of seven children was executed in front of 30,000 spectators in Kabul's Ghazi Sport stadium for murdering her husband (see right). She was imprisoned for three years and extensively tortured prior to the execution, yet she refused to plead her innocence in a bid to protect her daughter (reportedly the actual culprit).
- When a Taliban raid discovered a woman running an informal school in her apartment, they beat the children and threw the woman down a flight of stairs (breaking her leg), and then imprisoned her. They threatened to stone her family publicly if she refused to sign a declaration of loyalty to the Taliban and their laws.
- An Afghan girl named Bibi Aisha was promised to a new family through a tribal method of solving disputes known as baad. When she fled the violence girls often suffer under baad, her new family found her and a Taliban commander ordered her punished as an example, "lest other girls in the village try to do the same thing". Her ears and nose were cut off and she was left for dead in the mountains, but survived.
- Working women are threatened into quitting their jobs. Failure to comply with Taliban's threats has led to women being shot and killed as in the case of 22-year-old Hossai in July 2010.
- In 2013, an Indian author Sushmita Banerjee was shot dead by Taliban Militants for allegedly defying Taliban diktats. She was married to an Afghan businessman and had recently relocated to Afghanistan. Earlier she had escaped two instances of execution by Taliban in 1995 and later fled to India. Her book based on her escape from Taliban was also filmed in an Indian movie.

Many punishments were carried out by individual militias without the sanction of Taliban authorities, as it was against official Taliban policy to punish women in the street. A more official line was the punishment of men for instances of female misconduct: a reflection of a patriarchal society and the belief that men are duty bound to control women. Maulvi Kalamadin stated in 1997, "since we cannot directly punish women, we try to use taxi drivers and shopkeepers as a means to pressurize them" to conform. *Examples of the punishment of men:*

- If a taxi driver picked up a woman with her face uncovered or unaccompanied by a mahram then he faced a jail sentence and the husband would be punished.
- If a woman was caught washing clothes in a river then she would be escorted home by Islamic authorities where her husband/mahram would be severely punished.
- Tailors found taking female measurements faced imprisonment.

INTERNATIONAL RESPONSE

The protests of international agencies carried little weight with Taliban authorities, who gave precedence to their interpretation of Islamic law and did not feel bound by UN codes or human rights laws, legislation it viewed as instruments for Western imperialism.

After the Taliban takeover of Herat in 1995, the UN had hoped the gender policies would become more 'moderate' "as it matured from a popular uprising into a responsible government with linkages to the donor community". The Taliban refused to bow to international pressure and reacted calmly to aid suspensions.

- In November 1995, UNICEF suspended all aid to education in regions under Taliban control, as they argued the ban on mixing males and females in education was a breach of the Convention on the Rights of the Child. In the aftermath of the 1995 Beijing Women's Conference, this action moved to solidify UNICEF's role as a leading agency in matters concerning women and children.
- In 1996, Save The Children (UK) also withdrew support as communication with women, the primary child carers, was most difficult.
- UN Secretary General Boutros Boutros Ghali expressed his concern regarding the status of Afghan women.
- In 1999, US Secretary of State Madeleine Albright publicly stated "We are speaking up on behalf of the women and girls of Afghanistan, who have been victimised...it is criminal and we each have a responsibility to stop it".

In January 2006 a London conference on Afghanistan led to the creation of an International Compact, which included benchmarks for the treatment of women. The Compact includes the following point: "Gender:By end-1389 (20 March 2011): the National Action Plan for Women in Afghanistan will be fully implemented; and, in line with Afghanistan's MDGs, female participation in all Afghan governance institutions, including elected and appointed bodies and the civil service, will be strengthened." However, an Amnesty International report on June 11, 2008 declared that there needed to be "no more empty promises" with regard to Afghanistan, citing the treatment of women as one such unfulfilled goal.

PAKISTANI TALIBAN

Various Taliban groups have been in existence in Pakistan since around 2002. Most of these Taliban factions have joined an umbrella organization called Tehrik-i-Taliban Pakistan (TTP).

Although the Pakistani Taliban is distinct from Afghan Taliban, they have a similar outlook towards women. The Pakistani Taliban too has killed women accusing them of un-Islamic behavior and has forcibly married girls after publicly flogging them for illicit relations.

FEMALE INFANTICIDE IN CHINA

The People's Republic of China and its predecessors have a history of female infanticide spanning 2000 years. Worldwide, the practice of infanticide has been practiced since antiquity for the purpose of population control. It is an unsanctioned method offamily planning that has been condoned for centuries in the area until recent times. The phenomenon is also referred to as female gendercide; however, the word gendercide can be used for both sexes.

Background

The practice of female infanticide was far from wholly condoned in China. Buddhists wrote that the killing of young girls would bring bad karma, conversely those who saved a young girl's life either through intervening or through presents of money or food would earn good karma, leading to a prosperous life, a long life and success for their sons. However the Buddhist belief in reincarnationmeant that the death of an infant was not final as the child would be reborn, this belief eased the guilt felt over female infanticide.The Confucian attitude towards female infanticide was conflicted. By placing value on age over youth, Confucian filial piety lessened the value of children, whilst the Confucian belief of Ren led Confucian intellectuals to support the idea that female infanticide was wrong and that the practice would upset the balance between yin and yang.

When Christian missionaries arrived in China in the late sixteenth century, they witnessed newborns being thrown into rivers or onto rubbish piles. In the seventeenth centuryMatteo Ricci documented that the practice occurred in several of China's provinces and said that the primary reason for the practice was poverty. The practice continued into the 19th century and declined precipitously during the Communist era, but has reemerged as an issue since the introduction of the one-child policy in the early 1980s. The census of 1990 showed an overall sex ratio of 1.066, a normal sex ratio for all ages should be less than 1.02.

19th Century

During the 19th century the practice was widespread, readings from Qing texts show a prevalence of the term ni nü (to drown girls), and drowning was the most common method used to kill female children. Other methods used were suffocation and starvation. Leaving a child exposed to the elements was another method of killing an infant, the child would be placed in a basket which was then placed in a tree. Buddhist nunneries created "baby towers" for people to leave a child. In 1845 in the province of Jiangxi, a missionary wrote that these children survived for up to two days while exposed to the elements, and that those passing by, would ignore the screaming child. Missionary David Abeel reported in 1844 that between one third and one fourth of all female children were killed at birth or soon after.

In 1878 French Jesuit missionary, Gabriel Palatre, collated documents from 13 provinces and the Annales de la Sainte-Enfance (Annals of the Holy Childhood), also found evidence of infanticide in Shanxi and Sichuan. According to the information collated by Palatre the practice was more widely spread in the southeastern provinces and in the Lower Yangzi River region.

20TH CENTURY

In 1930, Rou Shi, a noted member of the May Fourth Movement, wrote the short story A Slave-Mother. In it he portrayed the extreme poverty in rural communities that was a direct cause of female infanticide. A white paper published by the Chinese government in 1980 stated that the practice of female infanticide was a "feudalistic evil". The state's official position on the practice is that it is a carryover from feudal times, and is not a result of the state's one-child policy. According to Jing-Bao Nie, it would be "inconceivable" to believe there is no link between the states family planning policies and female infanticide.

On 25 September 1980 in an "open letter", the Politburo of the Communist Party of China requested that members of the party, and those in the Communist youth league, lead by example and have only one child. From when the one-child policy was first proposed there were concerns that it would lead to an imbalance in the sex ratio. Early in the 1980s, senior officials became increasingly concerned with reports of abandonment, and female infanticide, by parents who were desperate for a son. In 1984, the government attempted to address the issue by adjusting the one-child policy to allow couples whose first child is a girl to have a second child.

CURRENT

Many Chinese couples desire to have sons because they traditionally carry on the family name and provide support and security to their aging parents later in life. On the contrary, a daughter is expected to leave her parents upon marriage to join and care for her husband's family. In rural households, which as of 2014 constitute almost half of the Chinese population, males are additionally valuable for performing agricultural work and manual labor.

A 2005 intercensus survey demonstrated pronounced differences in sex ratio across provinces, ranging from 1.04 in Tibet to 1.43 Jiangxi. Banister (2004), in her literature review on China's shortage of girls, suggested that there has been a resurgence in the prevalence of female infanticide following the introduction of the one-child policy. On the other hand, many researchers have argued that female infanticide is rare in China today, especially since the government has outlawed the practice. Zeng and colleagues (1993), for example, contended that at least half of the nation's gender imbalance arises from the underreporting of female births.

According to the Geneva Centre for the Democratic Control of Armed Forces (DCAF), the demographic shortfall of female babies who have died for gender related issues is in the same range as the 191 million estimated dead accounting for all conflicts in the twentieth century. In 2012 the documentary It's a Girl: The Three Deadliest Words in the World was released. It focused on female infanticide in India and China. As a result of female infanticide and sex-selective abortion combined, there are an estimated 30–40 million more men than women in China today. This female deficit is expected to generate a wide range of adverse social, political, and economic consequences.

VIOLENCE AGAINST WOMEN IN INDIA

Violence against women has become a prominent topic of discussion in India in recent years. Politicians and media have placed great focus on the issue due to continuously increasing trends during 2008–2012.

EXTENT

Year	Reported Violence
2008	195,856
2009	203,804
2010	213,585
2011	213,585
2012	244,270

According to the National Crime Records Bureau of India, reported incidents of crime against women increased 6.4% during 2012, and a crime against a woman is committed every three minutes. In 2012, there were 244,270 reported incidents of crime against women, while in 2011, there were 228,650 reported incidents. Of the women living in India, 7.5% live in West Bengal where 12.7% of the total reported crime against women occurs. Andhra Pradesh is home to 7.3% of India's female population and accounts for 11.5% of the total reported crimes against women. 65% of Indian men believe women should tolerate violence in order to keep the family together, and women sometimes deserve to be beaten.In January 2011, the International Men and Gender Equality Survey (IMAGES) Questionnaire reported that 24% of Indian men had committed sexual violence at some point during their lives.

MURDERS

Dowry Deaths

A dowry deaths is a murder or suicide of a married woman caused by a dispute over her dowry. In some cases, husbands and in-laws will attempt to extort a greater dowry through continuous harassment and torture which sometimes results in the wife committing suicide.

The majority of these suicides are done through hanging, poisoning or self-immolation. When a dowry death is done by setting the woman on fire, it is called bride burning. Bride burning murder is often set up to appear to be a suicide or accident. Dowry is illegal in India, but it is still common practice to give expensive gifts to the groom and his relatives at weddings which are hosted by the family of the bride.

Women are not always the only primary victims of dowry deaths. In some cases children are also killed alongside their mothers. In eastern India, on January 30, 2014, for example, a women and her one-year-old child were burned alive for dowry. 77 minutes. Incidents of dowry deaths have decreased 4.5% from 2011 to 2012.

Year	Reported Dowry Deaths
2008	8,172
2009	8,383
2010	8,391
2011	8,618
2012	8,233

In Uttar Pradesh, 2,244 cases were reported, accounting for 27.3% of the dowry deaths nationwide. In, Bihar, 1,275 cases were reported, accounting for 15.5% of cases nationwide.

Honour Killings

An honour killing is a murder of a family member who has been considered to have brought dishonor and shame upon the family. Examples of reasons for honor killings include the refusal to enter an arranged marriage, committing adultery, choosing a partner that the family disapproves of, and becoming a victim of rape. Honour killings are rooted to tradition and cannot be justified by any major world religion, because none of the major world religions condone honour-related crimes. The most prominent areas where honour killings occur in India are northern regions. Honor killings are especially seen in Punjab, Haryana, Bihar, Uttar Pradesh, Rajasthan,Jharkhand, Himachal Pradesh, and Madhya Pradesh. Honour killings have notably increased in some Indian states which has led to the Supreme Court of India, in June 2010, issuing notices to both the Indian central government and six states to take preventative measures against honour killings.

Honour killings can be very violent. For example, in June 2012, a father chopped off his 20-year-old daughter's head with a sword in pure rage upon hearing that she was dating a man who he did not approve of. Honour killings can also be openly supported by both local villagers and neighbouring villagers. This was the case in September 2013, when a young couple who married after having a love affair were brutally murdered.

Witchcraft-Related Murders

Murders of women accused of witchcraft still occur in India. Poor women, widows, and women from lower castes are most at risk of such killings.

Female Infanticide

Female infanticide is the elected killing of a newborn female child or the termination of a female fetus through sex-selective abortion. In India, there is incentive to have a son, because they offer security to the family in old age and are able to conduct rituals for deceased parents and ancestors. In contrast, daughters are considered to be a social and economic burden. An example of this is dowry. The fear of not being able to pay an acceptable dowry and becoming socially ostracized can lead to female infanticide for poorer.

Female Foeticide

Female foeticide is the elected abortion of a fetus, because it is female. Female foeticide occurs when a family has a strong preference for sons over daughters, which is a common cultural theme in India. Modern medical technology has allowed for the gender of a child to be determined while the child is still a fetus.

Once these modern prenatal diagnostic techniques determine the gender of the fetus, families then are able to decide if they would like to abort based on gender. If they decide to abort the fetus after discovering it is female, they are committing female feoticide. The foetal sex determination and sex-selective abortion by medical professionals is now a R.s 1,000 crore (US$244 million) industry. The Preconception and Prenatal Diagnostic Techniques Act of 1944 (PCPNDT Act 1994) was modified in 2003 in order to target medical professionals. The Act has proven ineffective due to the lack of implementation. Sex-selective abortions have totaled approximately 4.2-12.1 million from 1980-

2010. There was a greater increase in the number of sex-selective abortions in the 1990s than the 2000s. Poorer families are responsible for a higher proportion of abortions than wealthier families. Significantly more abortions occur in rural areas versus urban areas when the first child is female.

SEXUAL CRIMES

Rape

Rape is one of the most common crimes against women in India. Criminal Law (Amendment) Act, 2013 defines rape as penile and non-penile penetration in bodily orifices of a woman by a man, without the consent of the woman. In India, a woman is raped every 29 minutes. Incidents of reported rape increased 3% from 2011 to 2012. Incidents of reported incest rape increased 46.8% from 268 cases in 2011 to 392 cases in 2012.

Year	Reported Rapes
2008	21,467
2009	21,397
2010	22,172
2011	24,206
2012	24,923

Victims of rape are increasingly reporting their rapes and confronting the perpetrators. Although women are increasing their exposure to sexual harassment by leaving the home more often, they are becoming more independent. Women are becoming more independent and educated, which is increasing their likelihood to report their rape.

Although rapes are becoming more frequently reported, many go unreported or have the complaint files withdrawn due to the perception of family honour being compromised. Women frequently do not receive justice for their rapes, because police often do not give a fair hearing, and/or medical evidence is often unrecorded which makes it easy for offenders to get away with their crimes under the current laws.

Increased attention in the media and awareness among both Indians and the outside world is both bringing attention to the issue of rape in India and helping empower women to report the crime. After international news reported the gang rape of a 23-year-old student on a moving bus that occurred in Delhi, in December 2012, Delhi experienced a significant increase in reported rapes. The number of reported rapes nearly doubled from 143 reported in January–March 2012 to 359 during the three months after the rape. After the Delhi rape case, Indian media has committed to report each and every rape case.

Marital Rape

In India, marital rape is not a criminal offense. 20% of Indian men admit to forcing their wives or partners to have sex.

Marital rape can be classified into one of three types:

- *Battering rape:* This includes both physical and sexual violence. The majority of marital rape victims experience battering rape.
- *Force-only rape:* Husbands use the minimum amount of force necessary to coerce his wife.
- *Compulsive or obsessive rape:* Torture and/or "perverse" sexual acts occur and are often physically violent.

Gang Rape

Gang rape is defined as the rape of an individual by two or more perpetrators. The 2012 Delhi gang rape brought a lot of international attention to the issue of gang rape in India. On 16 December 2012, in Munirka, New Delhi, a 23-year-old was beaten and gang raped on a private bus. She died 13 days later. Following the rape, there was widespread national and international coverage of the incident as well as public protests against the government of India and the government of Delhi.

Insult to Modesty

Year	Assaults with intent to outrage modesty	Insults to the modesty of women
2008	40,413	12,214
2009	38,711	11,009
2010	40,613	9,961
2011	42,968	8,570
2012	45,351	9,173

Modesty-related violence against women includes assaults on women with intent to outrage her modesty and insults to the modesty of women. From 2011 to 2012, there was a 5.5% increase in reported assaults on women with intent to outrage her modesty.

Madhya Pradesh had 6,655 cases, accounting for 14.7% of the national incidents. From 2011 to 2012, there was a 7.0% increase in reported insults to the modesty of women. Andhra Pradesh had 3,714 cases, accounting for 40.5% of the national accounts, andMaharashtra had 3,714 cases, accounting for 14.1% of the national accounts.

Human Trafficking and Forced Prostitution

Year	Imported girls from foreign countries	Violations of the Immoral Traffic Act
2008	67	2,659
2009	48	2,474
2010	36	2,499
2011	80	2,435
2012	59	2,563

From 2011 to 2012, there was a 26.3% decrease in girls imported to India from another country. Karnataka had 32 cases, and West Bengal had 12 cases, together accounting for 93.2% of the total cases nationwide.

From 2011 to 2012, there was a 5.3% increase in violations of the Immoral Traffic (Prevention) Act of 1956. Tamil Nadu had 500 incidents, accounting for 19.5% of the total nationwide, and Andhra Pradesh had 472 incidents, accounting for 18.4% of the total nationwide.

DOMESTIC VIOLENCE

Domestic violence is abuse by one partner against another in an intimate relationship such as dating, marriage, cohabitation or a familial relationship. Domestic violence is also known as domestic abuse, spousal abuse, battering, family violence, dating abuse and intimate partner violence (IPV). Domestic violence can be physical, emotional, verbal, economic and sexual abuse. Domestic violence can be subtle, coercive or violent. In India, 70% of women are victims of domestic violence.

38% of Indian men admit they have physically abused their partners. The Indian government has taken measures to try to reduce domestic violence through legislation such as the Protection of Women from Domestic Violence Act 2005.

Year	Reported cruelty by a husband or relative
2008	81,344
2009	89,546
2010	94,041
2011	99,135
2012	106,527

Every 9 minutes, a case of cruelty is committed by either of husband or a relative of the husband. Cruelty by a husband or his relatives is the greatest occurring crime against women. From 2011 to 2012, there was a 7.5% increase in cruelty by husbands and relatives. In West Bengal, there were 19,865 cases, accounting for 18.7% of the national total, and in Andhra Pradesh, there were 13,389 cases, accounting for 12.6% of the national total. However the point to be noted here is that the Section 498a, which is called the anty dowry law is the most misused law in India. Many of these cases filed against men using 498a are false and no actions are usually taken against women even if they are proven wrong. This is one of the major factors for married Men's suicide in India which comes to 1 in every 9 minutes.

FORCED AND CHILD MARRIAGE

Girls are vulnerable to being forced into marriage at young ages, suffering from a double vulnerability: both for being a child and for being female. Child brides often do not understand the meaning and responsibilities of marriage.

Causes of such marriages include the view that girls are a burden for their parents, and the fear of girls losing their chastity before marriage.

ACID THROWING

Acid throwing, also called an acid attack, a vitriol attack or vitriolage, is a form of violent assault used against women in India. Acid throwing is the act of throwing acid or an alternative corrosive substance onto a person's body "with the intention to disfigure, maim, torture, or kill." Acid attacks are usually directed at a victim's face which burns the skin causing damage and often exposing or dissolving bone. Sulfuric acid and nitric acid are most commonly used for acid attacks. Hydrochloric acid is also used, but is less damaging. Acid attacks can lead to permanent scarring, blindness, as well as social, psychological and economic difficulties.

The Indian legislature has regulated the sale of acid. Compared to women throughout the world, women in India are at a higher risk of being victims of acid attacks. At least 72% of reported acid attacks in India have involved women. India has been experiencing an increasing trend of acid attacks over the past decade. In 2010, there was a high of 27 reported cases of chemical assaults. Scholars believe that acid attacks in India are being under-reported. 34% of acid attacks in India have been determined to be related to rejection of marriage or refusal by a women of sexual advances. 20% of acid attacks have been determined to be related to land, property, and/or business disputes. Acid attacks related to marriage are often spurred by dowry disagreements.

ABDUCTION

Year	Reported abductions
2008	22,939
2009	25,741
2010	29,795
2011	35,565
2012	38,262

Incidents of reported kidnappings and abductions of women increased 7.6% from 2011 to 2012. Uttar Pradesh had 7,910 cases, accounting for 22.2% of the total of cases nationwide.

HONOUR KILLING IN PAKISTAN

A form of gender-based violence, an honour killing is the homicide of a member of a family or social group by other members, due to the belief the victim has brought dishonorupon the family or community. The death of the victim is viewed as a way to restore the reputation and honour of the family.

In Pakistan, honour killing is known locally as karo-kari. Karo-kari is a compound word literally meaning "black male" (Karo) and "black female (Kari). Originally, Karo and Kari were metaphoric terms for adulterer and adulteress, but it has come to be used with regards to multiple forms of perceived immoral behavior. Once a woman is labeled as a Kari, family members consider themselves to be authorized to kill her and the co-accused Karo in order to restore family honour. In the majority of cases, the victim of the attacks is female with her attackers being male members of her family or community.

BACKGROUND

Karo-Kari is an act of murder, in which a person is killed for his or her actual or perceived immoral behavior. Such "immoral behavior" may take the form of alleged marital infidelity, refusal to submit to an arranged marriage, demanding a divorce, perceived flirtatious behaviour and being raped. Suspicion and accusations alone are many times enough to defile a family's honour and therefore enough to warrant the killing of the woman.

In patriarchal cultures, women's lives are structured through a strict maintenance of an honour code. In order to preserve woman's chastity, women must abide by socially restrictive cultural practices pertaining to women's status and family izzat, or honour, such as the practice of purdah, the segregation of sexes. Honour killings are frequently more complex than the stated excuses of the perpetrators. More often than not, the murder relates to inheritance problems, feud-settling, or to get rid of the wife, for instance in order to remarry. Human rights agencies in Pakistan have repeatedly emphasized that victims were often women wanting to marry of their own will. In such cases, the victims held properties that the male members of their families did not wish to lose if the woman chose to marry outside the family.

A 1999 Amnesty International report drew specific attention to "the failure of the authorities to prevent these killings by investigating and punishing the perpetrators." According to women's rights advocates, the concepts of women as property and honour are so deeply entrenched in the social, political and economic fabric of Pakistan that the government, for the most part, ignores the daily occurrences of women being killed and maimed by their families. The fact that much of Pakistan's Tribal Areas are semi-autonomous and governed by often fundamentalist leaders makes federal enforcement difficult when attempted.

PREVALENCE

In 2011, human rights groups reported 720 honour killings in Pakistan (605 women and 115 men). Some discrepancy exists between reports. For instance Pakistan's Human Rights Commission reported that in 2010 there were 791 honor killings in the country, while Amnesty International cited 960 incidents of women alone who were slain in honour killings that year.

Over 4,000 cases were reported in Pakistan between 1998 and 2004. Of the victims, almost 2,700 were women and just over 1,300 were men; and 3,451 cases came before the courts. The highest rates were in Punjab, followed by the Sindh province. Lesser number of cases have also been reported in North-West Frontier Province (NWFP) and inBalochistan. Nilofar Bakhtiar, advisor to Prime Minister Shaukat Aziz, stated that in 2003, as many as 1,261 women were murdered in honour killings.

Complications in Data

Data and its absence is difficult to interpret. One reason is the reluctance to report honor killings to official bodies. Another reason is that honor killings are occurring in cultural and social contexts which do not recognize the criminality of honor killings. The very nature of honor killings reflects deeply entrenched notions of "honour" and "morality," in which the perpetrator is upholding justice and order when the victim commits deplorable social acts. Honor killings thus inverts the roles of "right" and "wrong." The perpetrator becomes the champion of justice while the victim becomes the perpetrator and accused of the criminal act. Furthermore, human rights advocates are in wide agreement that the reported cases do not reflect the full extent of the issue, as honour killings have a high level of support in Pakistan's rural society, and thus often go unreported. Frequently, women killed in honour killings are recorded as having committed suicide or died in accidents.

SPECIFIC OCCURRENCES

In one of the most publicized honour killing cases committed in Pakistan, Samia Sarwar was murdered by her family in the Lahore office of well-known human rights activistsAsma Jahangir and Hina Jilani in April 1999. As Sarwar sought assistance for a divorce from her first cousin, her family arranged her murder after the shame felt in her attempt to marry a man of her choice. The police did not make any arrests or pursue prosecution as Sarwar's family is highly well known in elite, political circles. The 2000 award-winning BBC documentary, "License to Kill," covers Samia's killing in Pakistan.

Amnesty International reported that on 27 April 2010, Ayman Udas, a Pashtun singer from the Peshawar area, was shot to death apparently by her two brothers who "viewed her divorce, remarriage and artistic career as damaging to family honour." No one was prosecuted. In 2008, three teenage girls were buried alive after refusing arranged marriages.

A widely reported case was that of Taslim Khatoon Solangi, 17, of Hajna Shah village in Khairpur district, which was widely reported after her father, 57-year-old Gul Sher Solangi, publicized the case. He alleged his eight months' pregnant daughter was tortured and killed on March 7, 2008, by members of her village claiming that she had brought dishonour to the tribe. Solangi's father claimed that it was orchestrated by her father-in-law, who accused her of carrying a child conceived out of wedlock, potentially with the added motive of trying to take over the family farm. On 27 May 2014 a pregnant woman named Farzana Iqbal (née Parveen) was stoned to death by her family in front of a Pakistani High Court for eloping and marrying the man she loved, Muhammad Iqbal. Police investigator Mujahid quoted the father as saying: "I killed my daughter as she had insulted all of our family by marrying a man without our consent, and I have no regret over it." Muhammad Iqbal stated that it had been a prolonged engagement, and Farzana's father had become enraged only after Iqbal refused a demand for more money than the originally agreed amount of the bride price. Muhammad Iqbal strangled his first wife so that he would be free to marry Farzana, and police said he had been released after that murder when a "compromise" was reached with his first wife's family.

PAKISTANI LAW

An Amnesty International report noted "the failure of the authorities to prevent these killings by investigating and punishing the perpetrators." Honour killings are supposed to be prosecuted as ordinary murder, but in practice, police and prosecutors often ignore it. The Pakistani government's failure to take effective measures to end the practice of honor killings is indicative of a weakening of political institutions, corruption, and economic decline. In the wake of civil crisis, people turn to other alternative models, such as traditional tribal customs. In some rural parts of Pakistan, the male-dominated jirga, or tribal council, decides affairs and its executive decisions take primacy over state legislation. A jirga arbitrates based on tribal consensus and tribal values among clients. Tribal notions of justice often include violence on client's behalf.

Hudood Ordinance

In the 1970s, Pakistan experienced extensive legal, political,economic, and social changes which severely curtailed the rights of women. In 1977, military ruler GeneralMuhammad Zia-ul-Haq, initiated a series of repressive legal and political measures as part of his 'Islamization' agenda.

The Hudood Ordinance was a set of laws prescribing punishments for crimes such as rape, adultery, theft, use of alcohol and drugs. Haq intended to implement Islamic ShariaLaw by enforcing punishments mentioned in the Qur'an and Sunnah for zina, or extramarital sex. In the provisions of zina, a rape victim is liable to prosecution for adultery if she cannot produce four male witnesses (under Islamic law, a male's testimony is equivalent to two female's testimonies). This serves to reduce or totally exclude female evidence in courts. More importantly, the Hudood Ordinance diminishes women's legal abilities, as women become legally defined and situated as dependents of their biological family and community. Pakistani women in legal contexts are not defined as "sui juris", that is, within the bounds of personhood, autonomy, and independent decision-making. A conference held in May 2005 in Islamabad, Pakistan addressed whether Pakistani law, governments and international agencies were having any success in reducing honour killings in the country. They found that more cases of honour killing are being reported rather than hidden, and more women are having the courage to come forward. But, they found there was a severe lack of proper implementation of laws and assurances that men who commit honour killings are not given lighter sentences. The conference found primary fault with Pakistan's Zina laws that put women in an unfair disadvantage and inferior position, often at the mercy of men to prove their innocence.

1990 Qisas and Diyat Ordinance

Most honor killings are encompassed by the 1990 Qisas and Diyat Ordinance, which permits the individual and his or her family to retain control over a crime, including the right to determine whether to report the crime, prosecute the offender, or demand diyat (or compensation). This allows serious crimes such as honor killings to become "privatized" and to escape state scrutiny, shifting responsibility from the state to the individual. Under Islamic Sharia law, the punishment for murder, homicide or infliction of injury can either be in the form of qisas (equal punishment for the crime committed) or diyat (monetary compensation payable to the victims or their legal heirs). These concepts are applied in different ways in different Islamic systems.

In Pakistan, the right to waive qisas, or punishment, is given to the family of the victim. If and when the case reaches a court of law, the victim's family may 'pardon' the murderer (who may well be one of them), or be pressured to accept diyat (financial compensation). The murderer then goes free. Courts have used provisions like this to circumvent penalties for honor killings. Once such a pardon has been secured, the state has no further writ on the matter although often the killers are relatives of the victim. Human rights agencies in Pakistan have repeatedly emphasized that women falling prey to karo-kari were usually those wanting to marry of their own will. In many cases, the victims held properties that the male members of their families did not wish to lose if the women chose to marry outside the family. More often than not, the karo-kari murder relates to inheritance problems, feud-settling, or to get rid of the wife, for instance in order to remarry.

INTERNATIONALACTIVISM

Human rights are natural rights, fundamentally ensured to every human, regardless of nationality, race, gender, or ethnic group. Through the ongoing work of the United Nations, the universality of human rights has been clearly established and recognized in international law.

In March 1996, Pakistan ratified the CEDAW, or the Convention on the Elimination of All Forms of Discrimination against Women. By ratifying CEDAW, Pakistan promises to abolish discriminatory laws and establish tribunals and public institutions to effectively protect women. CEDAW, as a human rights treaty, notably targets culture and tradition as contributing factors to gender-based discrimination. In 1993, the United Nations General Assembly adopted the Declaration on the Elimination of Violence against Women, entreating states not to invoke custom, tradition, or religious consideration to avoid their obligation to eliminate violence against women.

According to Amnesty International, if a government is negligent in prosecuting perpetrators, it is liable and complicit in those abuses. The role of the modern nation-state is to ensure full protection of universal human rights. The prevalence of honour killings in Pakistan underscores the Pakistani government's systematic failure in ensuring fundamental human rights to women. However, international organizations and feminists globally have been criticized for upholding a Western-centric agenda when engaging in honour-killing activism. Long-standing discourses on the universality of human rights versus cultural relativism indicate tensions in international activism for women's rights. But cultural relativism can be partially resolved when local activists make clear that cultural customs are harmful to women and in violation of international human rights standard. Cultural and religious customs are constantly evolving and it is necessary to partner with regional activists in Pakistan to be at the forefront for demanding change.

PAKISTANI ACTIVISM

Human rights activists in Pakistan have been on the forefront of change and reform to end the practice of honor killings. Emphasizing universal human rights, democracy, and global feminism, Pakistani activists seek legal reform to criminalize the practice and protect victims from abuse. Asma Jehangir, chairperson of Human Rights Commission of Pakistan, and Hina Jilani are Pakistani lawyers reinvigorating civil society to become critical of the Pakistani state's failure to ensure fair rights and benefits to its female citizenry. Jehangir and Jilani founded Pakistan's first legal aid center in 1986 and a women's shelter called Dastak in 1991 for women fleeing from violence. Other notable Pakistani activists working on reporting and deterring honour killings include Aitzaz Ahsan, Anis Amir Ali, Ayaz Latif Palijo, and Shahnaz Bukhari.

Legal Reform

In September 2010, the Punjab law minister announced that violent crimes against women, including honour killings, would be tried under the country's Anti-Terrorism Act. On December 8, 2004, under international and domestic pressure, Pakistan enacted a law that made honour killings punishable by a prison term of seven years, or by the death penalty in the most extreme cases.

Women and human rights organizations were, however, skeptical of the law's impact, as it stops short of outlawing the practice of allowing killers to buy their freedom by paying compensation to the victim's relatives. This is problematic because most honour killings are committed by a close relative. In many cases, the family of the victim and the family of the accused are indistinguishable, so negotiating a pardon with the victim's family under the Islamic provisions becomes ineffective. Former judge Nasira Iqbal told IRINthe bill allowed close relatives of the deceased to escape punishment with ease. In March 2005 the Pakistani parliament rejected a bill, which sought to strengthen the law against the practice of honour killing declaring it to be un-Islamic. The bill was eventually passed in November 2006. However, doubts of its effectiveness remain.

4

Criminal Justice System of Asia

CRIMINAL JUSTICE SYSTEM OF JAPAN

Three basic features of Japan's system of criminal justice characterize its operations. First, the institutions—police, government prosecutors' offices, courts, and correctional organs—maintain close and cooperative relations with each other, consulting frequently on how best to accomplish the shared goals of limiting and controlling crime. Second, citizens are encouraged to assist in maintaining public order, and they participate extensively in crime prevention campaigns, apprehension of suspects, and offender rehabilitation programs. Finally, officials who administer criminal justice are allowed considerable discretion in dealing with offenders.

HISTORY

Until the Meiji Restoration in 1868, the Japanese criminal justice system was controlled mainly by daimyo. Public officials, not laws, guided and constrained people to conform to moral norms. In accordance with the Confucian ideal, officials were to serve as models of behavior; the people, who lacked rights and had only obligations, were expected to obey. Such laws as did exist were transmitted through local military officials in the form of local domain laws. Specific enforcement varied from domain to domain, and no formalpenal codes existed. Justice was generally harsh, and severity depended upon one's status. Kin and neighbors could share blame for an offender's guilt: whole families and villages could be flogged or put to death for one member's transgression.

After 1868 the justice system underwent rapid transformation. The first publicly promulgated legal codes, the Penal Code of 1880 and the Code of Criminal Instruction of 1880, were based on French models, i.e. the Napoleonic code. Offenses were specified, and set punishments were established for particular crimes. Both codes were innovative in that they treated all citizens as equals, provided for centralized administration of criminal justice, and prohibited punishment by ex post facto law. Guilt was held to be personal;collective guilt and guilt by association were abolished. Offenses against the emperor were spelled out for the first time.

Innovative aspects of the codes notwithstanding, certain provisions reflected traditional attitudes toward authority. The prosecutor represented the state and sat with the judge on a raised platform—his position above the defendant and the defense counsel suggesting their relative status. Under a semi-inquisitorial system, primary responsibility for questioning witnesses lay with the judge, and defense counsel could question witnesses only through the judge. Cases were referred to trial only after a judge presided over a preliminary fact-finding investigation in which the suspect was not permitted counsel. Because in all trials available evidence had already convinced the court in a preliminary procedure, the defendant's legal presumption of innocence at trial was undermined, and the legal recourse open to his counsel was further weakened.

The Penal Code was substantially revised in 1907 to reflect the growing influence of German law in Japan, and the French practice of classifying offenses into three types was eliminated. More important, where the old code had allowed very limited judicial discretion, the new one permitted the judge to apply a wide range of subjective factors insentencing.

After World War II, occupation authorities initiated reform of the constitution and laws in general. Except for omitting offenses relating to war, the imperial family, and adultery, the 1947 Penal Code remained virtually identical to the 1907 version. The criminal procedure code, however, was substantially revised to incorporate rules guaranteeing the rights of the accused. The system became almost completely accusatorial, and the judge, although still able to question witnesses, decided a case on evidence presented by both sides. The preliminary investigative procedure was suppressed. The prosecutor and defense counsel sat on equal levels, below the judge. Laws on indemnification of the wrongly accused and laws concerning juveniles, prisons, probation, and minor offenses were also passed in the postwar years to supplement criminal justice administration.

CRIMINAL PROCEDURE

The nation's criminal justice officials follow specified legal procedures in dealing with offenders. Once a suspect is arrested by national or prefectural police, the case is turned over to attorneys in the Supreme Public Prosecutors Office, who are the government's sole agents in prosecuting lawbreakers. Under the Ministry of Justice's administration, these officials work under Supreme Court rules and are career civil servants who can be removed from office only for incompetence or impropriety. Prosecutors presented the government's case before judges in the Supreme Court and the four types of lower courts: high courts, district courts, summary courts, and family courts. Penal and probation officials administer programs for convicted offenders under the direction of public prosecutors. After identifying a suspect, police have the authority to exercise some discretion in determining the next step. If, in cases pertaining to theft, the amount is small or already returned, the offense petty, the victim unwilling to press charges, the act accidental, or the likelihood of a repetition not great, the police can either drop the case or turn it over to a prosecutor. Reflecting the belief that appropriate remedies are sometimes best found outside the formal criminal justice mechanisms, in 1990 over 70 percent of criminal cases were not sent to the prosecutor.

JUVENILES

Police also exercise wide discretion in matters concerning juveniles. Police are instructed by law to identify and counsel minors who appear likely to commit crimes, and they can refer juvenile offenders and non-offenders alike to child guidance centers to be treated on an outpatient basis. Police can also assign juveniles or those considered to be harming the welfare of juveniles to special family courts. These courts were established in 1949 in the belief that the adjustment of a family's situation is sometimes required to protect children and prevent juvenile delinquency. Family courts are run in closed sessions, try juvenile offenders under special laws, and operate extensive probationary guidance programs. The cases of young people between the ages of fourteen and twenty can, at the judgment of police, be sent to the public prosecutor for possible trial as adults before a judge under the general criminal law.

CITIZENS

Arrest

Police have to secure warrants to search for or seize evidence. A warrant is also necessary for an arrest, although if the crime is very serious or if the perpetrator is likely to flee, it can be obtained immediately after arrest. Within forty-eight hours after placing a suspect under detention, the police have to present their case before a prosecutor, who is then required to apprise the accused of the charges and of the right to counsel. Within another twenty-four hours, the prosecutor has to go before a judge and present a case to obtain a detention order. Suspects can be held for ten days (extensions are granted in almost all cases when requested), pending an investigation and a decision whether or not to prosecute. In the 1980s, some suspects were reported to have been mistreated during this detention to exact a confession. These detentions often occur at cells within police stations, called daiyo kangoku.

Prosecution

Prosecution can be denied on the grounds of insufficient evidence or on the prosecutor's judgment. Under Article 248 of the Code of Criminal Procedure, after weighing the offender's age, character, and environment, the circumstances and gravity of the crime, and the accused's rehabilitative potential, public action does not have to be instituted, but can be denied or suspended and ultimately dropped after a probationary period. Because the investigation and disposition of a case can occur behind closed doors and the identity of an accused person who is not prosecuted is rarely made public, an offender can successfully reenter society and be rehabilitated under probationary status without the stigma of a criminal conviction.

Inquest of Prosecution

Institutional safeguards check the prosecutors' discretionary powers not to prosecute. Lay committees are established in conjunction with branch courts to hold inquests on a prosecutor's decisions. These committees meet four times yearly and can order that a case be reinvestigated and prosecuted. Victims or interested parties can also appeal a decision not to prosecute.

Trial

Most offenses are tried first in district courts before one or three judges, depending on the severity of the case. Defendants are protected from self-incrimination, forced confession, and unrestricted admission of hearsay evidence. In addition, defendants have the right to counsel, public trial, and cross-examination. Trial by jury was authorized by the 1923 Jury Law but was suspended in 1943. A new lay judge law was enacted in 2004 and came into effect in May 2009, but it only applies to certain serious crimes.

The judge conducts the trial and is authorized to question witnesses, independently call for evidence, decide guilt, and pass sentence. The judge can also suspend any sentence or place a convicted party on probation. Should a judgment of not guilty be rendered, the accused is entitled to compensation by the state based on the number of days spent in detention. Criminal cases from summary courts, family courts, and district courts can be appealed to the high courts by both the prosecution and the defense. Criminal appeal to the Supreme Court is limited to constitutional questions and a conflict of precedent between the Supreme Court and high courts.

The criminal code sets minimum and maximum sentences for offenses to allow for the varying circumstances of each crime and criminal. Penalties range from fines and short-term incarceration to compulsory labor and the death penalty. Heavier penalties are meted out to repeat offenders. Capital punishment consists of death by hanging and is usually imposed for multiple homicides. After a sentence is finalized, the only recourse for a convict to gain an acquittal is through a retrial. A retrial can be granted if the convicted person or their legal representative show reasonable doubt about the finalized verdict, such as clear evidence that past testimony or expert opinions in the trial were false.

Trial by Lay Judge

The first trial by citizen judge, "saiban-in", began August 3, 2009 under a new law passed in 2004. Six citizens became lay judges and joined three professional judges to determine the verdict and sentence the defendant. Japan belongs to an inquisitory system of criminal process. Therefore, a judge oversees the proceedings and also determines the guilt and the sentence of the accused. The citizen lay judges as well as professional judges are allowed to put forth questions to defendants, witnesses and victims during the trial. The new system aims to invite participation of the wider community and also provide a speedier, more democratic justice system, according to Eisuke Sato, the justice minister. The first trial by lay judge lasted four days, while some comparable criminal cases may last years under the old system. The historic trial of 72-year-old Katsuyoshi Fujii who stabbed his 66-year-old neighbor to death had substantial media attention. The selected lay judges must be voters, at least 20 years old, and possess a secondary level education. Professional lawyers and politicians may not serve as lay judges in the new system. At least one judge must concur with the majority vote from the lay judges in regards to a guilty verdict, however a majority not guilty verdict by the lay judges will stand. During the inaugural case, the citizens relied on the professional judges to help ascertain a sentence for the verdict decided upon, but felt confident in their interpretation of the trial arguments presented by prosecution and defence.

CONVICTION RATE

One of the main features of the Japanese criminal justice system well known in the rest of the world is its extremely high conviction rate, which exceeds 99%. Some in the common law countries argue that this is to do with elimination of the jury system in 1943, however, trials by jury were rarely held as the accused had to give up the right to appeal. Lobbying by human rights groups and the Japan Federation of Bar Associations resulted in the passing of a judicial reform bill in May, 2004, which introduced a lay-judge system in 2009, which is often confused with jury system in common law countries.

J. Mark Ramseyer of Harvard Law School and Eric B. Rasmusen of Indiana University examine if the accusation is in fact warranted. In their paper ("Why Is the Japanese Conviction Rate So High?") they examined two possibilities. One is that judges who come under the control of central bureaucracy are pressured to pass a guilty verdict, ensuring high conviction. Another possibility is that, given that the non-jury system under inquisition system has predictable ruling on guilt, Japan's understaffed prosecutors working on low budgets only bring the most obviously guilty defendants to trial, and do not file indictments in cases in which they are not certain they can win.

All Japanese court rulings are accessible in digital format; the two academics examined every case after World War II in which the court found the defendant not guilty. The result is mixed. Simple statistical analysis shows that the judge's later career tends to be negatively affected by a non-guilty verdict. However, by examining the individual cases, the two academics found that all of those cases which negatively affected judges' careers had political implications (such as labour law or electoral law) and that the facts of the case (i.e. the defendants committing the accused deed) itself were never in dispute. However, judges delivered 'not guilty' verdicts on technicalities such as statutes of limitation or constitutional arguments, which were subsequently reversed in a higher court. In cases in which the judge delivered a 'not guilty' verdict because they ruled that there was insufficient evidence to ascertain that the defendants did the accused deed, the judge suffered no negative consequence. For this reason, the paper argued that Japanese judges are politically conservative in legal interpretation but are not biased in matter of fact.

In the matter relating to Japanese prosecutors being extremely cautious, the paper found ample evidence for it. In Japan, 99.7% of all the cases brought to court resulted in conviction, while in the U.S. the figure is 88%. According to a cited research, in the U.S. the accused contest guilt in 22% of federal cases and 11% of state cases, while in Japan, the ratio is modestly less. The paper attributes this difference to greater predictability of the outcome in Japanese cases. This is due to two reasons.

One is that it is the judge rather than the jury who determines the verdict. As judges "have seen it all before" and the lawyers on both sides "have seen them seeing it", as they can read the judge's previous ruling (which includes written reasoning for the previous verdict), the way that the judge thinks and argues is very predictable.

Secondly, Japanese trials before the institution of the current lay judge system, were discontinuous. The defense and the prosecutor would first gather in front of the judges and present the issue. Then, the court would enter recess and both sides would go back to prepare their case. As they reconvened on different dates, they would then present each case which the judges examined, the court would be put in recess again and each side would go back to gather further evidence. Some complex trials took years or even a decade to conclude which is impossible under jury system. During the questioning of evidence, judges were explicit about their opinions by the way they questioned the evidence, which gave greater predictability about the final verdict.

For this reason, the prosecutor is far more likely to bring in the case where conviction is assured and the accused is far more likely to settle. Moreover, the paper found that Japanese prosecutors have a far more pressing need to be selective. In the U.S., the federal government employs 27,985 lawyers and the states employ another 38,242 (of which 24,700 are state prosecutors). In Japan, with about a third of U.S. population, the entire government employs a mere 2,000. Despite Japan having a low crime rate, such numbers create a significant case overload for prosecutors. In the U.S., there are 480 arrests (96 serious cases) per year per state prosecutor. (The actual figure is lower as some are prosecuted in federal court). In Japan, the figure is 700 per year per prosecutor. In the U.S., a rough estimate is that 42% of arrests in felony cases result in prosecution - while in Japan, the figure is only 17.5%.

In murder, U.S. police arrested 19,000 people for 26,000 murders, in which 75% were prosecuted and courts convicted 12,000 people. In Japan, 1,800 people were arrested for 1,300 murders, but prosecutors tried only 43%. Had the allegation that Japanese prosecutors use weak evidence mostly based on (forced) confessions to achieve convictions been true, the larger proportion of arrests would have resulted in prosecutions and eventual conviction. But the opposite is true. In fact, the data indicates that Japanese prosecutors bring charges only when the evidence is overwhelming and likelihood of conviction is near absolute, which gives a greater incentive for the accused to confess and aim for a lighter sentence, which, in turn, results in a high rate for confession.

The Japanese criminal justice system, despite retaining the death penalty, is relatively lenient in sentencing by the standard of the United States. Outside capital cases, many of those sentenced to life sentences are paroled within 15 years. Those convicted of less heinous murder and manslaughter are likely to serve less than 10 years.

Those convicted of rape will often serve less than two to five years. It is even possible for someone convicted of murder to serve a suspended sentence if the defense successfully argues for mitigating circumstances. Moreover, in Japanese criminal proceedings the conviction and sentencing phase are separate. In the Japanese criminal justice system, these are distinct phases, echoing that of common law jurisdictions where sentencing is usually remitted to a later hearing after a finding of guilt. The court proceedings first determine guilt, then a second proceeding takes place to determine the sentence. Prosecutors and defense teams argue each phase. Defense lawyers, given the predictability of the outcome in term of guilt once the charge is brought, together with leniency of punishment (except in death penalty cases), often advise the accused to confess their guilt in trial. Remorse is seen as a mitigating factor which tends to bring reduced sentences.

CONFESSION IN JAPANESE CRIMINAL INVESTIGATION

Many Western human rights organizations alleged that the high conviction rate is due to rampant use of conviction solely based on confession. Confessions are often obtained after long periods of questioning by police as those arrested may be held for up to 23 days. This can, at times, take weeks during which time the suspect is in detention and can be prevented from contacting a lawyer or family. Article 38 of Japan's Constitution categorically requires that "no person shall be convicted or punished in cases where the only proof against suspect is his/her own confession," In practice, this constitutional requirement take a form of safeguard known as "revelation of secret" (Himitsu no Bakuro, lit "outing of secret"). Because suspects are put through continuous interrogation which could last up to 23 days as well as isolation from the outside world, including access to lawyers, both the Japanese judiciary and the public are well aware that confession of guilt can easily be forced. Consequently, the court (and the public) take the view that mere confession of guilt alone is never any sufficient ground for conviction.

Instead, for confession to be a valid evidence for conviction, the Japanese court requires confession to include revelation of verifiable factual matter which only the perpetrator of the crime could have known such as the location of an undiscovered body or the time and place the murder weapon was purchased, a fact about the crime scene, etc. Furthermore, to safeguard against the possibility that the interrogator implanting such knowledge into confession, the prosecutor must prove that such revelation of secret was unknown to the police until the point of confession. For example, in the Sachiura murder case which happened in 1948, the conviction was initially secured by the confession of the location of the body which was yet to be discovered. However, it later transpired that the police likely knew the location of the body and this created a possibility that the confession of the location of the body could be forged and implanted by the investigating police, resulting in the higher court declaring the confession unsafe and reversing the verdict. While it is impossible for an innocent suspect to reveal relevant information about a crime even under severe torture, a guilty suspect is likely to crack under prolonged interrogation in isolation and make a damning confession. Activists claim that the Japanese justice system (and Japanese public to some extent) consider that prolonged interrogation of suspect in isolation without access to lawyers is justified to solve the criminal cases without risking the miscarriage of justice.

In addition, the requirement that the revelation of relevant information by the accused was unknown to the police and that the prosecutor examines the police investigation before the case is brought to the court, is seen as an extra layer of safeguard for the validity of confession as evidence.

However, most miscarriage of justice cases in Japan are, indeed, the results of conviction solely based on the confession of the accused. In these case, (1) the record of sequence and timing of the police discoveries of evidence and the timing of confession is unclear (or even faked by the police) (2) the contents of the revelation of secret has only weak relevance to the crime itself or that (3) the revelation of secret to be actually vague enough that it is apply only loosely to the elements of crime (Prosecutor's fallacy). Serious miscariage of justice cases in Japan involve police deliberately faking the police evidence (and insufficient supervision by the prosecutor to spot such rogue behaviour) such as where the police already knew (or suspected) the location of the body or the murder weapon but they fake the police record to make it appear that it is the suspect who revealed the location. During the 1970s, a series of reversals of death penalty cases brought attention to the fact that some accused, after intensive interrogation signed as-yet unwritten confessions, which were later filled in by investigating police officers. Moreover, in some cases, the police falsified the record so that it appear that the accused confessed to the location where the body was buried, yet the truth was that the police had written in the location in the confession after the body was discovered by other means. These coerced confessions, together with other circumstantial evidence, often convinced judges to (falsely) convict.

Currently the Japanese Federation of Bar Associations is calling for the entire interrogation phase to be recorded to prevent similar incidents occurring. The International Bar Association, which encompasses the Japanese Federation of Bar Associations, cited problems in its "Interrogation of Criminal Suspects in Japan". Japan's current Minister of Justice, Hideo Hiraoka, has also supported videotaping interrogations. Police and prosecutors have traditionally been opposed to videotaping interrogations, stating that it would undermine their ability to get confessions. The current office of prosecutors has, however, reversed their previous opposition to this proposal. Proponents argue that without the credibility of confessions supported by electronic recordings, the lay judges may refuse to convict in a case when other offered evidence is weak. It is also argued that recording of interrogation may allow lowering standard in the "revelation of secret" that confession must contain the element of crime which police and prosecutor did not know. Once the recording is introduced, it would become impossible for the police to forge confession. Then, it may become possible to bring conviction based on confession of elements of crime which only perpetrator "and" police knew.

In October 2007, the BBC published a feature giving examples and an overview of "'Forced confessions' in Japan". The case was called "Shibushi Case". In addition, Hiroshi Yanagihara, who was convicted in November 2002 for attempted rape and rape due to forced confession and the identification by the victim despite an alibi based on the phone record, was cleared in October 2007 when the true culprit was arrested for an unrelated crime. The two cases damage the credibility of Japanese Police.

To Japanese citizens and police, however, the arrest itself already creates the presumption of guilt which needs only to be verified via a confession. The interrogation reports prepared by police and prosecutors and submitted to the trial courts often constitute the central evidence considered when weighing the guilt or innocence of the suspect.

CRIMINAL JUSTICE SYSTEM OF CHINA

China is a large country with a total land area of 9.6 million square kilometres, and more than 1 billion people which amounts to one fourth of the world population. People's Republic of China was established as a socialist country in 1949. Since then, efforts have been made to enact basic laws concerning criminal justice administration. It was in 1979, after the period of "Cultural Revolution" which lasted for ten years, that the Criminal Law and Criminal Procedure Law were enacted. At the same time, laws concerning the organization and function of the courts and public prosecution were also re-organized. Basic laws with regard to the lawyers, arrest and detention of the suspects, civil suit procedures, marriages, etc. have been established.

The Chinese Criminal Law takes the concept of Marxism, Leninism and Mao Zedong as its guide. It proclaims that its tasks are to use criminal punishments to struggle against all counter-revolutionary and other criminal acts in order to safeguard the system of the people's democratic dictatorship and the smooth progress of the course of socialist construction.

The Law takes the Constitution as its basis. Article 28 of the Constitution stipulates that "The State maintains public order and suppresses treasonable and other counter-revolutionary activities; it penalizes acts that endanger public security and disrupt the socialist economy and other criminal activities, and punishes and reforms criminals".

Since 1979, higher legal education has considerably developed through universities and other institutions. High priority is being given to publicizing information on the legal system through, eg. the China Law Journal, and many provincial and municipal journals, magazines and newspapers. Law education has been introduced in the primary, middle and other schools. Studies, symposia and public lectures are often organized in factories, mines, rural communes and brigades in order to give increased publicity to the Constitution and other laws.

The age for bearing criminal responsibility is sixteen. Minors under the age of fourteen are entirely exempted from criminal responsibility, even if they commit acts harmful to society. Minors aged fourteen but under the age of sixteen shall partially bear criminal responsibility, that is to say they are responsible criminally only in cases involving murder and manslaughter, serious injury, robbery, arson, habitual theft or other acts seriously undermining social order. For delinquents aged fourteen to seventeen but younger than eighteen, the Law requires a lenient punishment - to be specific, a lessor penalty within the range of the legally-prescribed punishment. When minors are not punished because they are under sixteen, the heads of their families or their guardians are to be ordered to subject them to discipline or when necessary, the minors may be given shelter or rehabilitation by the Government.

The crime rate in China has shown a drastic increase in recent years. Still China remains one of the countries with the lowest crime rate in the world. Of all the crimes reported, theft accounted for about 80%, but the violent crimes like murder and robbery were also up. Crimes associated with gangs abroad, such as trafficking in narcotics, smuggling of gold and relics, and counterfeiting of currency and credit cards also increased during 1988.

SANCTIONS

The Criminal Law provides that Principal Punishments are classified as control, criminal detention, fixed term imprisonment, life imprisonment and death penalty. Control is a criminal penalty imposed for minor offences. The offender continues to work in his place of employment and continues to receive his normal wages, while undergoing the supervision of the public security organs (police) and the masses. He is required to make periodical reports on his circumstances to the public security organ concerned.

Criminal detention is a criminal penalty imposed for relatively minor offences, and totally different from pre-trial detention. The criminal on whom this penalty is imposed is deprived of his freedom and confined in a detention house by the local organ of public security rather than being put in prison. He may go home for one or two days each month and be paid for work. The term of fixed-term imprisonment is not less than six months and nor more than fifteen years. An offender sentenced to fixed term imprisonment or life imprisonment is to have his sentence executed in prison or in other place for reform through labour. Reform through labour is to be carried out on any offender who is imprisoned, as long as he has the ability to labour.

The death penalty is only to be applied to those offenders who commit the most heinous crimes. The Criminal Law provides for two types of death penalty viz. death penalty with two year suspension of execution and death penalty without suspension of execution. The Law stipulates that in the case of a criminal who should be sentenced to death, but for whom immediate execution is not essential, a two-year suspension of execution may be pronounced at the time the sentence of death is imposed; the criminal will be put into prison and reform-through-labour carried out and the results observed. If the criminal truly repents during the period of suspension, he is to be given a reduction of sentence to life imprisonment upon the expiration of the two-year period; and, if he not only truly repents but also demonstrates meritorious service, he is to be given a reduction of sentence to not less than fifteen years and not more than twenty years of fixed-term imprisonment upon the expiration of the period. Only those who have resisted reform in an odious manner, provided the evidence of such behaviour is verified, are to be executed upon a ruling or an approval of the Supreme Court. The Criminal Law provides for the following supplementary punishments: fines, deprivation of political rights, and confiscation of property. These supplementary punishments may also be applied independently.

PROSECUTION

The people's procuratorates (public prosecutors) are responsible for initiating public prosecution. The people's procuratorates have the power to investigate criminal cases as well as the power to make decisions of prosecution, non-prosecution or exemption from prosecution in each criminal case considering the evidence of the case and nature and circumstances of the crime.

JUDICIARY

The people's courts are responsible for adjudication, and no other bodies are given the power to adjudicate criminal cases. The number of professional judges as of 31 December 1986 was 137,066, out of which 19,897 were female judges. More than 144,000 employees are working in the judicial system.

PRISONS

In Chinese prison services, there have been various new ways of mobilizing public participation in helping re-mould prisoners. For example, famous scholars, writers, educators, artists, musicians and sportspeople are invited to call on prisoners, and encourage them to make more efforts to reform themselves; former prisoners who have been already integrated into the society after release are organized to persuade current inmates to re-mould themselves; family members, relatives and friends of the prisoners are encouraged and provided with every facility to admonish and educate them.

NON-INSTITUTIONAL SERVICES

In China, supervision of offenders both during the suspension of execution of sentence and after release on parole is carried out by the public security organ (police). Probationers and parolees are turned over by the public security organ to a work unit or a basic level organization. The policeman in charge of the community shall supervise their daily life, their work and ideological trend and encourage their consciousness to become law-abiding citizens. Meanwhile the policeman shall keep in touch with their neighbours if they conduct any law- breaking activities.

PRE-TRIAL DETENTION

The Criminal Procedure Law stipulates that, in hearing a case of public prosecution, the people's court shall announce judgement within one month after accepting the case, and it may extend one month and one-half at the latest. Accordingly, pre-trial detention is not considered to pose any serious problem.

DIVERSION

There are several diversion schemes to imprisonment. Police are empowered to give warnings or to impose a certain limited amount of fines (not more than 200 yuan) to the criminals who have committed minor offences (Security Control and Enforcement Law). This warning and fine are regarded as a final sanction imposed by the police and they need not send the case to either the public prosecutor nor the court. This system is applicable to various types of minor offences including theft, embezzlement, fraud, assault, gambling, violations of traffic regulations and various types of public disturbances. If the person who receives this summary sanction is dissatisfied with the disposition, he/she can appeal to the higher police organ and finally to the courts. This scheme is fully utilized as an alternative and diversion to the formal criminal justice procedure and imprisonment.

At prosecution stage, public prosecutors are empowered to grant exemption from prosecution, considering the gravity of the crime and other circumstantial factors, even if there is enough evidence to convict the suspect. According to the Criminal Law, suspension of sentence may be pronounced for an offender who has been sentenced to criminal detention or to fixed-term imprisonment for not more than three years according to the circumstances of his/her crime and his/her demonstration of repentance, and where it is considered that applying a suspended sentence will not result in further harm to society.

An offender sentenced to fixed term imprisonment of which not less than half has been executed, or an offender sentenced to life imprisonment of which not less than ten years have been actually executed, may be granted parole if he/she demonstrates true repentance and will not cause further harm to society. If special circumstances exist, the above restrictions relating to the term executed need not be imposed. During the period of suspension of sentence and parole, the offender is placed under the supervision of the public security organ (police), and the public security organ utilizes the mass organization of the community to help watch the offender's daily behaviour and lead him/her to become a law-abiding citizen. It is said that the number of the revocation of suspension of sentence and parole because of the committal of new crime is very small, and that this type of community based treatment has been proving very successful, although clear statistics are not available in this regard.

REFORM THROUGH LABOUR

Offenders who have been sentenced to detention, fixed-term imprisonment, life imprisonment or the death penalty with suspension of execution, provided that they can work, are obligated to work. Under the basic policy of "reform through labour", emphasis is placed on educating and redeeming prisoners to law abiding citizens through daily labour in the institutions. The purpose of this policy is considered to re-mould their ideology, freeing them from bad influence and habits, and to resocialize them into someone who can live on their own labour and are useful to society. Labour is considered to be a principal measure of reforming criminals, though it is not the only one.

The system of reform-through labour has been said to be effective and successful over the past forty years. It is reported that, according to some sample statistics, among those who have served a term of imprisonment, 4-6% of them committed a crime again after release.

CRIMINAL JUSTICE SYSTEM IN INDIA

The Criminal Justice System in India has many loop holes. With my last assignment with Human Rights Law Network (HRLN) on Prisoner's Rights I came to know about several problems existing in the system. I witnessed so many cases where for petty crimes people are in jails for more than 3, 4 years. Many un-dertrials are detained because they have no money to get a bail or hire a lawyer to assist them. If he is unable to furnish surety, he cannot get bail and spends years in a prison. Quite often, the surety amount asked by the court is large that the poor cannot furnish it as a result he goes to the prison. And the speed of justice delivery system has given rise in Prison population which resulted in overcrowding.

Criminal Law of India is a replica of colonial times. It is hostile to the poor and the weaker sections of society. The law still serves and protects the needs of the haves and ignores the have-nots. Such biasness has resulted in rich people escaping law and the jail is more often full of the unprivileged class of society. The hierarchy of courts and with appeals after appeal have led to a situation where the poor cannot reach the temple of justice due to heavy cost of its access. In other words one can state that granting justice at a higher cost indirectly means the denial of justice. Such circumstances lead to a clear violation of the Supreme Court judgement which held, legal aid to a poor is a constitutional mandate not only by virtue of Article 39A but also Articles 14, 19, 21 which cannot be denied by the government.

When we think about prisons the image that comes to our mind is that of hard core criminals who were imprisoned for committing crimes. But in actual fact 64.7% of prisoners in Indian jails are undertrials who may or may not be punished. Thousands of them, arrested on suspicion of committing petty crimes, languish in jails for a much longer period than the maximum punishment under the law for the crime which they have committed. The presence of higher number of undertrials in the prison results in their over-crowding, which in turn causes many socio economic problems in the society.

As understood by a layman an, 'undertrial'is a person who is currently on trial or who is imprisoned on remand whilst awaiting trial. As defined in the Oxford Dictionary, 'A person who is on a trial in a court of law'. The 78th Report of Law Commission also includes a person who is in judicial custody on remand during investigation in the definition of an 'undertrial'.

The presence of large number of undertrial prisoners and their continuing stay for longer period definitely indicates the slow pace of trials which will leads to the overcrowding of prisons. In the National Human Rights Commissions view, unnecessary and unjustified arrests made by the police and the slow judicial processes causing congestion of undertrial prisoners are the main causes of overcrowding in jails. The poor are particularly worse off when confronted with criminal justice system. When prison population goes beyond its authorized capacity of accommodation, it is known as Over-crowding. Overcrowding in the Prisons is an important human rights issue as it results in deterioration of the general living conditions of the prisoners. It also creates hindrances in the reformation process. Prison officers find it difficult to initiate and continue correctional measures. Overcrowding contributes to a greater risk of disease, higher noise levels, which affect the health of the prisoners, and adversely affect the hygienic conditions, surveillance difficulties, which increase the danger level. This apart, life is more difficult for inmates and work is more onerous for staff when prisoners are in over capacity.

The system of imprisonment has originated in the first quarter of the 19th century. In the initial stages the prisons were used as a place for detention of the undertrials. It has undergone a radical change and the penology of the present day has become centered on imprisonment as a measure of rehabilitation of the criminals. But unfortunately even now the prisons are crowded with under-trial prisoners. Many of them are innocent persons who are caught in the web of the law eagerly waiting for their trial date and several of them are prepared to confess their crime and accept their sentence

There is a law where undertrials can get justice but the implementation is an issue. In one of the study the data compiled by the National Crime Records Bureau (NCRB) at the end of 2013, the total number of convict prisoners was 1,29,608 and under-trial prisoners was 2,78,503 in jails of the country, there were 1,92,202 Hindu, 57,936 Muslim, 11,666 Sikh, 12,406 Christian, 4,293 Other under-trial prisoners in jails at the end of 2013. In terms of societal strata there were 59,326 Scheduled Caste, 31,581 Scheduled Tribe, 87,848 OBC and 99,748 Other under-trial prisoners at the end of 2013.

Supreme Court of India in its order dated 5.9.2014 in Writ Petition No. 310/2005 –Bhim Singh Vs Union of India & Others relating to under-trial prisoners, has directed for effective implementation of Section 436A of the Code of Criminal Procedure by directing the jurisdictional Magistrate/Chief Judicial Magi-strate/Sessions Judge to hold one sitting in a week in each jail/prison for two months commencing from 1st October, 2014 for the purposes of effective implementation of section 436A of the Code of Criminal Procedure. In its sittings in jail, the above judicial officers shall identify the under-trial prisoners who have completed half period of the maximum period or maximum period of Imprisonment provided for the said offence under the law and after complying with the procedure prescribed under Section 436A pass an appropriate order in jail itself for release of such under-trial prisoners who fulfill the requirement of section 436A of Cr PC.

One of the serious concerns for these undertrials is their family. In the absence of the main breadwinner, many families are forced into destitution. This combined with the social stigma and ostracism that they face, leads to circumstances propelling children towards delinquency and exploitation by others. It is a vicious circle. The problems become acute when they belong to the socio-economically marginalized and exploited sections of the society. One of the horrible plights a person can undergo is spending years in a jail as undertrials and at the end he was found not guilty. In such a situation can anyone compensate them for the mental agony and torture they and their family have suffered or give back to them the lost years, the loss of honour and reputation. The undertrials should not be kept in the jails as far as possible. If unavoidable then they should be kept separately with in the prison so that they are not allowed to mix with the convicts. Within the undertrials also a classification should be made so that the first and young offenders should be kept away from the hard core criminals thereby preventing contamination.

There are hundreds of examples where court acquitted people from criminal charges after spending more than 10 years in Jail. There are no proper policies for their rehabilitation. No one can compensate them the time they spent and the things they lose during the period. But to respect their human rights governments should form a policy to adequately rehabilitate them.

In order to mitigate the conditions of the undertrial prisoners the first and foremost thing that has to do is to bring down their population drastically. This cannot happen unless all the branches of the criminal jus-tice system work hand in hand. The presence of large number of undertrial prisoners is really shame to any criminal justice administration .For this we have to take these undertrials out of the prison or not to keep them for a long period as well as not to sent more undertrials to the prison.

BAHRAIN

POLICE AND THE CRIMINAL JUSTICE SYSTEM

The Ministry of Interior has overall responsibility for public security and law and order. Under the ministry, the national police has primary responsibility for maintaining public order and preventing and investigating crimes. The National Guard—a semiautonomous body—has guard duties on the border and at oil fields, utilities, and other strategic locations. The guard acts as a reserve for the regular forces and reinforces the metropolitan police as needed.

Police selected for officer rank attend a three-year program at the Police Academy. National Guard officer candidates attend the Kuwaiti Military College, after which they receive specialized guard training. Women work in certain police departments, such as criminal investigation, inquiries, and airport security.

The principal police divisions are criminal investigation, traffic, emergency police, nationality and passports, immigration, prisons, civil defense, and trials and courtsmartial . The criminal investigation division is responsible for ordinary criminal cases; Kuwait State Security investigates security-related offenses.

Both are involved in investigations of terrorism and those suspected of collaboration with Iraq.

The Kuwaiti judicial system generally provides fair public trials and an adequate appeals mechanism, according to the United States Department of State's Country Reports on Human Rights Practices for 1991. Under Kuwaiti law, no detainee can be held for more than four days without charge; after being charged by a prosecutor, detention for up to an additional twenty-one days is possible. Persons held under the State Security Law can be detained. Bail is commonly set in all cases. The lowest level courts, aside from traffic courts, are the misdemeanor courts that judge offenses subject to imprisonment not exceeding three years. Courts of first instance hear felony cases in which the punishment can exceed three years. All defendants in felony cases are required to be represented by attorneys, appointed by the court if necessary. Legal counsel is optional in misdemeanor cases, and the court is not obliged to provide an attorney. Kuwaiti authorities contend that the rate of ordinary crime is low, and data available through 1986 tended to bear this out. Of more than 5,000 felonies committed in that year, only 5 percent were in the category of theft. The number of misdemeanors was roughly equal to the number of felonies, but only 10 percent were thefts. Offenses involving forgery, fraud, bribery, assaults and threats, and narcotics and alcohol violations were all more common than thefts. Two separate State Security Court panels, each composed of three justices, hear crimes against state security or other cases referred to it by the Council of Ministers. Trials in the State Security Court initially are held in closed session but subsequently are opened to the press and others. They do not, in the judgment of the Department of State, meet international standards for fair trials. Military courts, which ordinarily have jurisdiction only over members of the armed services or security forces, can try offenses charged against civilians under conditions of martial law.

Martial law was imposed for the first time after the liberation of the country from Iraqi occupation. About 300 persons suspected of collaboration with Iraq were tried by military courts in May and June 1991, and 115 were convicted. Twenty-nine received sentences of death, later commuted to life imprisonment after international criticism of the trials. Human rights groups drew attention to the failure to provide adequate legal safeguards to defendants and an unwillingness to accept the defense that collaboration with Iraqi forces had been coerced. Many of the accused alleged that their confessions had been extracted under torture.

CRIMINAL JUSTICE SYSTEM IN BANGLADESH

Criminal Justice System refers to judicial process or procedure of adjudicating criminal issues of which depends on vast knowledge in the Criminal matter and its practice. Easily it may be said Criminal Justice in concerned with the punishment of the wrong other than civil wrong which in Criminal Proceeding is know as crime.

The main objective of the Criminal Proceeding is to punish wrongdoer. Criminal Justice brought only for rendering punishment of the accused for the allegation alleged against him subject to the proof that the offence or crime has been committed by him or not.

DEFINITION

In this research the following words and expressions have the following meanings:

- Bangladesh is a unitary, independent, sovereign Republic to be known as the People's Republic of Bangladesh.
- Advocate used with reference to any proceeding in any Court means an advocate or a mukhtar authorized under any law for the time being in force to practice in any such Court and includes any other person appointed with the permission of the Court to act in such proceeding.
- Bailable offence means an offence shown as bailable in the second schedule, or which is made bailable by any other law for the time being in force; and "non-bailable offence" means any other offence.
- Charge includes any head of charge when the charge contains more heads than one.
- Clerk or Staffs of the State includes any officer specially appointed by the Chief Justice to discharge the functions given by this Code to the Clerk of the State.
- Complaint means the allegation made orally or in writing to a Magistrate, with a view to his taking action under this Code that some person whether known or unknown, has committed an offence, but it does not include the report of a police-officer.
- High Court Division" means the High Court Division for criminal appeal or revision.
- Inquiry includes every inquiry other than a trial conducted under this Code by a Magistrate or Court.
- Investigation includes all the proceedings under this Code for the Collection of evidence conducted by a police-officer or by any person (other than a Magistrate) who is authorized by Magistrate in this behalf.
- Judicial proceeding includes any proceeding in the course of which evidence is or may be legally taken on oath.
- Offence means any act or omission made punishable by any law for the time being in force.
- Officer in charge of a police-station includes, when the officer in charge of the police-station is absent from the station-house or unable from

illness or other cause to perform his duties, the police-officer present at the station house who is next in rank to such officer and is above the rank of constable or, when the Government so directs, any other police-officer so present.

- Place includes also a house, building, tent and vessel.
- Police-station means any post or place declared, generally or specially, by the Government to be a police-station, and includes any local area specified by the Government in this behalf.
- Public Prosecutor means any person appointed under section 492, and includes any person acting under the directions of a Public Prosecutor.
- Special law is a law applicable to a particular subject.
- Section denotes one of those portions of a chapter of this Code which are distinguished by prefixed numeral figures.
- *Act denotes as well a series of acts as a single act:* The word
- Omission" denotes as well a series of omissions as a single omission.
- Dishonestly -whoever does anything with the intention of causing wrongful gain to one person or wrongful loss to another person, is said to do that thing "dishonestly".
- Moveable properties are intended to include corporeal property of every description, except land and thing attached to the earth or permanently fastened to any thing which is attached to the earth.
- Court of Justice denote a Judge who is empowered by law to act judicially alone, or a body of Judges which is empowered by law to act judicially as a body, when such Judge or body of Judges is acting judicially.
- Judge" denotes not only every person who is officially designed as a Judge, but also every person,-
- who is empowered by law to give, in any legal proceeding, civil or criminal, a definitive judgment, or a judgment which, if not appealed against, would be definitive, or a judgment which, if confirmed by some other authority, would be definitive, or who is one of a body of persons, which body of persons is empowered by law to give such a judgment.
- Government" denotes the person or persons authorized by law to administer executive Government in Bangladesh, or in any part thereof.
- Public includes any class of the public or any community.
- Person includes any Company or Association, or body of persons, whether incorporated or not.
- *Man denotes a male human being of any age:* The word "woman" denotes a female human being of any age.

RATIONAL OF THE STUDY

Everyman has a criminal mentality. Whenever he gets chance or needs to take benefit he just use that and as a result crime committed and which tends criminal justice to be adjudicated. Bangladesh is a development country which because of its economic, political and geographical position is full of crime but does not seek justice properly.

Criminal Justice System of the country is only showing uniformed theoretically but practically it suffers much disability. Criminal violation to a person is much painful and non-bearable. The rational of the study is to bring out reason behinds failure to seek justice and the steps which may reasonably be able to suppress its disabilities.

OBJECTIVES OF THE STUDY:

The main objective of the Criminal Justice is to punish the wrong door with penalty which intent to deter peoples to not engaged in crime and suppress crime. The main objective of the study is to find out the reason why Criminal Justice is not ensured yet after having all the body of enforcing and almost uniformed judicial system.

We have the law, administrative body, legislative body, Executive Authorities and Judiciary everything to suppress crime and to ensure justice if it committed but hence there are lots of cases where no justice is ensured and moreover crime is increasing day by day .So the study objects to find out reason of such incapability and to find out some practical doings which may reasonably reduce crime.

Following are the main objective of the study:

- Find out the problems behind failure to justice, and
- Point out suggestions to reform the failure.

SCOPE OF THE STUDY

The fieldwork on which this thesis is based was carried out from 01st April 2013 to 1st September 2013. In order to gain a broad perspective on and nuanced understanding of the criminal justice system my original aim was to find out the present condition of the criminal justice system of the country by considering the origin of the laws of the country. And on that's reason I spend about 5 months on gathering information from the cases pending or adjudicated in various criminal court within the territory and from the communication with jurists, lawyers, staffs, police, plaintiff and accused also.

METHODOLOGY OF THE STUDY

The methodology of the present research work include- Review of related literature and examination of important principle document, law Book and Based, Journals, law ripcord DLR, ILR, Periodicals and Judicial precedence concern with Criminal Justice System. The work also includes- Case study, data collection, concerning cases instituted in and disposed of every year and interviewing of litigant, Lawyers, Law officers and Judges. Where necessary and expending data would be collected from primary sources litigants, Lawyers and Judges would be selected for interview. On the basic of convenience and expedience, in cases of need other related work such as using web side, on visiting library could also be carried out. Basically the work would be a combination of description and anilities. Further the work also is a work of theoretical or operational research.

In final, as regards approach the work would be blend of to approaches-

- Historical Approaches
- Analytical Approaches

LIMITATION OF THE STUDY

Every good work is restricted by certain restriction. Research on criminal justice system is also a good work because the criminal justice system of the country are suffering from much disabilities and through this research problem behind the criminal justice system shall be definitely specify as well as reasonable remedial measures may be drawn from critical analysis on such disabilities and from the suggestion proposed by the jurists, lawyer, judges etc.

Besides the research was subjected to some others technical limitation also. For example while working on this research I had to go through various limitations those are termed in this research as limitation of the study.

As a researcher I had to go through following limitations namely,

- Analysis or research on criminal justice system is a vast and wide doings. It is hard to complete the research within this short period of time granted by the 6 months.
- The research is subjected to the vast knowledge in the criminal justice system and as a researcher I had to suffer from the reference of book,
- It was hard to communicate or have the appointment of the jurists on criminal justice system,
- The criminal justice system of Bangladesh is a vast matter which can not be exactly or completely analyzed with in 200 pages,
- Finally, due to time constraint many of the aspects could not be discussed and presented in the assigned report.

CRIME, CRIMINAL JUSTICE SYSTEM AND CAUSE OF CRIME: BANGLADESH PERSPECTIVE

CRIME

Literally crime means an act or omission that constitutes an offense that may be prosecuted by the state and is punishable by law. Crime is "an action or an instance of negligence that is deemed injurious to the public welfare or morals or to the interests of the state and that is legally prohibited"

The term crime does not, in modern times, have any simple and universally accepted definition, but one definition is that a crime, also called an offence or a criminal offence, is an act harmful not only to some individual, but also to the community or the state (a public wrong). Such acts are forbidden and punishable by law.

The idea that acts like murder, rape and theft are prohibited exists all around the world, and probably has universal moral basis. What precisely is a criminal offence is defined by criminal law of each country. While many have a catalogue of crimes called the criminal code, in some common law countries no such a comprehensive statute exists.

The state (government) has the power to severely restrict one's liberty for committing a crime. Therefore, in modern societies, a criminal procedure must be adhered to during the investigation and trial. Only if found guilty, the offender may be sentenced to punishment such as community sentence, imprisonment, life imprisonment or, in some jurisdictions, even death. To be classified as a crime, the act of doing something bad (actus reus) must be usually accompanied by the intention to do something bad (mens rea), with certain exceptions (strict liability).

While every crime violates the law, not every violation of the law counts as a crime. Breaches of private law (torts and breaches of contract) are not automatically punished by the state, but can be enforced through civil procedure. Whether a given act or omission constitutes a crime does not depend on the nature of that act or omission. It depends on the nature of the legal consequences that may follow it. An act or omission is a crime if it is capable of being followed by what are called criminal proceedings. Thus crime is an unlawful act or omission from doing an act which he is bound to do or under the obligation to do so but acted or omitted.

CRIMINAL

The word criminal was used first in the 15th century and derived from Late Latin word criminalis .The word literally means A person who has committed a crime. A criminal is a person who has acted or omitted himself from doing an act for which he was bound to do or omit him from doing under obligation imposed by any law or whose duty it was to do or omit himself from doing. Thus criminal means a person who committed a crime is the criminal himself for such act.

CRIMINAL JUSTICE SYSTEM

Criminal justice system is a generic term for the procedure by which criminal conduct is investigated, arrests made, evidence gathered, charges brought, defenses raised, trials conducted, sentences rendered, and punishment carried out. It also means the system of law enforcement, the bar, the judiciary, corrections, and probation that is directly involved in the apprehension, prosecution, defense, sentencing, incarceration, and supervision of those suspected of or charged with criminal offenses.

The criminal justice system consists of three main parts: (1) Legislative (create laws); (2) adjudication (courts); and (3) corrections (jails, prisons, probation and parole). In the criminal justice system, these distinct agencies operate together both under the rule of law and as the principal means of maintaining the rule of law within society.

The criminal justice system is the set of agencies and processes established by governments to control crime and impose penalties on those who violate laws. There is no single criminal justice system in the United States but rather many similar, individual systems. How the criminal justice system works in each area depends on the jurisdiction that is in charge: city, county, state, federal or tribal government or military installation. Different jurisdictions have different laws, agencies, and ways of managing criminal justice processes.

SYSTEM COMPONENTS

Most criminal justice systems have five components-law enforcement, prosecution, defense attorneys, courts, and corrections, each playing a key role in the criminal justice process.

The system of law enforcement, the bar, the judiciary, corrections, and probation that is directly involved in the apprehension, prosecution, defense, sentencing, incarceration, and supervision of those suspected of or charged with criminal offenses.

Law Enforcement: Law enforcement officers take reports for crimes that happen in their areas. Officers investigate crimes and gather and protect evidence. Law enforcement officers may arrest offenders, give testimony during the court process, and conduct follow-up investigations if needed.

Prosecution: Prosecutors are lawyers who represent the state or federal government (not the victim) throughout the court process-from the first appearance of the accused in court until the accused is acquitted or sentenced. Prosecutors review the evidence brought to them by law enforcement to decide whether to file charges or drop the case.

Prosecutors present evidence in court, question witnesses, and decide (at any point after charges have been filed) whether to negotiate plea bargains with defendants. They have great discretion, or freedom, to make choices about how to prosecute the case. Victims may contact the prosecutor's office to find out which prosecutor is in charge of their case, to inform the prosecutor if the defense attorney has contacted the victim, and to seek other information about the case.

Defense Attorneys: Defense attorneys defend the accused against the government's case. They are ether hired by the defendant or (for defendants who cannot afford an attorney) they are assigned by the court. While the prosecutor represents the state, the defense attorney represents the defendant.

Courts: Courts are run by judges, whose role is to make sure the law is followed and oversee what happens in court. They decide whether to release offenders before the trial. Judges accept or reject plea agreements, oversee trials, and sentence convicted offenders.

Corrections: Correction officers supervise convicted offenders when they are in jail, in prison, or in the community on probation or parole. In some communities, corrections officers prepare pre-sentencing reports with extensive background information about the offender to help judges decide sentences. The job of corrections officers is to make sure the facilities that hold offenders are secure and safe. They oversee the day-to-day custody of inmates. They also oversee the release processes for inmates and sometimes notify victims of changes in the offender's status.

CAUSE FOUND IN SCIENTIFIC METHOD:

People are not bad by nature, but sometimes simply too timid to resist the vicious demons that play on their weaknesses and cut their bond with the source of their Power. Humans are good by default, but not everyone is made of steel so as to defend themselves against the demonic forces – destructive emotions and detrimental attitudes: fear, ignorance, hatred, worry, revenge, envy, attachment, greed, lust, selfishness, doubt, prejudice, pride, vanity, impatience, sloth, discrimination, arrogance, ambition, addiction, gluttony, criticism, blame, anxiety, frustration and so on.

We all get attacked by those faulty ethereal goblins of our minds and hearts, but most of us succeed to resist them. It's easy to act on anger, greed, revenge or any of highlighted above, but it takes courage and strength to determine that there is something more important than that.

There are two core reasons why weakness prevails with some:

1. Lack of faith, not believing enough in the power of one's own internal weapons (against inner demons), such as: courage, tolerance, understanding, forgiveness, mercy, honesty, sincerity, integrity, honor, modesty, humbleness, generosity, love, compassion, kindness, detachment, patience, self-discipline, temperance, etc. As a result of not trusting inner resources, there is no enough motivation to develop them and use them. Art Solutions – get the free crime cure; watch inspirational films and read inspirational stories of good qualities conquering the bad ones.
2. Imbalance – most criminals are simply too strong physically, pumping up the body muscles, but not enough the mental and emotional

muscles. The reason why their strength becomes weakness is because they are not balanced.

Art Therapy Solutions – get the free artistic crime cure; watch the movie trilogy 'Samurai' by legendary Japanese director Hiroshi Inagaki. It tells the story of the greatest Samurai warrior in Japan – Musashi Miyamoto, his journey from being just a tough warrior to a true hero, equally strong on all three accounts: physical skills, mental calmness and emotional state. Watch all three films online here for free. (Titles: Samurai One, Samurai Two, Samurai Three)

Underneath all the weaknesses is a genuine human desire to do well. When we decline ourselves from our source (Higher Power), we find ourselves either in a wrong relationship or in a wrong job, or simply in a wrong place at wrong time, but also in a wrong state of mind – causing us to do the wrong things, on the wrong side of tracks.

POOR JUDGMENT

Lack of proper education and great role-models causes many to fail to distinguish right from wrong. In most cases offenders don't think they are doing something wrong, it seems right from their point of view. Poor judgment is also reflected in knowing its wrong, but thinking they could get away with it, not getting caught.

Art Therapy Solutions – get the free crime cure. Lack of love being raised in a dysfunctional family, or coming from a disadvantaged background, or feeling discriminated; none of it alone can cause crime. There are so many others in the world with such conditions, but nevertheless don't turn to crime. However they cause the lack of love and respect for others. That, endorsed with some other factors, can be a major issue related to crime.

POVERTY

Poverty is often blamed for leading to crime, however underneath is something more vital – society bombards us with commercial values, making us want more and more material things, to the point when some would do anything (including criminal acts) to get them. Unemployment is another factor in this category that contributes to crime through looking ways to earn money by any means possible. Art Therapy Solutions – get the free crime cure; – find the best powerbroker (presented also here in the top of the right column) to help you out of poverty into wealth.

Deprived neighborhoods economically impoverished neighborhoods breed criminal minds Solution: if moving out is out of the question, then keep away from the guys in the hood by making yourself busy with putting your new show on the road. Do you have the strength to distance yourself from the harmful influences of your neighbors? If not, find the strength from the power behind your new thing, which you can discover in the illustrated guide 'Jump'.

TV VIOLENCE

Being a victim in a chain of events sometimes individuals don't mean to cause harm, but are drawn into it by a chain of events that are beyond their control or influence.

Poor parenting skills erratic or harsh discipline, lack of parental control, supervision and monitoring, parental conflict, family dysfunction/breakdown, criminal, anti-social and or alcoholic parent/s Read more about it from BBC indoor.

The Independent Father lessens is also one of underestimated cause of crime. Read more about it by clicking here. *Consider these facts:*

- 85% of all children that exhibit behavioral disorders come from fatherless homes (U.S. Center for Disease Control);
- 90% of all homeless and runaway children are from fatherless homes (U.S. Bureau of the Census);
- 80% of rapists motivated with displaced anger come from fatherless homes (Criminal Justice & Behavior, Vol 14, p. 403-26, 1978);
- 70% of juveniles in state-operated institutions come from fatherless homes (U.S. Dept. of Justice, Special Report, Sept 1988);
- 85% of all youths sitting in prisons grew up in a fatherless home (Texas Dept. of Corrections 1992).

Ecological it has long been known by police officers that cold winter nights keep criminals off the streets and crime levels down. Crime scientists speculate that one of the hidden consequences of global warming will be an increase in street crime during mild winters.

Studies have suggested that warmer temperatures boost aggression hormones such as epinephrine and testosterone. Fraudulent Supreme Court rulings Defective court rulings are one cause of the extra crimes. American FBI has devised a list of the factors which contribute to crime. Source:

Bureau's "Uniform Crime Report":

- Population density and degree of urbanization.
- Variations in composition of the population, particularly youth concentration.
- Stability of population with respect to residents' mobility, commuting patterns and transient factors.
- Modes of transportation and highway systems.
- Economic conditions, including median income, poverty level and job availability.
- Cultural factors and educational, recreational and religious characteristics.
- Family conditions with respect to divorce and family cohesiveness.
- Climate.
- Effective strength of law enforcement agencies.

ORIGIN & DEVELOPMENT OF CRIMINAL JUSTICE SYSTEM IN THE UNITED KINGDOM

GENERAL

The law of United Kingdom is uniform and specific compare to others country of the world. They are the most law abiding country of the world and that's the reason to foot them to highest step of success. Though it is most law abiding country but in past there was no uniform law to regulate them but they adopt it in need of time.

ORIGIN AND NATURE OF LAWS OF UNITED KINGDOM

The main source and origin of laws of United Kingdom is Common law. Thus common law is the foundation of laws of UK as common law was the only system of adjudicating dispute among peoples of the country. Afterwards Equity and Statue law developed and make revolutionary changes in judicial system.

Considering from origin and nature of laws the law of United Kingdom are of three types:

- Common Law
- Equity and
- Statute law

COMMON LAW

The Common Law is therefore, a body of rules which had never been ordained by any Monarch or enacted by any legislative body. It grew by decision and in the British system. In particular, it covers the general principles of the law of contracts and civil wrongs. The criminal law, too, was the Common Law. Though most of it has now been put into statutory form.

So Englishmen one of the most-abiding nations in the world and the Common Law was in origin a judge-made lad. The Common Law is a body of rules which had never been ordained by any Monarch, or enacted by any legislative body the criminal law, too, was the Common Law. Common Law, arising from ancient customs, finds its origin to about eight hundred years back, Before the Norman conquest there was no uniform legal system. The courts were local bodies and the laws had varied a great deal in different places.

The Norman and Angevin Kings were determined to unite the nation and "to make the strength of Monarchy felt, or, in the legal phrase, to make the King's writ run," throughout the length and breadth of the land. They found that their judicial power was the most effective instrument for this purpose, and their practice was to send their judges to tour the country and to see that it was being properly governed. In the beginning, the traveling judges listened to cases in the local courts and applied the customs which they found in different places.

Gradually, they began to iron out the differences and applied the same principles every where much regarded for particular local custom. By the process of unification the judges built a system of rules which was the same or "common" for the whole of the realm.

B.EQUITY

With the lapse of time, however, the Common Law became sufficiently inflexible as to give rise to serious complaints. Judges ceased to adapt it to the changing needs of British society. There were many cases in which the Common Law provided no remedy and sometimes there were manifest injustices because of rigid adherence to precedence. Feudalism was disappearing and money was taking its place about the fifteenth century. The country at that time was passing through a period of social, economic and political instability in which justice often required a procedure less technical and dilatory and method of enforcement more summary, than those that the Common Law was providing. The development of Equity, the second strand in English Law, provided remedies for deficiencies in to Common Law and saved the situation

The law had always regarded the Kings as the fountain of justice, and the court were his courts. If his courts failed to give justice an aggrieved subject was entitle to the King and to pray him to grant a remedy out to deal with each petition on merit, giving the matter his personal attention and sometimes discussing it with his Council. But he soon found that if he kept on dealing with the entire petition himself, he would have time for nothing else

Equity was rooted not in custom but in conscience. "It was based on the belief that law should correspond to the moral standard of the community" Since Equity provided remedies where the Common Law could only impose penalties, and as it recognized the existence of new problems to which the law had not been adapted, much business came to the Chancellors was framed a body of rules knows as an addition to it. Equity included such principles as following:

"Equity will not suffer a wrong to be
Without a remedy.
He who seeks equity must do equity
Delay defects equity.
Equality is equity.
Equity looks to the intent, rather than
To the form."

So, Equity consists of a miscellaneous collection of principles, "not systematically related to one another, but each tending to make this or that of the Common Law more equitable than would otherwise be". Equity simply added to the rules of the Common Law in order to make it more equitable and thereby to remove the rigidity or inadequacy of law

STATUTE LAW

The Statute Law is composed of Acts passed by Parliament and this is by far the largest source of law in modern time .Until the nineteenth century almost all civil and criminal law was Common Law and Equity. Even when the civil and criminal law had been embodied in the Acts of Parliament their basis still remained Common Law. It must, however, be noted that Statute Law overrides the Common Law. This is unlike Equity, because it does not contradict Common Law. It simply mitigates Common Law or meets its deficiencies.

In case of a conflict between Statute and Common Law , the former is always upheld. For the Statute Law has final voice, whatever the Common Law , or past Statutes, or, decisions based on them may have prescribed, that can be altered by a new Statute. In fact the need for Statutory Law was felt to remove the anomalies by the precedents which did not fulfill changing needs of society and were in conflict with the new standards.

When we turn from the sources to the contents of law, the most important distinction is the one between civil and criminal law. The object of civil proceedings, which is called "action", is give redress, usually, in the form of pecuniary damages, to some private party whose rights another has infringed, on the other hand, in criminal proceedings or "prosecutions" the law does not regard the wrong act as directed to a particular person only. It considers that there is a public interest at stake and its aim is to protect society against such acts by punishing the offender.

SOME CRIMINAL LAWS ENFORCEABLE IN UNITED KINGDOM

Every judicial system is directed and administered through some rule, procedure and Act. United Kingdom for administering criminal judicial system has enacted different criminal rules and Act besides they follow common laws and hardly believe in equity. For example for the purpose of fixing specific procedure of appeal they have enacted "Criminal Appeal Act, 1968".

Some of the criminal law enforceable in United Kingdom are mentioned bellow:

- Juries Act 1974
- Road Traffic Act 1988
- Theft Act 1968
- Offences against the Person Act 1861
- Suicide Act 1961
- Prison Security Act 1992
- Criminal Justice Act 1991
- Misuse of Drugs Act 1971
- Drug Trafficking Act 1994
- Terrorism Act 2000
- Criminal Damage Act 1971
- Firearms Act 1968

- Child Abduction Act 1984
- Sexual Offences Act 1956

CLASSIFICATION OF CRIMINAL COURTS

United Kingdom has adopted and moderate their court system or structure of the court time to time as it demands.

Classification of criminal courts may be made in considering two period of time. they are:

- The structure of courts in the Ancient legal system
- The structure of courts in the contemporary legal system

A The structure of courts in the Ancient legal system: Following courts were existing during ancient United Kingdom judicial system:

PETTY CASES COURTS

Acting single, Justices of Peace and Magistrates have jurisdiction over petty cases. Punishment by a fine of not more than twenty shillings or by imprisonment for not more than fourteen days.

PETTY SESSION COURT

More serious cases than petty cases are tried by a Benches of two or more Justices or a Magistrate, its called a Court of Petty Session .The courts have summary jurisdiction. Punishment may impose maximum fines ranging from 50 to 100 or even 500 in certain specified cases, or By imprisonment may impose a sentence up to six months or in a very few cases, a year. If the offence is punishable by imprisonment for more than three months, the accused may be tried by Jury.

QUARTER SESSIONS COURT

The Court of Quarter Sessions composed of two or more of the Justices from the whole of county. In the larger towns it is presided over by a single paid Magistrate, the Recorder, appointed by the Home Secretary. All indictable offences, save the most serious, can be tried here, and appeals from the Courts of Summary Jurisdiction are heard. In fact, it is the court in which majority of grave crimes are tried.

Court of Assizes

Court of Assizes is branches of the High Court of Justice. They are held in the country towns and in certain big cities three times a year. A Queen's Benches judge is the presiding officer of the court assisted by a jury. The Assistant Judges work on circuits covering England and Wales, and travel from one country to another in the course of their duties and try any indictable offence committed in the country.

The Judge at a criminal trial, in English law it is not the function of a judge to discover the truth. He observed the rules and both sides to the cases have fair play. The truth will be known when the jury gives their verdict. If the jury returns the verdict of not guilty, the accused is forthwith discharged. If on the other hand, it finds him guilty, the judge pronounces judgment. If the jury cannot agree , there may be a new trial with a different set of juries.

The House of Lords

The House of Lords is the highest Court, as stated previously, both in civil and criminal cases. But its criminal business is quite exceptional. Since 1948 the House of Lords has voted away the historic rights of its members to tried for treason or felony by a jury of Peers of their owe or higher rank. The House no longer exercises any original jurisdiction.

THE STRUCTURE OF COURTS IN THE CONTEMPORARY LEGAL SYSTEM

A working knowledge of the court structure is required for the understanding of the location of adjudication, the types of dispute handled and the interaction of culture and personnel. You should learn the jurisdiction of each type of court (i.e. what kinds of case it can deal with), how it fits into the hierarchy of courts, how it compares with other courts in terms of workload and how it is organized (e.g. where it sits; who the judges are). The relevant courts are, beginning with the lowest:

Magistrates' Courtsu
County Courtsu
the Crown Courtu
the High Courtu
the Court of Appealu
the Supreme Courtu
the Judicial Committee of the Privy Councilu
the European Court of Justice.u

Magistrates' Courts

Magistrates' Courts have a wide and varied jurisdiction. They are involved in some way in virtually all criminal prosecutions; magistrates hear cases concerning young persons (when constituted as a Youth Court), family or 'domestic' proceedings, as well as enforcement of income tax or local tax. Magistrates' Courts are therefore of enormous importance in the criminal justice decision-making process. They also grant (or refuse) licensees for the sale of alcoholic liquor, betting, etc. Aside from their breadth of jurisdiction, the most important feature of Magistrates' Courts is the extensive involvement of lay people (non-professionals) as judges.

There are approximately 26,000 magistrates who sit as unpaid, part-time lay judges; in inner London, by contrast, there are professional 'stipendiary magistrates' (recently renamed District Judges, Magistrates' Court), advised by a professionally qualified clerk. The fact that professional judges sit in Magistrates' Courts in inner London is largely an accident of history.

County Courts

There are almost 250 County Courts in England and Wales. As a result most medium sized and large towns contain this court of first instance in the civil justice process. As of January 1999, the County Court will normally hear cases on contract and tort to a limit of £25,000, and certain property and other matters to a limit of £30,000. Claims in contract or tort between £25,000 and £50,000 can either be heard in the County Court or High Court, while claims over £50,000 will be heard in the High Court

The Crown Court

Although predominantly a court of first instance for the trial of the more serious criminal offences, the Crown Court also has significant appellate and civil business. The most controversial aspect of the Crown Court's jurisdiction concerns the extent to which an accused person should have the right to insist upon trial by jury.

The relationship between the Crown Court and Magistrates' Courts as higher and lower trial courts for criminal cases raises questions similar to those mentioned above relating to civil courts. But the relationship between the criminal courts is more complex, because jury trial is available in criminal cases only in the Crown Court; any proposal to adjust this relationship will necessarily raise sensitive questions about extending/removing the right to jury trial.

The High Court

The High Court is based in London, with various provincial 'branches'. Some knowledge of its historical development is essential to understand the modern arrangement of the High Court. Note that the High Court is merely one part of the Supreme Court of England and Wales

THE HIGH COURT HAS THREE BRANCHES

The Chancery (the historic successor to the Chancellor's Court) dispensing equity. It mainly deals with trust matters, conveyance, mortgages, contested probate, intellectual property other than that covered by the Patents Court (one of the four specialist courts of the High Court) bankruptcy and appeals from decisions of Commissioners of Inland Revenue The Queen's Bench, which mainly deals with personal injury, contract and tort claims The Family Division, which hears divorce cases and ancillary matters, and Children Act cases.

The Court of Appeal

It is only necessary for you to understand what decisions may be the subject of an appeal to the Court of Appeal Civil Division or to the Court of Appeal Criminal Division, and how the Court is constituted to hear them.

The Supreme Court

The Supreme Court came into being in October 2009, replacing the Appellate Committee of the House of Lords, and assuming the devolution jurisdiction of the Judicial Committee of the Privy Council. The Supreme Court is now the highest court in the UK. The court is staffed by 12 'independently appointed judges' – Justices of the Supreme Court. The Court's jurisdiction extends over appeals on matters of law raising issues of 'great public importance' in civil cases from the UK. It also has a similar jurisdiction over criminal law in cases from England, Wales and Northern Ireland. The powers of the court also cover issues in raised by devolution – as specified under the Scotland Act 1998, the Northern Ireland Act 1998, and the Government of Wales Act 2006.

The Judicial Committee of the Privy Council

Primarily a Commonwealth court, the Judicial Committee is of interest mainly in relation to the doctrine of precedent. It has played an important role in drawing together the common law legal family, although the number of common law countries that have it as their highest court is declining.

The European Court of Justice

An important recent feature of the English legal system is the increasing use made of two courts, the first of which " the European Court of Justice (ECJ) " takes its jurisdiction from the United Kingdom's entry into the European Union, while the second " the European Court of Human Rights (ECtHR) " takes its jurisdiction from the United Kingdom's signing the European Convention on Human Rights.

PROCEDURE REGARDING JURY

One of the basic features of the criminal court of United Kingdom is jury. Jury is the body to administer justice like court but hold some difference in formation. Every jury is formed or consisted of twelve to twenty three presiding judges to deal with any dispute place before them. The fundamental of this jury system is that two or more judges presided over it. The jury system is more successful and the decision of it is more justifiable because there exist co operation between the judges and whenever the judgment is made by twelve to twenty three consciences it becomes justifiable.

The laws of United Kingdom has give it importance and that's why the decision pronounce by it is more acceptable. The gentle United Kingdom has adopted law to specify its power and function and other procedure. The Act is known as "The Juries Act, 1974".

A FINDING THROUGH RESEARCH IN JURY

Thomas, Professor at the Centre for Empirical Legal Studies at University College London. The survey included more than 1,000 jurors at Crown Courts and a separate study of over 68,000 jury verdicts. In newspaper comments Professor Thomas summarized the findings:

This research shows that juries in England and Wales were found to be fair, effective and efficient – and should lie to rest any lingering concerns that racially-balanced juries are needed to ensure fairness in trials with BME defendants or racial evidence. But it is also clear from the research that jurors want and need better information to perform this crucial role. The study recommends that all sworn jurors be issued with written guidelines explaining what improper conduct is, including use of the Internet, and how and when to report it.

SUMMARY TRIAL

Course of a Summary Trial

The course of a summary trial is, to a large extent, identical to the course of trial on indictment. As this is not a law of evidence course, we shall be exploring aspects of the course of trial, both summarily and on indictment, so as to highlight some of the key issues for discussion. The key distinction is that in a summary trial the magistrates are tries of both fact and law. By contrast, a trial on indictment will be heard by a jury who decide on questions of fact and before a judge who will advise the jury on issues of law. Following are the steps of a summary trial by the courts of magistrate:

The Plea:

As the summary trial begins, the clerk of the court will put the information to the accused. The accused must then plead either guilty or not guilty. If the accused stays silent, a not guilty plea will be entered. If the accused pleads guilty, the magistrates move to the process of sentencing, which we shall deal with later.

Prosecution Case:

If the accused pleads not guilty, the prosecution has to prove that the accused did commit the offence with which he or she is charged. The prosecution can give an opening statement, but given the magistrates' experience in trying cases this is unlikely to be long. The prosecution will then examine their witnesses in chief, who will then be cross examined by the defense. If any matters are raised during cross-examination, the prosecution has the right to re-examine their witnesses. There may also intermittently be questions from the bench. Written statements can be used under s.9 of the Criminal Justice Act 1967.

Submission of No Case

Once the prosecution has outlined its case, the defense may decide to make a Submission of no case to answer. This should be upheld if there is no evidence to prove an essential element of the offence charged, or if the evidence presented by the prosecution has been so discredited by the defense that it is manifestly unreliable and no reasonable tribunal would convict on it. If a submission of no case is upheld the accused goes free. If not, the trial continues.

Defense Case

Under rule 37.1 CrimPR, if there is a case to answer the defense may wish to call evidence, but does not have to. The defendant is a competent witness, and therefore can give evidence, but is never compellable, so cannot be forced to give evidence. Once the defense evidence has been presented the defense can deliver a closing speech. The prosecution does not have the right to deliver a closing speech, but the relative informality does permit them to ask questions when and if they become relevant.

Verdict

If the summary trial is being presided over by a district judge, the judge will usually announce his or her decision immediately. Lay magistrates tend to retire to consider their verdict.

Unlike the jury in a trial on indictment, the judge at summary trial must deliver a verdict based on the offence charged. Under s.142 of the Magistrates' Courts Act 1980, if the magistrates then have second thoughts they can direct that the case be re-heard by different justices.

A pre-trial review involves the magistrates ordering the steps that need to be taken for Trial. This can include special measures directions for vulnerable witnesses and rules

Committal for Sentencing:

Once a defendant has pleaded guilty or has been found guilty by the magistrates' Court, the magistrates will then proceed to sentence. They will follow a procedure (Described in Chapter 14). In doing this they are limited by the restrictions on their powers of punishment. Under s.154 of the Criminal Justice Act 2003, the maximum prison sentence that the magistrates can impose in respect of any one offence is twelve months. The maximum aggregate term for two or more offences is 65 weeks. All of this is done in line with the new 'custody plus' arrangements.

Appeal:

The procedure of appeal in criminal justice system is described and specified in criminal appeal Act, 1968.This is the English man who enacts laws regarding every navel matters. So it can be said that appeal process of the criminal court is unitary. Following are the process as to appeal from an inferior court to the higher court in criminal justice system of United Kingdom:

APPEALS FROM THE MAGISTRATES' COURTS

There are three ways in which a decision of a magistrates' court can be challenged. These are:

- Appeal to the Crown Court
- Appeal to the High Court by way of case stated
- Appeal to the High Court for judicial review.

An appeal to the Crown Court can only take place if a person has been convicted, whereas an appeal to the High Court by way of case stated or for judicial review can be made by anyone who is 'aggrieved' by the magistrates' court decision.

Appeal to the Crown Court

This is the most important process of the three for this course. It is governed by ss.108–110 of the Magistrates' Courts Act 1980 and Part 63 of the Criminal Procedure Rules 2005. If a person is convicted by a magistrates' court, they may only appeal in certain prescribed circumstances. If that person pleaded not guilty, they can appeal against their conviction or their sentence. But if they pleaded guilty, they can only appeal against their sentence. This latter process is governed by s.108 (1) of the Magistrates' Courts Act 1980. Under s.108 (3) an appeal against sentence can be brought in respect Of any order made. There is an express prohibition on appealing an order to pay costs. As has already been indicated, a plea of guilty at trial in the magistrates' court will Prohibit an appeal against conviction. There are three exceptions to this rule.

Pleas equivocal when made. This is where the defendant says 'guilty' but adds things like 'I did it to defend myself'. The law would normally demand that this accused change their plea to 'not guilty' but if they do not, appeal is possible. This will usually result in the case being remitted by the Crown Court for full hearing on a not guilty plea.

Pleas subsequently shown to be equivocal. This is where a plea is made unequivocally but is then rendered equivocal by additional information provided by the defendant before the magistrates pass sentence. A good example would be where the defendant pleads guilty to breaking into someone's house but then, in mitigation, tells the magistrates that he had broken in by mistake, believing it to be his friend's house, and that the friend would not have minded him breaking in. This would make the guilty plea inconsistent with the mitigation. Pleas entered under duress. Even if a plea of guilty was unequivocal when made and this was still the case prior to the passing of sentence, this will not prevent appeal if the plea was subsequently discovered to have been entered under duress. A good example would be where two people are jointly charged with theft and one party would have argued that they were forced to undertake the theft, fearing serious harm to them or their loved ones, and they were likewise forced to enter the plea of guilty because the other party had decided that a guilty plea would result in a lesser sentence. Finally, the Criminal Cases Review Commission can refer a conviction in the magistrates' court to the Crown Court even if it is based upon a guilty plea.

Appeal to the High Court by Case Stated

This process is one where an appeal takes place on a point or points of law. The clerk of the magistrates' court prepares the document for appeal with the co-operation of the magistrates. This appeal is then filed with the High Court. These appeals are governed by s.111 of the Magistrates' Courts Act 1980, Part 64 of Criminal Procedure Rules 2005, and Order 56, Rules of the Supreme Court 1965.

Procedure on Appeal

An application for appeal on this process must be made within 21 days. It must be in writing and should identify the question of law or jurisdiction on which the High Court's opinion is sought. The application is then sent to the clerk of the relevant magistrates' court. If it is felt to be a frivolous appeal, then under s.111(5) of the Magistrates' Courts Act 1980 a certificate will be issued by the magistrates explaining that the application has been refused. If this happens, the defendant can apply to the High Court for an order which compels the magistrates' court to state a case.

The magistrates will then draft a letter stating the case by identifying the key facts of the case, but not the evidence that led to these facts being established. The charge or charges heard are then outlined and the contentious issues relating to questions of law or jurisdiction are raised along with any authorities raised or the magistrates' decision. Once this has happened the letter is sent to the appellant, who then has to lodge it within ten days. If it is not lodged within ten days it will be struck out. If a custodial sentence has been passed, bail may be granted.

Appeals from the Crown Court

Historically, if a person was convicted on indictment there was no general right of appeal. This was changed by the Criminal Appeal Act 1907, which created the Court of Criminal Appeal. The Court of Criminal Appeal was then abolished by the Criminal Appeal Act 1966, which transferred its jurisdiction to the Court of Appeal (Criminal Division). The primary function of the Court of Appeal (Criminal Division) is to hear appeals by the defense against the accuser's conviction or sentence.

Other functions include a procedure whereby the Attorney-General can increase an over-lenient sentence by referring the case to this court. It is also possible for the court to give an opinion on a point of law which arose during the trial that led to an acquittal.

The Lord Chief Justice is President of the Criminal Division. When Considering an appeal, there must be at least three judges sitting. There may be more, but this is rare. This panel can deliver majority decisions.

Besides this the legal system of united kingdom has clear and specific provision as to appeal in different exception .for example Criminal legal system of united kingdom does not exclude following matters of appeal:

- Appeal from the High Court to the House of Lords
- Appeals against conviction(Section 2(1) of the Criminal Appeal Act 1968)
- Appeal in case of Errors in a trial
- Effect of an appeal (Under s.2(2) of the Criminal Appeal Act 1968)
- Appeals against sentence.(Under s.9 of the Criminal Appeal Act 1968)

SENTENCING

The Criminal judicial system of United Kingdom has adopted an Act to deal with the sentencing pronunciation procedure. They adopt Powers of Criminal Courts (Sentencing) Act 2000.

According the very Act Sentencing in United Kingdom are two forms:

- Custodial sentences
- Fines
- Others Sentence

Custodial Sentence

If an adult is faced with a custodial sentence, this means that he or she is facing a period of imprisonment. For a sentence of imprisonment to be passed the offender must be aged 21 or over. Offenders under 21 years of age are awarded a sentence of detention rather than imprisonment. Both terms suggest that the offender's liberty will be limited and they will be allocated to a prison. There are two main types of prison: closed and open prisons. Closed prisons have boundary walls or fences and the parameter is secure. Open prisons, by contrast, enjoy a far more relaxed regime.

Prisons may also be local, which means that they house prisoners who are on remand or long-term prisoners who are being allocated to a training prison. Training prisons are either open or closed and usually provide useful working facilities.

They have far better conditions than local prisons:

- When deciding that a custodial penalty is to be imposed, the court has to abide by certain statutory requirements.
- These include the following:
- All prisoners have to be legally represented or must have been offered such representation.
- The criteria laid out in s.152 of the Criminal Justice Act 2003 must be met before a custodial sentence is passed.
- A pre-sentence report should be obtained before a custodial sentence is passed (s.156 of the Criminal Justice Act 2003).
- All aggravating and mitigating factors must be considered by the court before a Custodial sentence is passed.
- The court must state its reasons for passing a custodial sentence.

SENTENCING FOR STATUTORY OFFENCES

Whilst all common law offences (most notably manslaughter) are prima facie. Punishable with life imprisonment, statute has defined the maximum penalty for a Number of key offences. Prisons are the usual forum for custodial sentences and are classified according to the Level of security imposed. All offenders under the age of 21 are detained, whereas all Offenders over 21 are imprisoned.

Fines:

If a community sentence is not appropriate and the threshold is not met, a fine may be the appropriate non-custodial sentence. If the offence is an indictable one, there is no maximum limit placed on the Crown Court with regard to the size of the fine. However, fines are by far the most common penalty for summary offences and each offence will be allocated to a level which caps the limit of the fine.

The levels of fine are:

Level 1 £200

Level 2 £500

Level 3 £1,000

Level 4 £2,500

Level 5 or either way offence £5,000.

To impose a fine the magistrates need to consider the seriousness of the offence under s.164 of the Criminal Justice Act 2003. Having considered aggravating and mitigating factors, the court will then decide, on means testing grounds, whether the fine should be level A (assessed on 50% of weekly take home pay), level B (assessed on 100% of weekly take home pay) or level C (assessed on 150% of weekly take home pay). page 246 University of London International Program. At the time of issuing the fine, the court must make clear the term of imprisonment that will be imposed if the offender defaults and does not pay. The court imposing the fine must give the offender time to pay. Fines can be combined with the community sentence if it is appropriate.

Other Sentences:

Endorsement and disqualification from driving If a traffic offence is suitably serious, the offending driver may find themselves Disqualified from driving, under the Road Traffic Act 1988. This is a good example of Incapacitation at work as it demands that the offender be prevented from committing the offence again by rendering them unable to do so. Lesser traffic offences Involve the driver's license being endorsed with penalty points. When the penalty Points add up to 12, the license is confiscated and the defendant is disqualified for at least six months.

If the offender is convicted of:

- Causing death by dangerous driving
- Careless driving whilst under the influence of alcohol or drugs
- Trying to drive whilst under the influence of alcohol or drugs or
- Dangerous driving

They will be automatically disqualified. A minimum period of 12 months must pass before they are allowed to hold a driving license again.

Forfeiture and Compensation Orders

Under s.143 of the Powers of Criminal Courts (Sentencing) Act 2000, a forfeiture order can be made if the court is satisfied that the offender used the property to be confiscated to commit or facilitate the offence. Section 130 of the Powers of Criminal Courts (Sentencing) Act 2000 provides for the order where an offender has to pay compensation to the victim of his offence.

Restitution and Confiscation Orders

Under s.148 of the Powers of Criminal Courts (Sentencing) Act 2000, goods which have been stolen can be recovered where the court orders anyone having possession or control of the goods to restore them to the original owner. Under the Proceeds of Crime Act 2002 it is now possible for the Crown Court to utilize its power to confiscate the assets of those convicted of criminal offences.

Recommendation for Deportation

If a convicted offender is not a British citizen, then under s.3 of the Immigration Act 1971 a recommendation can be made to the Home Secretary that he be returned to his country of origin.

Hospital Order

Sections 37–43 of the Mental Health Act 1983 cover the provision of hospital orders where the court decides that an individual should be admitted and detained in Hospital where they can receive treatment for their mental disorder. The effect of the order is to authorize the offender's move to a hospital where they will be housed for about six months before the review begins.

Anti-Social Behavior Order (ASBO)

An ASBO can be awarded under s.1 of the Crime and Disorder Act 1998. Here the court protects the local community from the anti-social behavior that others have engaged in by preventing the 'offenders' from disrupting others' lives.

Registration Under the Sex Offenders Act 1997

As a result of this legislation, some offenders are required to notify the police of their whereabouts so that supervision in the community can take place.

Disqualification from Working with Children

If an offender has been convicted of an offence involving a child, they can be disqualified by the court from working with children in future.

BAIL

Bail is the release of a person who is subject to a duty to surrender to custody at an appointed time and place. Bail is the process of getting release from the custody legally. The gentle United Kingdom has adopted a specific Act for determining procedure on bail. the Act is known as the Bail Act 1976.

Some remarkable development on Bail by the Act is pointed out bellow:

- Remand on bail or in custody
- Principles governing the decision to grant or refuse bail
- Custody time limits
- The imposition of conditions for bail(Section 3 of the Bail Act 1976)
- Duty to surrender to custody
- Sureties
- Deposit of security

REGULATION OR PROCEDURE REGARDING POLICE:

Power, function and others procedure regarding police has been specified by several enactments of Acts. Among them Police and Criminal Evidence Act 1984 is the most efficient:

Summery of the Police and Criminal Evidence Act 1984

The majority of police powers involved in the detection of crime are to be found in the Police and Criminal Evidence Act 1984. These statutory provisions are accompanied by extensive Codes of Practice which provide substantial guidance as to the way in which police powers should be exercised. A criminal charge can be brought about in two particular ways. For serious offences an arrest followed by detention in a police cell can take place before a decision to charge is taken. For less serious offences the process of issuing a summons is used.

The Act does not forget to include the followings procedure:

- The power to arrest without warrant(s.24 and s.24A of PACE)
- Detention without charge is dealt with under ss.40–44 of PACE and there is a timetable which the police are expected to follow to reach a resolution as to whether or not to charge.
- The main milestones of detention without charge are as follows:
- Within 6 hours A review takes place to decide whether it is necessary to hold the detainee.
- Within 15 hours Nine hours after the first review a second review takes place.
- Within 24 hours here a detainee must be charged or released unless the continued detention has been authorized by the station superintendent.
- Within 36 hours Here a detainee must be charged or released unless a magistrates' court has issued a warrant of further detention.
- After 72 hours the magistrates' court can extend the detention for a further 36 hours after the first 36 hours.
- After 96 hours The magistrates' court can extend the detention for a further 24 hours after the first two periods of 36 hours. At the end of this period the detainee must
- Right to a solicitor(s.58(1) of PACE)
- Recording what the suspect says
- Powers of stop and search(ss.1–3 of PACE)
- Powers to search premises(Section 8 of PACE)
- Statutory safeguards(ss.15–16 of PACE)

ORIGIN & DEVELOPMENT OF CRIMINAL JUSTICE SYSTEM UNDER HINDU PERIOD, MUSLIM PERIOD, BRITISH PERIOD & PAKISTAN PERIOD

Criminal Judicial System Under Hindu Period:

The subject of Legal History comprises the growth, evolution and development Of the legal system of a country; it sets forth the historical process where by a legal system has come to be what it is over.

Hindu Period: these period extents for nearly 1500 years before and after the beginning of the Christian era. The ancient India was divided into several independent states and the King was the supreme authority of each state. As far as the administration of justice is concerned the King was considered the fountain of justice. He was entrusted with the supreme authority of the administration of justice in his kingdom. The essential features of judicial system of this period were as follows:

Organization of Court Structure:

Following courts were exist during the ancient Hindu period:

The King's Court:

The Kings court was the highest court of appeal in the state. It was also a court of original jurisdiction for cases of vital importance to the state. In Kings Court the King was advised by learned Brahmins, The Chief Justice and other judges, ministers, elders and representatives of the trading community.

The Chief Justice's Court:

The Chief Justices Court which consisted of the Chief Justice and a board of judges to assist the Chief Justice. All the judges in the board belonged to three upper castes preferable Brahmins.

Special Tribunal:

Sometimes separate tribunals with specified territorial jurisdiction used to be formed from among judges who were members of the board of the Chief Justice's court.

TOWN OR DISTRICT COURT:

In towns and districts courts were run by the government officials to administer justice under the authority of the king.

VILLAGE COUNCIL:

The local village councils or Kulani was constituted at village level .This councils consisted of a board of five or more members for administration of justice to villagers. The councils dealt with civil and criminal matters.

JUDICIAL PROCEDURE:

Stages of a Suit:-

A suit or trial consisted of four stages the plaint, the reply and investigation and finally the verdict or decision of the court.

Bench of More than One Judges:-

The courts were functioning on the principle that justice should not be administered by a single judge. Generally a bench of two or more judges would administer justice. Even the King decided cases in his council.

Appointment of Judges and Judicial Standard:-

In the appointment of the Chief Justice and other judges the question of caste consideration played vital role. The Chief Justice was mandatory appointed from Brahmins. A sudra was forbidden to be appointed as a judge. Appointments were made from among the persons who were highly qualified and learned in law. Women were not allowed to hold the office of a judge. Judges were required to take the office of a judge. Judges were required to take the oath of impartiality when deciding disputes between citizens.

DOCTRINE OF PRECEDENT:–

The decisions of the King's court were binding on all lower courts. The principles of law declared by higher courts were taken into consideration by the lower courts while deciding cases.

Evidence:

During the course of proceeding both the parties were required to prove their case by producing evidence. Ordinarily, evidence was based on any or all the three sources, namely, documents, witnesses, and the possession of incriminating objects. In criminal cases, sometimes circumstantial evidence was sufficient to punish the criminal or acquit him.

Trial by Ordeal:

Ordeal which was a kind of custom based on religion and faith in God was a means of proof to determine the guilt of the person. The application of trial by ordeal was limited only to the cases where any concrete evidence on either side was not available. This system ordeal was very painful and dangerous to the accused, and sometimes the person giving ordeal died during the ordeal. Some common ordeals are described below:

Ordeal by Fire: According to the Hindu myth fire is considered to be God and it has purifying qualities. According to the ordeal of fire, the accused was directed to walk through or stand or sit in fire for some specified time. If the accused comes out from the fire without any harm, he was considered to innocent. Sometime the accused was asked to carry a red hot iron ball in his hand and walk a few paces. If he had no signs of burns after the ordeal, he was considered to be innocent. *Ordeal by water:* Water seen as a sign of purity under the Hindu mythology was used to test the guilt of the accused. The accused was required to stand in waist- deep water and then to sit down in the water, as an archer shot to an arrow. If the accused remained in the water during the time limit, he was held to be innocent,. Alternatively the accused was required to drink water used in bathing the idol. If he had no harmful effects within next fourteen days, he was declared to be innocent.

Ordeal by Poison:-

This method was also based on the view that God protects innocent people. The accused was required to drink poison without vomiting it. If he survived, he was declared to be innocent.

Ordeal by Rice- Grains:-

The accused was required to chew un- husked rice and then asked to spit out. If blood appeared in his mouth, he was considered to be guilty, otherwise not.

Ordeal by Lot:-

Two lots of the same type representing Right (Dharma) and Wrong (Adharma) were placed in a jar. The accused was asked to draw a lot, if the accused drew Dharma he was declared innocent.

Trial by Jury:

The jury system existed in ancient India but not in the same from as understood in today's world. There is evidence that the community members used to assist the administration of justice. They were merely examiners of the case of conflict and placed true facts before the judge though the verdict was declared by the presiding judge and by the jury.

Crimes and Punishments:

The philosophy of crime and punishment was based on the idea that the punishment removed impurities from the accused person and his character is reformed. Before punishment was to be awarded the judge had to consider the motive and nature of the offence, time and place, strength, age, conduct, learning and monetary position of the offender.

There were four methods of punishment- by gentle admonition, by severe reproof, by fine and by corporal punishment. These punishments could be inflicted separately or together depending upon the nature of the offence. Judges always considered the relevant circumstances before deciding actual punishment. The severity of punishment depended on caste as well.

Certain classes of persons were exempted from punishment:

- Old people over eighty
- Boys below sixteen
- Women and persons suffering from diseases were to be given half of the normal punishment.
- A child below five was considered to be immune from committing any crime and therefore was not liable to be punished.
- In adultery and rape, punishment was awarded on the basis of the caste consideration of the offender and of the woman.
- In abuse or contempt case every care was taken to see that each higher caste got due respect from persons of lower caste.

For example:- If a person of a lower caste set with a person of higher cast, the man of the lower caste was to be branded on the breech. For committing murder the murder was to pay 1000 cows for killing a Kshatriya, 100 for a Vaisyo and 10 for a Sudra. These cows were given to the King to be delivered to the relatives of the murdered person. A bull was given to the King as a fine for murder. If a Brahmin was killed a person of lower caste, the murderer would be put to death and his property confiscated. If a Brahmin was killed by another Brahmin he was to be branded and banished. If a Brahmin killed a person from lower caste, he was to compound for the harem of the King, adding the King's enemy, creating revolt in the army, murdering ones father or mother or committing serious arson, capital punishment was given in varied forms, namely, roasting alive, drowning, trampling by elephants, devouring by dogs, cutting into pieces, impalement etc.

The above discussion on crime and punishment gives a necessary idea that infliction of punishment was not based on any broad principle rather on whim and caste consideration which was completely devoid of humanity and ethics.

CRIMINAL JUDICIAL SYSTEM UNDER MUSLIM PERIOD:

A Judicial System in Medieval India

This period starts with the invasion by Turkish Muslims in the Indian Sub-continent in 1100 A.D. The Hindu kingdoms began to disintegrate gradually with the invasion of Turkish race in the end of eleventh and the beginning of the twelfth century. When Muslim conquered the states, they brought with them the. Turkish idea of administration. The theory of Muslims was based on Quran, their religious book. According to the Quran, sovereignty lies in Allah (God) and the King is His humble servant to carry out His will on the earth. The ruler was regarded as trustee, being the Almighty's chosen agent.

The whole Muslim period in India may be divided into two sub-periods-the Sultanate of Delhi and the Mughal Empire. By the end of twelfth century Muslim Sultanate was established at Delhi by Muhammad Ghor. This period existed for thirty, years beginning from 1206 till 1526. On the other hand, in 1526 Delhi Sultanate came to an end when Delhi was captured by Zahiruddin Babar. Babar founded the Mughal Empire in India which existed until 1857.

Legal System Under the Sultanate

The Sultan or the King was the supreme authority to administer justice in his kingdom. The judicial system under the Sultanate was organized on the basis of administrative divisions. A systemic classification and gradation of the courts existed at the seat of the capital, in Provinces, Districts, Parganahs, and villages. The powers and jurisdiction of each court were clearly defined.

Courts at Centre: The courts established at the capital of the Sultanate were as follows: The King's Court, Diwan-e-Mazalim, Diwan-e-Risalat, Sadre Jehan's court, Chief Justice's court and Diwan-e-Siyasat.

- The King's court was presided over by the Sultan himself. This court exercised both original and appellate jurisdiction in all kinds of cases. It was the highest court of appeal in the realm. In discharging judicial functions the Sultan was assisted by two reputed Muftis highly educated and expert in law.
- The court of Diwan-e-Mazalim and court of Diwan-e-Risalat were the highest courts of criminal and civil appeals respectively. Though the Sultan nominally presided over these courts, in the absence of the Sultan the Chief Justice (Qazi-ul Quzat) presided over these courts. Quazi-ul Quzat was the actual head of the judiciary and he tried all types of cases. Qazi-ul Quzat was appointed by the Sultan from amongst the most virtuous of the learned men in his kingdom. In 1248, Sadre Jahan was appointed by Sultan Nasiruddin. This post was superior to post of Qazi-ul Quzat. Now he became defacto head of the judiciary. The offices of Sadre Jahan and Chief Justice remained separate for a long period, but these were amalgamated by emperor Ala Uddin. However, these were again separated by Sultan Firoz Tuughlaq.
- The court of Diwan-e-Siyat was constituted to decide the cases of rebels and high treason etc. Its main purpose was to deal with criminal prosecutions.

Some of the other officers attached to the court of Chief Justice were as under:

- *Mufti:* He was selected by the Chief Justice and appointed by the Sultan. He acted as legal expert and in case of difference of opinion between the mufti and judge, the difference was referred to the Sultan for decision.
- *Pandit:* He was a Brahmin learned in law of Hindu and he acted as expert of law in civil cases of non-Muslims and his position was similar to the Mufti.
- *Mohtasib:* He was entrusted with the prosecution for the violation of cannon law.
- *Dadbak:* He was the registrar or the clerk of the court and his duty was to ensure attendance of persons summoned by the court. Sometimes he was also entrusted with the task of trying of petty civil cases.

Provincial Courts: In each Province (Subah) at the Provincial Headquarters four courts were established, namely Adalat Nazim-e-Subah, Adalat Qazi-e-Subah, Governor's Bench (Diwan-e-Subah) and Sadre-e- Subah.

Adalat Nazim Subah: This court was presided over by the Nazim. In the Province the Sultan was represented by him and like the Sultan he exercised both original and appellate jurisdiction. In original cases he usually sat as single judge. From his judgment an appeal lay to the Central Appeal Court at

Delhi. While exercising appellate jurisdiction, the Nazim sat with the Qazi-e-Subah constituting a Bench to hear appeals. From the decision of this Bench, a final second appeal lay before the Central Court at Delhi.

Adalat Qazi-e-Subah: This court was presided over by the Chief Qazi of the Province. This court tried all cases of civil and criminal matters. It also heard appeals from the courts of District Qazis. Appeals from this court lay to the Adalat Nazim-e-Subah.

This court also had the supervisory jurisdiction over the administration of justice in his province and to see that the Qazis in districts were properly functioning. Qazi-e-Subah was appointed by the Sultan, but selected by the Chief Justice amongst persons who had established reputation for learning and scholarship of law and possessed a high character and was a man of unimpeachable integrity. Four officers namely Mufti, Pandit, Mohtasib and Dadbak were attached with this court too.

Diwan-e-Subah: This court had both original and appellate jurisdiction in all revenue matters. It had the final authority in the Province over all cases concerning revenue.

Sadre-e-Subah: This was the Chief Ecclesiastical court in the province. This court dealt with the matters relating to grant of stipend, lands etc.

District Courts: In each District, at the District Headquarter, following courts were established:

- *The District Qazi's Court:* This court had the jurisdiction to try all civil and criminal matters. It also heard appeals from the decisions of the Parganah Qazis, Kotwals and village panchayats. This court was presided over by the Qazi who was appointed by the Sadre Jahan on the recommendation of the Qazi-e-Subah. This court was also assisted by same four officials as mentioned above.
- *Faujder Court:* This court had jurisdiction to try petty criminal cases concerning security and suspected criminals.Appeal from this court lay with the court of Nazim-e-Subah.
- *Court of Mir Adils:* This court dealt with land revenue matters. Appeal from this court lay before the Court of Diwan-e-Subah.
- *Court of Kotwals:* This court was authorised to try police and municipality cases.

Parganah's Courts: The Courts of Qazi-e-Parganah and Kotwals were constituted at each Parganah Headquarter. The Court of Kazi-e-Parganah had all powers of a District Kazi in all civil and criminal cases except hearing appeals. The Kotwal was authorised to try petty criminal cases. He was also the principal executive officer of the town.

Village Courts: For each group of villages, a panchayat was functioning to look after the executive and judicial functions. The panchayat decided petty civil and criminal cases of purely local nature.

B Legal System Under The Mughal Administration

During the Mughal period (1526-1857) the Mughal emperor was considered the 'fountain of justice'. The emperor created a separate department of justice (Mahakuma-e-Adalat) to regulate and see that justice was administered properly. The important courts functioning during this period were as follows:

Courts at Capital

Three important courts were functioning at the capital city of Delhi. *They were as follows:*

a. *The Emperor's Court:* The Emperor's court presided over by the emperor himself, was the highest court of the empire. This court had jurisdiction to hear both civil and criminal cases. The Emperor while hearing the cases as a court of first instance, was assisted by Daroga-e-Adalat, Mufti and Mir Adil. While hearing appeal the Emperor presided over a Bench consisting of the Chief Justice (Qazi-ul-Quzat) and other Qazis of the Chief Justice's court. The Emperor referred points for – opinion regarding authoritative interpretation of law on a particular point to the Chief Justice's court.
b. *The Court of Chief Justice:* This was the second important court at the capital, This court presided over by the Chief Justice was assisted by two Qazies of great importance who were attached to this court as puisne judges. This court had jurisdiction to try original, civil and criminal cases and also to hear appeals from the Provincial courts. It had also supervisory power over the working of the Provincial courts.
c. *Chief Revenue Court:* This was the third important court in Delhi. It was the highest court of appeal to decide revenue cases. This court was also assisted by the same four officials as mentioned below.

In each court, as stated above, four officials were attached- Daroga-e-Adalat, mufti, Muhtasib and Mir Adil. Apart from the above-stated three important courts, there were also two courts in Delhi. The court of Qazi-e-Askar was a special court to decide military matters. This court moved from place to place with troops. Another court was the court of Qazi of Delhi which sat in the absence of the Qazi-ul-Quzat to decide local civil and criminal matters.

Provincial Courts

In each Province there were following three types of courts:

a. *The Governor's Court (Adalat-e-Nazim-e-Subah):* The Governor or Nazim presided over this court and he had original jurisdiction in all cases arising in the Province. This court had also jurisdiction to hear appeals from the subordinate courts. Further appeal from this court lay to the Emperor's court. This court had also supervisory power over the administration of justice in the Province. One Mufti and a Daroga-e-Adalat were attached to this court.

b. *The Provincial Chief Appeal Court (Qazi-i-Subah's Court):* This court heard appeals from the decisions of the Qazis of the districts. The powers of Qazi-i-subah were co-extensive with those of Governors. This court had original civil and criminal jurisdiction as well. The officers attached to this court were, Mufti, Mohtasib, Daroga-e-Adalat-e-Subah, Mir Adil, Pandit, Sawaneh Nawis and Waqae Nigar.
c. *Provincial Chief Revenue Court (Diwan's Court):* This court presided over by Diwan-e-Subah had original and appellate jurisdiction in all revenue matters. An appeal from this court lay to the Diwan-e-Ala at the Imperial capital. Four officers attached to this court were-Peshker, Darogha, Treasurer and Cashier.

District Courts

In each district there were following four courts:

a. *District Qazi:* The chief civil and criminal court of the district was presided over by the Qazi-e-Sarkar. This court had jurisdiction to try all civil and criminal matters. Appeal from this court lay to the Qazi-e-Subah. Qazi-e-Sarkar was the principal judicial officer in the District. Six officers were attached to this court- Darogha-e-Adalat, Mir Adil, Mufti, Pandit, Mohtasib and Vakil-e-Sharayat.
b. *Faujdar Adalat:* This court presided over by a Faujdar had jurisdiction to try cases concerning riots and state security. An appeal lay to the court of Governor from the decisions of this court.
c. *Kotwali Court:* This court presided over by a FCotwal-e-Shahar decided all petty criminal cases. Appeals from this court lay to the Qazi-e-Sarker.
d. *Amalguzari Kachari:* This court presided over by an Amalguzar decided revenue matters. An appeal from this court lay to Diwan-e-Subah's adalat.

Parganah's Court

In each Parganah there were three courts:

a. *Qazi-e-Parganah's Court:* This court had jurisdiction over all civil and criminal cases arising within its original jurisdiction. This court had no appellate jurisdiction. Appeal from this court lay to the court of District Qazi.
b. *Court of Kotwal:* This court decided all petty criminal cases. Appeals from this courts' decision lay to the Court of District Qazi.
c. *Amin-e-Parganah:* This court presided over by an Amin decided all revenue matters. An appeal from this court lay to the District Amaguzar.

Village Courts

In each village two types of courts were working- court of village panchayat and the court of Zaminder. The village panchayat consisted of five persons headed by a headman. The panchayat had the power to decide petty local civil and criminal matters. No appeal was allowed from the decision of a panchayat. In the late Mughal period, Zaminder's courts were empowered to try petty criminal and civil matters.

Crime and Punishment in the Mughal Administration

A systematic judicial procedure was followed by the courts during the Mughal period. The judicial procedure was regulated by two Muslim Codes namely Fiqh-e-Firoz Shahi and Fatwai-i-Alamgiri. Evidence was classified into three categories- (a) full corroboration; (b) testimony of a single individual; and (c) admission including confession.

The court always preferred full corroboration to other classes of evidence. The Muslim criminal law broadly classified crimes under three heads: (i) crimes against God; (ii) crimes against the King; and (iii) crimes against private individual. During the Muslim period trial by ordeal as existed in Hindu period was prohibited. Instead three forms of punishments were executed by the courts under Muslim law for above three types of crimes.

a. *Hadd (fixed penalties):* This is the form of punishment which was prescribed by the cannon law and could not be reduced or modified by human agency. Hadd meant specific punishments for specific offences. It thus provided a fixed punishment as laid down in Sharia for crimes like theft, robbery, whoredom (zinah), apostasy (ijtidad), defamation and drunkenness. It was equally applicable to Muslims and non-Muslims. The state was under a duty to prosecute all those who were guilty under Hadd. "No compensation was granted under it. For instance, stoning to death was prescribed for adultery or drinking wine, cutting off the right hand for theft etc. All offences for which Hadd was prescribed as punishment are characterised as offences against God, in other words, against 'public justice'.
b. *Tazir (Discretionary Punishment):* This was another form of punishment which meant prohibition and it was applicable to all crimes which were not classified under Hadd. Offences. for which tazir was fixed were all offences against God. It included crimes like gambling, causing injury, minor theft etc. Under Tazir the kind and amount of punishment was left entirely with the judge's wish; courts were free to even invent new methods oi punishing the criminals e.g. cutting out the tongue, impalement etc. The object was to reform the criminal.
c. *Qisas (retaliation) and Diya (blood money):* Qisas meant, in principle, life for life and limb for limb. Qisas was applied to cases of willful

killing and certain types of grave wounding or maiming which were characterisd as offences against human body. Qisas was regarded as the personal right of the victim or his next of kin, to inflict a like injury on the wrong-doer as he had inflicted on his victim. Under Qisas the relatives or successors of the murdered person could excuse the murderer. Qisas became Diya when the next of kin of the victim was satisfied with money as compensation for the price of blood. This also could not be reduced or modified either by the Q*. zi or the Emperor. In cases where Qisas was available, it could be exchanged with diya or blood money.

Defects of Muslim Administration of Justice

The Muslim administration of justice particularly the criminal justice in medieval India suffered from many defects. The British people who gradually took over to administer justice here always had an owl-look over the Muslim criminal law. Warren Hastings declared it to be a more barbarous law than anything.

The inherent defects of Muslim administration of justice were as follows:

- The judicial administration was defective in the sense that there was no separation between the executive and judiciary. The emperor who was the head of the government was also the fountain of justice and administered justice directly.
- In many cases Muslim criminal law was not certain and uniform. In practice it was discovered that the law laid down in Hidaya and Fatwa-e-Alamgiri was mostly conflicting. There were differences of opinions among Muslim jurists which gave the Qazis a good deal of leeway to interpret the law and apply it to a specific fact before him. Thus in each case the interpretation of law depended on the Qazi.
- The Muslim criminal law did not draw any distinction between public law and private law. Criminal law was regarded as a branch of private law. It had not developed the idea that crime was an offence not only against the injured individual but also against the society as well.
- Muslim criminal law suffered from much illogicality. This is because crimes against God were regarded crimes of an atrocious character. Crimes against men were regarded as crimes of a private nature and punishment was regarded as private right of the aggrieved party.
- The most defective provision in Muslim criminal law was the provision of Diya. In many cases the murderer escaped simply by paying money to the dependants of the murdered person. Many evil practices developed out of it.
- In cases where murdered person left no heirs to punish the murderer or to demand blood-money no specific provisions was available in

Muslim law. A minor heir was to wait till he attained majority for punishing the murderer or demanding the blood-money.

- Though Muslim law tried to distinguish between murder and culpable homicide, it did not rest on the intention or want of intention of the culprit. It rested on the method of weapons employed in committing the crime. This was peculiar and generated grave injustice.
- The law of tazir which provided for discretionary punishment was also very vague which gave too much power to the judges. On the one hand, even innocent persons were punished by the courts while on the other hand, it led to corruption and injustice. Punishment could be unduly severe or ridiculously light as there was no standard or measure for them.
- The law of evidence under Muslim law was very defective unsatisfactory, and of primitive nature which made conviction of offenders quite difficult. For example, no Muslim could be given capital punishment on the evidence of an infidel. In other cases evidence of one Muslim was regarded as being equivalent to those of two Hindus. Evidence of two women was regarded as being equal to that of one man. Again, evidence was to be direct; no circumstantial evidence was allowed. To convict a man for rape, for example, it was necessary to have four witnesses who would swear that they had actually seen the accused in the very act of committing the offence. A thief would be convicted only on the evidence of two men, or of one man and two women. It was an invariable case rule to exclude the evidence of women in all cases under haddor qisas.
- The nature of punishment of stoning, mutilation etc were so cruel and inhuman that no flesh and blood could even think of it in a civilized society. The punishment of mutilation meant slow, cruel and lingering death to the unfortunate person who had to undergo it, for he could not adopt any means of livelihood. The manner was one to give gooseflesh in ones body. The culprit was tied down. The executioner took a blunt hatchet and hacked off the hand by the joint of a wrist and the foot by the joint of an ankle. The bleeding stump was immediately immerged into a pot of boiling butter (ghee) in order to stop bleeding.

CRIMINAL JUDICIAL SYSTEM UNDER BRITISH PERIOD:

A Modernization of Ancient Indian Law

The modernisation of ancient Indian law took place in the hand of the British people who came in India as a trading company under a series of Royal Charters. The pace of the development of the administration of justice in British India may be divided into following five periods:

a. Early Administration of Justice until the Charter of 1726;
b. Administration of Justice from the Charter of 1726 till the Regulating Act of 1773;
c. Administration of Justice from the Regulating Act of 1773 till the era of Unification in 1861; and
d. From 1861 till the Independence in 1947.

First Period: Early Administration of Justice Until the Charter of1726

This period marks the beginning of the British involvement into the administration of justice in India. In another sense, this period deals with the intervention of the Company into the- administration of justice in India as opposed to intervention by the British Queen. The East India Company gradually took possession of three factories and settlements at Bombay, Madras and Calcutta. Starting as trading stations, these settlements became known as the Presidency Towns and the territories around these towns came to be known as Mufassil. Till'1726 the administration of justice in three Presidency Towns was haphazard. The Company participated in administration of justice in cooperation with the local Mughal authorities. Some changes were brought in the administration of justice in three Presidency Towns with the intervention of some Charters issued from time to time by the Company though these changes were fringe and different in three Presidency Towns. For example, the first Mayor's court in India was established at Madras by the Company's Charter of 1687.

This was a Company's court as opposed to the Crown's court and no specific rules of law and procedure was laid down for this court by the Company. On the other hand, the Company first acquired the territorial acquisition of Bengal, Bihar and Orissa in 1765 as Mufassil area as opposed to Presidency Towns. Though the Company took the full control of Diwani and military power, the administration of both civil and criminal justice.were left to the indigenous machinery at the hand of natives until 1772. The development of adalat system in Mufassil area will be discussed in a different heading.

Second Period: The Era of the Mayor's Court: Administration of Justice from the Charter of 1726 till the Regulating Act of 1773

This period may be divided into two parts: from the Charter of 1726 till the Charter of 1753; and from the Charter of 1753 till the Regulating Act of 1773. The first part of this period marks the beginning of the intervention by the British Crown in the administration of justice in India. The Charter of 1726 issued by King George I by way of granting Letters Patent to the Company was the first gateway of the introduction of English law in India. The Charter of 1726 established a corporation for each Presidency towns. Following changes in the administration of justice were made by this Charter:

CRIMINAL JUDICIARY:

a. *Justices of the Peace:* Under the Charter the criminal justice was fully executive dominated. In each Presidency town the criminal justice was vested in the Governor and five senior members of the Council of the Company. Each of them was to act in the same manner, and to have the same powers, as the justices of the peace in England. A justice of the peace could arrest persons accused of committing crimes, punish those who were guilty of minor crimes, and commit the rest to be tried by the Quarter Sessions.

b. *Court of Quarter Session:* Three justices of the peace collectively were to form a court of record and they were to hold quarter sessions four times a year to try and punish each and every criminal offence, except high treason, committed in the Presidency Towns. Trial at these session courts were to be held with the help of grand jury and petty jury. All technical forms and procedures of the English criminal justice were introduced in the Presidency Towns as it was explicitly laid down in the Charter.

Governor-in-Council: Under the Charter criminal justice was vested in the Governor and five senior members of the Council of the Company. They had both original and appellate jurisdiction in some specified criminal matters, e.g. high treason and serious crimes like murder etc.

Defects of the Judicial System Under the Charter of 1726

- The criminal justice was fully executive dominated as it was at the hand of the Governor-in-Council.
- The Mayor's courts were not free from the executive influence. The aldermen were either Company's servants or other English traders who depended upon the Company's permission to stay in India and were at the mercy of the local government. In other words, the Governor and Council were the maker and unmaker of the judges.
- Judges were non-professionals. The Company had a policy of confining administration of justice to its servants and hence it avoided appointing lawyers.
- The Mayor's court was constituted to work independently. But its relationship with the executive was not stated clearly and there emerged an unhappy clash between the executive and the judiciary. This clash is evident from some important cases like Shrimpy's case, Arab Merchant's case, Pagoda Oath case etc.
- The Charter did not mention anything about the jurisdiction of the Mayor's court. When the Mayor's court decided that it was empowered to decide cases where both the parties were native Indians, it created great dissatisfaction and unrest among native

Third Period: The Era of the Supreme Court: Administration of Justice from the Regulating Act of 1773 Till the Era of Unification in1861

Though the Charter of 1753 was issued with a view to removing the defects of the Charter of 1726, the Mayor's Court suffered from certain drawbacks having far-reaching consequences. In 1772 the House of Commons appointed a secret committee to prove into the affairs of the Company. The committee reported, inter alia, that the Mayor's court had degenerated into an engine of oppression rather than acting as a court of justice.

On the basis of report of the committee the House of Commons intervened and passed the Regulating Act 1773. The Act empowered the King to establish by Charter a Supreme Court at Calcutta. Accordingly the King issued the Charter of 1774 establishing the Supreme Court at Calcutta. Subsequently Supreme Courts were established in Madras in 1801 and in Bombay in 1824 abolishing the Mayor's Court.

After the establishment of the Supreme Court under the Regulating Act of 1773 the judicial reform took the following shape:

- A Supreme Court was established in place of Mayor's Court in each Presidency Town of Calcutta, Bombay and Madras,
- Three Courts of Requests in three cities were retained and they were made subordinate to the Supreme Court. However, in 1850 these Courts of Requests were abolished and in their place Small Causes Courts were established in three Presidency Towns.
- The Supreme Court consisted of a Chief Justice and three other puisne judges. They were to be all professional barristers sent out to India from England. They held office during the pleasure of the King.
- The Supreme Court was empowered to supervise the Court of Collector, Quarte ession, Justice of Peace and the Court of Requests. Under this supervisory jurisdiction the Supreme Court could issue various prerogative writs.
- The general jurisdiction of this court was limited within the geographical limits of the PresidencyTown. Beyond the Presidency Towns, the court exercised a personal jurisdiction over three categories of persons- British subjects and persons employed directly or indirectly to the service of the Company.
- The Supreme Court had both original, appellate, civil, criminal, ecclesiastical and admiralty jurisdiction. It heard appeal from the decisions of the Mufassil courts and Company's courts.
- A second appeal from the decision of the Supreme Court where the cause of action exceeded 1000 pagodas lay with the King-in-Council within six months from the decision of the Supreme Court. In criminal cases the Supreme Court had full and absolute discretion to allow or deny permission to make an appeal to the King-in-Council.

- In 1850 the Courts of Requests were abolished and in their place Small Causes Courts were established in three Presidency towns.

Defects with the Working the Supreme Court

- In actual functioning both the judiciary and the executive came into serious conflicts and dissatisfaction arose between them under the following points:
- There appeared huge debate over the point of jurisdiction. In Patna and Cossijurah's cases the Supreme Court came into an open conflict with the Company on the issue whether the Indian Zaminder and farmers of revenue came under the jurisdiction of the Supreme Court or not.
- There emerged conflict between the Supreme Court and the Company's court. This was because neither the Regulating Act nor the Charter of 1774 clarified the question of relationship between the Supreme Court and the Company's Courts.
- There occurred conflicts on point of superiority between the Council and the Supreme Court. There was a great deal of vagueness in the crucial area of relationship between the Company and the Supreme Court.
- The two distinct and parallel judicial systems- the Supreme Court in the Presidency Towns and Adalat in the Mufassil area soon gave rise to conflict over the question of jurisdiction. For example, the Supreme Court cliamed jurisdiction over the whole native population which was opposed by the Council of the Company.
- Raja Nandkumar's, Radha Charan, Kamaluddin, Saropchand, Patna, Cossijurah etc cases provide glaring examples of lacunae and defective provisions of the Regulating Act and the Charter of 1774.

Thus though the Supreme Court was designed to be independent in discharging its functions, two fundamental things- shortcomings in the Regulating Act and the Charter and the violent interference of the executive- did not allow it to work independently.

Fourth Period: Era of Unification: From 1861 till the Independence in 1947 (Judicial Reform Under the Direct British Rule).

This period may be divided into two sub-heads: from 1861 till 1935 (the era of High Court); and from 1935 till 1947 (the era of High Court and the Federal Court). As a result of severe clash between the executive and the Supreme Court, within only seven years time the Supreme Court came to be a body disliked by all. Petitions in the form of allegation were submitted to the King of England not only by the Governor-General but also by the inhabitants of Bengal which followed by the appointment of a Select Committee in 1780 to enquire into administration of justice in Bengal. The Committee's report led to the passage of the Act of Settlement, 1781 which in fact curtailed the power of the Supreme Court to accommodate the Council's opinion. The Supreme Court now was deprived of its jurisdiction in revenue matters and Company's Court.

Though the plan did away with the clash between the executive and judiciary, it virtually undermined the position and prestige of the Supreme Court as a highest court and also as a court of record, for no longer was it in a position to control the executive. Secondly, the Supreme Court continued its interpretation of 'constructive inhabitancy' whereby it exercised jurisdiction over many persons residing outside Presidency Towns. Again, Mufassil courts had jurisdiction over these persons. Third, problems continued to arise regarding concurrent jurisdiction of the two sets of courts. At times the Supreme Court and Mufassil Courts passed conflicting decrees. Fourth, serious conflicts arose in execution proceedings. The process of the Supreme Court ran through the Mufassil where it could execute it in Presidency Towns. On the other hand, the Mufassil courts could not execute its decree in Presidency Towns. To execute it in the Presidency Towns separate suit was to be filed in the Supreme Court for its recognition. Against the background of this unsatisfactory state of affair, gradually opinion began to crystallise in favour of merger and consolidation of the two rival systems.

The first important step to unite the two sets of courts was taken in 1853, where the first Law Commission was established in India and an all India Legislature was created whose laws were to be binding on all courts whether established by the Royal Charter or the Company's authority. The second step was the appointment of the second Law Commission which was assigned to formulate a scheme of amalgamation of the Sadar Adalats and the Supreme Court and also to prepare codes of procedure to be applied to all courts.

The third step was the dissolution of the company and the taking over the Government of India by the British Crown in 1858 following the event of mutiny in 1857. This ultimately paved the way of unification much easier. The final step was taken with the enactment of three uniform codes (Civil Procedure Code, Criminal Procedure Code and Penal Code). With the achievement of these common legal fabric, the stage was set for the union of the two judicial systems and this was finally done by the British Parliament in 1861. By enacting the Indian High Courts Act which provided for the creation of the High Courts in three Presidency Towns by merging the Supreme Court and Sadar Adalats. The Charter for the Calcutta High Court was issued in 1862 and the High Court was established on 2nd July 1862.

Judicial System After the Unification

- Two parallel judicial systems, namely, the Company's courts in Mufassil areas and three Supreme Courts (King's Courts) in three Presidency Towns were merged into a unified system under three High Courts of Judicature at three Presidency Towns.

- The Supreme Courts and the Courts of Sadar Diwani Adalat and Sadar Nizamat Adalat were abolished.
- The ordinary original jurisdiction of the High Court was limited to the local limits of the Presidency Towns. Its predecessor the erstwhile Supreme Court d! in fact exercise a broader jurisdiction in the sense that in certain circumstances persons and property beyond the local limits of the presidency towns fell within its jurisdiction.
- In its ordinary civil jurisdiction the High Court was empowered to try and determine suits of every description except those falling within the jurisdiction of the Small Causes Courts.
- The High Court had original criminal jurisdiction within the local limits of its civil jurisdiction.
- The High Court exercised its appellate jurisdiction to hear appeals from both civil and criminal courts from which appeals were preferred to the Sadar Diwani and Sadar Nizamat Adalats. To be more specific, the original side of the High Court was the immediate successor to the Supreme Court and the appellate side of the High Court was the immediate successor of the Sadar Diwani Adalat and Sadar Nizamat Adalat.
- The High Court had supervisory jurisdiction over all subordinate courts both civil and criminal.
- Unlike the erstwhile Supreme Court, the High Court was empowered to exercise jurisdiction over revenue.
- A further appeal from the decision of the High Court involving a sum not less than Rs. 10,000 lay to the Privy Council. The High Court was also empowered to certify that the case was fit one for appeal to the Privy Council.

Criminal Judicial System Under Pakistan Period:

As mentioned earlier, with the adoption of the Constitution of 19 the highest court in Pakistan became the Supreme Court of Pakistan the High Courts were retained at provinces as earlier. The subordinate courts were the same as in 1947. After the adoption of the Constitution of 1962 the'whole judicial structure was the same as under the Constitution of 1956.

PROVISION OF THE LAW CONCERNING CRIMINAL JUSTICE SYSTEM IN BANGLADESH

General:

Legal system of Bangladesh is a mixer or collection of the rules and laws followed in the other country of the world. Bangladesh got its independence on 16th December 1971. Before the independence it passed through different period of administration process e.g. Hindu, Muslim, British, Pakistan etc. So it enacts its law in considering the history and enacting law which it thought necessary for its administration. As a result in every laws even in the constitution of Bangladesh reflects taste of the ancient period.

Origin and Nature of Laws of Bangladesh:

The present legal and judicial system of Bangladesh owes its origin mainly to two hundred years British rule in the Indian Sub-Continent although some elements of it are remnants of Pre-British period tracing back to Hindu and Muslim administration. It passed through various stages and has been gradually developed as a continuous historical process. The process of evolution has been partly indigenous and partly foreign and the legal system of the present day emanates from a mixed system which has structure, legal principles and concepts modeled on both Indo-Mughal and English law. The Indian sub-continent has a known history of over five hundred years with Hindu and Muslim periods which proceeded the British period, and each of these early periods had a distinctive legal system of its own.

Some Criminal Laws Enforceable in Bangladesh:

Administration of justice is necessary and essential for a country to be run. Every country has enacted law or regulation for administration of justice. Bangladesh has also enacted several Acts for its own self. For the proper management of criminal justice system it enacted different laws. For example penal code, 1860 for the determination or affixing the punishment of criminal offences committed with in the territory of the country.

Thus following are some of the criminal laws enforceable in Bangladesh which is supervising criminal justice system of the country:

- Code of criminal Procedure, 1898
- Penal Code, 1860
- Nari O Shishu Nirjaton Domon Ain,2000
- Special Powers Act, 1974
- Police Act, 1864
- The Evidence Act, 1882
- The Arms Act,1878
- The Drugs Act, 1940
- The Explosive Substances Act 1908

Classification of Criminal Courts:

The ordinary criminal courts have their legal basis in the Code of Criminal Procedure, 1898. The classes of courts, power and function as to the courts, and appointment of the judges are found in this very code. Section- 6 of the code of criminal procedure deals with the court which will exist in the whole territory. Section-6 of the code of criminal procedure, 1898 is as follows:

Section-6: Classes of Criminal Courts

1. Besides the Supreme Court and the Courts constituted under any law for the time being in force, other than this Code, there shall be two classes of Criminal Courts in Bangladesh, namely:-
   a. Courts of Sessions; and
   b. Courts of Magistrates.
2. There shall be two classes of Magistrate, namely: –
   a. Judicial Magistrate; and
   b. Executive Magistrate.
3. here shall be four classes of judicial Magistrate, namely: –
   a. Chief Metropolitan Magistrate in Metropolitan Area and Chief judicial Magistrate to other areas;
   b. Magistrate of the first class, who shall in Metropolitan area, be known as Metropolitan Magistrate;
   c. Magistrate of the second class; and

Explanation: For the purpose of this sub-section, the word “Chief Metropolitan Magistrate” and “Chief judicial Magistrate” shall include “Additional Chief Metropolitan Magistrate” and “Additional Chief judicial Magistrate” respectively.

Following are the courts in criminal justice system in Bangladesh in the modern contemporary period to administer justice:

- Supreme Court
  – Appellate Division
  – High Court Division
  – Court of Sessions
  – Court of Sessions
  – Additional Court of Session
- Chief Metropolitan Magistrate or Chief Judicial Magistrate
- Additional Chief Metropolitan Magistrate or Additional Chief Judicial Magistrate
- Metropolitan Magistrate or Magistrate of 1st class
- Executive Magistrates
- District Magistrate
- Additional District Magistrate
- Other Executive Magistrate
- Special Magistrates

A The Supreme Court:

Article–94: Establishment of Supreme Court:

1. There shall be a Supreme Court for Bangladesh (to be known as the Supreme Court of Bangladesh) comprising the Appellate Division and the High Court Division.

2. The Supreme Court shall consist of the Chief Justice, to be known as the Chief Justice of Bangladesh, and such number of other Judges as the President may deem it necessary to appoint to each division.
3. The Chief Justice, and the Judges appointed to the Appellate Division, shall sit only in that division, and the other Judges shall sit only in the High Court Division.
4. Subject to the provisions of this Constitution the Chief Justice and the other Judges shall be independent in the exercise of their judicial functions.

B Courts of Sessions:

Section-6 of the Code of Criminal Procedure, 1898 has classified the criminal courts in two heads session and magistrate court; it has categorized Session courts in section-9 of the code. Section-9 of the code of criminal procedure is as follows:

Section-9: Court of Sessions

1. The Government shall establish a Court of Session for every sessions division, and appoint a judge of such Court; and the Court of Session for [a] Metropolitan Area shall be called the Metropolitan Court of Session.]
2. The Government may, by general or special order in the official Gazette, direct at what place or places the Court of Session shall hold its sitting; but, until such order is made, the Courts of Session shall hold their sittings as heretofore.
3. The Government may also appoint Additional Sessions Judges and Assistant Sessions Judges to exercise jurisdiction in one or more such Courts.

3A. The members of the Bangladesh Judicial Service shall be appointed as Sessions Judge, Additional Sessions Judge and Joint Sessions Judge in accordance with the rules framed by the President under the proviso to Article 133 of the constitution to exercise jurisdiction in one or more of such areas.]

4. A Sessions Judge of one sessions division may be appointed by the Government to be also an Additional Sessions Judge of another division, and in such case he may sit for the disposal of cases at such place or places in either division as the Government may direct.
5. All Courts of Session existing when this Code comes into force shall be deemed to have been established under this Act.

As Section-9 stated, the session courts will include the following:

- Court of Session
- Additional Sessions Judge
- Joint Sessions Judge

C Courts of Magistrates:

Section-6 of the code of criminal procedure, 1898 has classified the criminal courts which will conduct its judicial power with in the territory Bangladesh. It has established Court of Magistrate as the one of the branch of adjudicating judicial dispute.

Section-6 of the code introduces following classification as to Magistrate courts:
There shall be two classes of Magistrate, namely:

a. Judicial Magistrate; and
b. Executive Magistrate

......Section-6(2) of code of criminal procedure, 1898

Judicial Magistrate:

There shall be four classes of judicial Magistrate, namely: –

a. Chief Metropolitan Magistrate in Metropolitan Area and Chief judicial Magistrate to other areas;
b. Magistrate of the first class, who shall in Metropolitan area, be known as Metropolitan Magistrate;
c. Magistrate of the second class; and
d. Magistrate of the third class

.........Section-6(3) of Code of criminal procedure, 1898

Executive Magistrate:

Section-10 of the code of criminal procedure, 1898 dealt with the provision regarding executive magistrate. Section-10 of the code says as:

Section-10: Executive Magistrates:

1. In every district and in every Metropolitan Area, the Government shall appoint as many persons as it thinks fit to be Executive Magistrates and shall appoint one of them to be the District Magistrate.
2. The Government may also appoint any Executive Magistrate to be an Additional District Magistrate, and such Additional District Magistrate shall have all or any of the powers of a District Magistrate under this Code or under any other law for the time being in force, as the Government may direct.
3. Whenever in consequence of the office of a District Magistrate becoming vacant, any officer succeeds temporarily to the chief executive in the administration of the district, such officer shall, pending the orders of the Government, exercise all the powers and perform all the duties respectively conferred and imposed by this Code on the District Magistrate.
4. The Government may, or subject to the control of the Government, the District Magistrate may, from time to time, by order define local

areas within which the Executive Magistrate may exercise all or any of the powers with which they may be invested under this Code and, except as otherwise provided by such definition, the jurisdiction and powers of every such Executive Magistrate shall extend throughout the district.

5. The Government may, if it thinks expedient or necessary, appoint any persons employed in the Bangladesh Civil Service (Administration) to be an Executive Magistrate and confer the powers of an Executive Magistrate on any such member.
6 Subject to the definition of the local areas under sub-section (4) all persons appointed as Assistant Commissioners, Additional Deputy Commissioners or Upazila Nirbahi Officer in any District or Upazila shall be Executive Magistrates and may exercise the power of Executive Magistrate within their existing respective local areas.
7. Nothing in this section shall preclude the Government from conferring, under any law for the time in force, on a Commissioner of Police, all or any of the powers of an executive Magistrate in relation to a Metropolitan area.]

Thus section-10 declares following as executive magistrates:

- District Magistrate
- Additional District Magistrate
- Executive Magistrate

Power and Functions of the Courts:

Powers of the court here refers the sentence or punishment which may the court grant to the victim or complainant for the criminal offences or violation committed against him.

The powers of the court in commencing sentence may be discussed in two heads:

A. Powers of the Magistrate Court and
B. Powers of the court of Sessions and High Court Division

A Powers of the Magistrate Court:

The sentence or punishment which a magistrate court may pronounce in adjudicating any criminal dispute place before his learned court is specified in section-32, section-33 and section-33A of the code of criminal procedure, 1898.

They are as follows:

Section-32.Sentences which Magistrates May Pass:

1. The Courts of Magistrates may pass the following sentences namely:-
   a. *Courts of Metropolitan Magistrates and] of Magistrates of the first class:* Imprisonment for a term not exceeding five years],

including such solitary confinement as is authorized by law; Fine not exceeding ten thousand taka]; Whipping.

   b. Courts of Magistrates of the second class: Imprisonment for a term not exceeding three years], including such solitary confinement as is authorized by law; Fine not exceeding five thousand taka];
   c. Courts of Magistrates of the third class: Imprisonment for a term not exceeding two year]; Fine not exceeding two thousand taka].
2. The Court of any Magistrate may pass any lawful sentence, combining any of the sentences which it is authorized by law to pass.

Section-33: Power of Magistrates to Sentence to Imprisonment in Default of Fine:

1. The Court of any Magistrate may award such terms of imprisonment in default of payment of fine as is authorized by law in case of such default:

Provided that-

   a. The term is not in excess of the Magistrate's powers under this Code;
   b. In any case decided by a Magistrate where imprisonment has been awarded as part of the substantive sentence, the period of imprisonment awarded in default of payment of the fine shall not exceed one-fourth of the period of imprisonment which such Magistrate is competent to inflict as punishment for the offence otherwise than as imprisonment in default of payment of the fine.

2. The imprisonment awarded under this section may be in addition to a substantive sentence of imprisonment for the maximum term awardable by the Magistrate under section 32.

POWERS OF THE COURT OF SESSIONS AND HIGH COURT DIVISION:

Sentencing power of the Sessions court and High Court Division has been settled by section-31 of the code of criminal procedure, 1898. Section-31 states as follows:

Section-31: Sentences which High Court Division and Sessions Judges May Pass:

1. The High Court Division] may pass any sentence authorized by law.
2. A Sessions Judge or Additional Sessions Judge may pass any sentence authorized by law; but any sentence of death passed by any such Judge shall be subject to confirmation by the High Court Division.

3. A (Joint) Sessions Judge may pass any sentence authorized by law, except a sentence of death or of transportation for a term exceeding [ten] years or of imprisonment for a term exceeding 2 [ten] years

Appointment of Magistrates and judges:

Procedure of Appointment of the Magistrates, judges is specified in section- of the code of criminal procedure, 1898 and the appointment of chief justice and other judges of Supreme Court are specified in or followed by Article 95 of the constitution of Bangladesh.

APPOINTMENT OF JUDGES OF THE SUPREME COURT:

Article-95: Appointment of Judges:

1. The Chief Justice shall be appointed by the President, and the other Judges shall be appointed by the President after consultation with the Chief Justice.
2. A person shall not be qualified for appointment as a Judge unless he is a citizen of Bangladesh and –
   a. Has, for not less than ten years, been an advocate of the Supreme Court ; or
   b. Has, for not less than ten years, held judicial office in the territory of Bangladesh ; or
   c. Has such qualifications as may be prescribed by law for appointment as a Judge of the Supreme Court.
3. In this article, "Supreme Court" includes a court which at any time before the commencement of this Constitution exercised jurisdiction as a High Court in the territory of Bangladesh.

Appointment of the Magistrates and Judges in Session Divisions:

Appointment of magistrate or subordinate courts is established through Article 115 &116 of the constitution of Bangladesh and section 9, 11 & 18 of the code of criminal procedure, 1898.

[115. Appointments to subordinate courts Appointments of persons to offices in the judicial service or as magistrates exercising judicial functions shall be made by the President in accordance with rules made by him in that behalf.]
116. Control and discipline of subordinate courts The control (including the power of posting, promotion and grant of leave) and discipline of persons employed in the judicial service and magistrates exercising judicial functions shall vest in the [President] [and shall be exercised by him in consultation with the Supreme Court].

Section 9, 11 & 18 of the code of criminal procedure, 1898 are as followes:
Section-9: Court of Sessions:

- The Government shall establish a Court of Session for every sessions division, and appoint a judge of such Court; and the Court of Session for a] Metropolitan Area shall be called the Metropolitan Court of Session.]
- The Government may, by general or special order in the official Gazette, direct at what place or places the Court of Session shall hold its sitting; but, until such order is made, the Courts of Session shall hold their sittings as heretofore.
- The Government may also appoint Additional Sessions Judges and Assistant Sessions Judges to exercise jurisdiction in one or more such Courts.
- The members of the Bangladesh Judicial Service shall be appointed as Sessions Judge, Additional Sessions Judge and Joint Sessions Judge in accordance with the rules framed by the President under the proviso to Article 133 of the constitution to exercise jurisdiction in one or more of such areas.]
- A Sessions Judge of one sessions division may be appointed by the Government to be also an Additional Sessions Judge of another division, and in such case he may sit for the disposal of cases at such place or places in either division as the Government may direct.
- All Courts of Session existing when this Code comes into force shall be deemed to have been established under this Act.

Section-11: Judicial Magistrates:

1. In every district outside a Metropolitan Area, the Chief Judicial Magistrates, Additional Chief Judicial Magistrates and other Judicial Magistrates shall be appointed from the persons employed in the Bangladesh Judicial service in accordance with the rules framed by the President under the proviso to Article 133 of the constitution.
2. An Additional Chief Judicial Magistrate shall have all or any of the powers of the Chief Judicial Magistrate under this Code or any other law for the time being in force, as the Government may direct.
3. The Government may, or subject to the general or special orders issued by the Government in consultation with the High Court Division, the Chief Judicial Magistrate may, from time to time, define local areas within which the Judicial Magistrates may exercise all or any of the powers with which they may be invested under this Code, and except as otherwise provided by such definition, the jurisdiction and powers of every such Magistrate shall extend throughout the district.
4. Notwithstanding anything contained in this section, the Government may require any Executive Magistrate to perform the functions of a

Judicial Magistrate for a period to be determined in consultation with the High Court Division and during such period, the Magistrate shall not perform the functions of an Executive Magistrate.]

Section-18: Appointment of Metropolitan Magistrates:

1. In every Metropolitan Area, the Chief Metropolitan Magistrate, Additional Chief Metropolitan Magistrate and other Metropolitan Magistrates shall be appointed from among the persons employed in the Bangladesh judicial Service.]
2. The Government may appoint one or more Additional Chief Metropolitan Magistrates, and such Additional Chief Metropolitan Magistrates shall have all or any of the powers of the Chief Metropolitan Magistrate under this Code or under any other law for the time being in force, as the Government may direct.

Illustration, Nature and Salient Features of Some Criminal Laws of Bangladesh:

The chapter intends to illustrate some criminal laws of the territory to have knowledge of their nature and salient features. The country has adopted and chosen laws for her administration of justice. Most of the law of the country is adopted from the sub continent of India and somehow the laws and their nature are connected with Laws exist in the ancient period e.g. Hindu, Muslim, British and Pakistan Period. The knowledge of criminal laws of the territory is so much essential to justify or evaluate criminal justice system of the country. Here elaboration of some law considering their nature, objects and features are described bellow:

Code Of criminal Procedure, 1898:

Code of criminal procedure, 1898 is one of the essential code of the country in dealing with the criminal administration of justice. The only law of the country dealt with the procedure for determining power and function of the country and other procedural matter which is connected with criminal judicial system of the country.

- Nature:
- Objects:
- Fundamental procedures
- Evaluation

Nature:

CrPC is a branch of procedural law. Adjective of procedural criminal law provides machinery for the punishment of offenders against substantive criminal laws, e.g. the penal code and other statutes. However, CrPC is not the only procedural law for punishing offenders; it is the main general law of procedure for criminal proceedings but any other statute or special law may determine aspects of procedural law. The CrPC though mainly an adjective or procedural law deals with many other aspects: it deals with the constitution of criminal courts, classifies them, defines their powers etc. there are provisions in the CrPC which provide for substantive law by creating offences.

For instance, section 250 creates a separate offence in case of false, frivolous and vexatious accusations in cases tried by magistrates. In addition to offences created by section 203 and 211 in the penal code, section 250 of the CrPC creates another offence of false accusation and punishment has been prescribed in that very section also. Likewise, section 485A of the CrPC creates another offence with punishment for non-attendance by a witness in obedience to summons. If any witness fails, without just excuses, to appear before a court in response to a summon, the court before which the witness is to appear may try him summarily and sentence him to fine not exceeding two hundred taka and fifty.

Objects:

The main objects of the code are to determine and specify the machinery for the punishment of offenders against substantive criminal laws enforceable in the country. The law itself the main general law of the country supervise the formation, function and other procedure requires for administration of criminal justice. Thus CrPC is the main law of procedure but not the only.

Fundamental Procedures:

The Code of Criminal Procedure, 1898 is the main general law of procedure of the country in criminal justice system. The very code does not preclude anything which is needed for the determining of machinery of ensuring criminal justice. It is in considering of law is most uniform and clear. The code successfully elaborate structure of the courts to functions of the court, pre trial stage to commencing of sentences and their execution, other procedures related with the administration of criminal justice. The knowledge of the code is essential for the criminal justice system because this is the main procedural law of the country to deal with the criminal justice system.

FOLLOWING ARE SOME FUNDAMENTAL FEATURES OF THE CODE:

Classification of the Courts:(Section-6 of CrPC)

The code of criminal procedure itself clearly defines the court which will regulate its jurisdiction over the people of the country. Section-6 of the code has clearly classified the courts which will exist in adjudication of criminal disputes within the country.

According to section-6 of the code following are the courts in criminal justice system of Bangladesh in the modern contemporary period to administer justice:

- Supreme Court
- Appellate Division
- High Court Division
- Court of Sessions
- Court of Sessions
- Additional Court of Session
- Joint Session Court
- Court of Magistrates
- Judicial Magistrates
- Chief Metropolitan Magistrate or Chief Judicial Magistrate
- Additional Chief Metropolitan Magistrate or Additional Chief Judicial Magistrate
- Metropolitan Magistrate or Magistrate of 1st class
- Executive Magistrates
- District Magistrate
- Additional District Magistrate
- Other Executive Magistrate
- Special Magistrates

Determining Power and Functions of the Courts:(Section-31 to Section-33A of the Cr.PC):

The maximum Power of sentencing In adjudicating a criminal matter before the courts exist in the territory have been specified in section-31,32,33 and 33A of the code of criminal procedure. The maximum power of sentencing court is drawn in the table bellow:

POWER OF THE MAGISTRATES COURT

Section-32.Sentences which Magistrates May Pass:

The Courts of Magistrates may pass the following sentences namely:-

a. *Courts of Metropolitan Magistrates and] of Magistrates of the first class*: Imprisonment for a term not exceeding five years], including such solitary confinement as is authorized by law; Fine not exceeding ten thousand taka]; Whipping.
b. *Courts of Magistrates of the second class:* Imprisonment for a term not exceeding three years], including such solitary confinement as is authorized by law; Fine not exceeding five thousand taka];
c. *Courts of Magistrates of the third class:* Imprisonment for a term not exceeding two year];

Fine not exceeding two thousand taka].

(2) The Court of any Magistrate may pass any lawful sentence, combining any of the sentences which it is authorized by law to pass.Section-33: Power of Magistrates to sentence to imprisonment in default of fine:

The Court of any Magistrate may award such terms of imprisonment in default of payment of finė as is authorized by law in case of such default:

Provided that-

a. The term is not in excess of the Magistrate's powers under this Code;
b. In any case decided by a Magistrate where imprisonment has been awarded as part of the substantive sentence, the period of imprisonment awarded in default of payment of the fine shall not exceed one-fourth of the period of imprisonment which such Magistrate is competent to inflict as punishment for the offence otherwise than as imprisonment in default of payment of the fine.

(2) The imprisonment awarded under this section may be in addition to a substantive sentence of imprisonment for the maximum term awardable by the Magistrate under section 32.

Powers Of the High Court Division or Session CourtSection-31: Sentences which High Court Division and Sessions Judges may pass:

1. The High Court Division] may pass any sentence authorized by law.
2. A Sessions Judge or Additional Sessions Judge may pass any sentence authorized by law; but any sentence of death passed by any such Judge shall be subject to confirmation by the High Court Division.
3. A (Joint) Sessions Judge may pass any sentence authorized by law, except a sentence of death or of transportation for a term exceeding [ten] years or of imprisonment for a term exceeding 2 [ten] years.Power of the Special MagistratesSection-33A: Higher powers of certain Magistrates:

The Court of a Magistrate, specially empowered under section 29C, may pass any sentence authorized by law, except a sentence of death or of transportation or imprisonment for a term exceeding seven years.]

Provision as to Arrest:(Section-46 to Section-67 and Section-75 to Section-86)

Arrest is the beginning of imprisonment. Its purposes may be classified as preventive, punitive, and protective. There is no necessary assumption that arrest will be followed by a charge.

A constable who reasonably suspects a person of involvement in an offence may arrest that person with a view to interrogating him in the more formal atmosphere of a police station.

Thus arrest is the legal detention of a person which does not demand for necessary charge but mere reasonably suspicion of involvement of an offence is enough.

ARREST IN GENERAL:

Section 46 to 53 provides procedure of how an arrest can be made. The whole procedure may be described in the following steps:

Effecting Arrest by Touching the Body of the Arrestee:

Section-46: Arrest how made:

1. In making an arrest the police-officer or other person making the same shall actually touch or confine the body of the person to be arrested, unless there be a submission to the custody by word or action.

Resisting Endeavour to Arrest:

2. If such person forcibly resists the endeavor to arrest him, or attempts to evade the arrest, such police-officer or other person may use all means necessary to effect the arrest.
3. Nothing in this section gives a right to cause the death of a person who is not accused of an offence punishable with death or with [transportation for life].

Search of Place Entered by:

While making the arrest under warrant or in case of a warrantable case the police officer may ask free ingress to any residence or place where he has reason to believe that the person to be arrested is hiding or has entered into (Section-47) If ingress to such place can not be obtained under section 47 it shall be lawful for the police officer to break into the house or residence to effect the arrest (Section-48)

If such a breaking into the house is to be done into a zanana, the police officer must to give the women inside the zanana opportunity to withdraw themselves from it (Section-48) The person arrested shall not be subjected to more restraint than is necessary to prevent his escape (Section-49).

4. Arrest without Warrant: (Section-54-67):

Section 54 to section 67 of the code dealt with the procedure regarding arrest without warrant. Among them section-54 of the code provides unbeaten power to the police to arrest peoples without warrant.

Section-54: When police may arrest without warrant:

Any police-officer may, without an order from a Magistrate and without a warrant, arrest- firstly , any person who has been concerned in any cognizable offence or against whom a reasonable complaint has been made or credible information has been received, or a reasonable suspicion exists of his having been so concerned; secondly , any person having in his possession without lawful excuse, the burden of proving which excuse shall lie on such person, any implement of house breaking; thirdly, any person who has been proclaimed as an offender either under this Code or by order of the Government; fourthly, any person in whose possession anything is found which may reasonably be suspected to be stolen property and who may reasonably be suspected of having committed an offence with reference to such thing; fifthly, any person who obstructs a police-officer while in the execution of his duty, or who has escaped, or attempts to escape, from lawful custody; sixthly, any person reasonably suspected of being a deserter from the armed forces of Bangladesh.

Seventhly , any person who has been concerned in, or against whom a reasonable complaint has been made or credible information has been received or a reasonable suspicion exists of his having been concerned in, any act committed at any place out of Bangladesh, which, if committed in Bangladesh, would have been punishable as an offence, and for which he is, under any law relating to extradition or under the Fugitive Offenders Act, 1881, or otherwise, liable to be apprehended or detained in custody in Bangladesh; eighthly , any released convict committing a breach of any rule made under section 565, sub-section (3); ninthly, any person for whose arrest a requisition has been received from another police-officer, provided that the requisition specifies the person to be arrested and the offence or other cause for which the arrest is to be made and it appears therefore that the person might lawfully be arrested without a warrant by the officer who issued the requisition.

Besides the Code Includes:

Section-55: Arrest of vagabonds, habitual robbers, etc

Section-57: Pursuit of offenders into other jurisdictions

Section-59: Arrest by private persons and procedure on such arrest

Section-60: Person arrested to be taken before Magistrate or officer in charge of police-station

Section-61: Person arrested not to be detained more than twenty-four hours

Section-64: Offence committed in Magistrate's presence

Section-65: Arrest by or in presence of Magistrate

Warrant of Arrest:

Provision regarding arrest of a person under warrant against any person who committed an act criminal in nature or arrest of the person as require or for whose arrest an order of the court or reasonable authority are mentioned in section-75 to section-86 of the code of criminal procedure, 1898.

Search Warrant:(Section-94 to Section-106 of CrPC):

Section-96 to Section-99G of the code of criminal procedure dealt with the provision regarding issuing search warrant and procedure regarding execution of such warrant.

Section-96: When search- warrant may be issued

Section-97: Power to restrict warrant

Section-98: Search of house suspected to contain stolen property, Forged document, etc

Section-99: Disposal of things found in search beyond jurisdiction

Section-100: Search for persons wrongfully confined

Section-102: Person in charge of closed place to allow search

Disputes as to Immoveable Property:(Section-145 to Section-148 of the CrPC):

Section 145 to section 148 deals with the disputes as to immovable property. Section 145 of the code states procedure where dispute concerning land, etc. is likely to cause breach of peace and state that party in possession to retain possession until legally evicted. Section 146 of the code deals with the provision regarding attachment of disputed property subject to exceptions.

Section-145: Procedure where dispute concerning land, etc, is likely to cause breach of peach:

- Whenever a District Magistrate, or an Executive Magistrate specially empowered by the Government in this behalf] is satisfied from a police-report or other information that a dispute likely to cause a breach of the peace exists concerning any land or water of the boundaries thereof, within the local limits of his jurisdiction, he shall make an order in writing, stating the grounds of his being so satisfied, and requiring the parties concerned in such dispute to attend his Court in person or by pleader, within a time to be fixed by such Magistrate, and to put in written statements of their respective claims as respects the fact of actual possession of the subject of dispute.
- For the purposes of this section the expression "land or water" includes buildings, markets, fisheries, crops or other produce of land, and the rents or profits of any such property.
- A copy of the order shall be served in manner provided by this Code for the service of a summons upon such person or persons as the Magistrate may direct, and at least one copy shall be published by being affixed to some conspicuous place at or near the subject of dispute. Inquiry as to possession
- The Magistrate shall then, without reference to the merits or the claims of any of such parties to a right to possess the subject of dispute, peruse the statements so put in, hear the parties, receive all such evidence as may be produced by them respectively, consider the effect of such evidence, take such further evidence (if any) as he thinks necessary, and, if possible, decide whether any and which of the parties was at the date of the order before mentioned in such possession of the said subject:

- Provided that, if it appears to the Magistrate that any party has within two months next before the date of such order been forcibly and wrongfully dispossessed, he may treat the party so dispossessed as if he had been in possession at such date:
- Provided also, that if the Magistrate considers the case one of emergency, he may at any time attach the subject of dispute, pending his decision under this section.
- Nothing in this section shall preclude any party so required to attend, or any other person interested, from showing that no such dispute as aforesaid exists or has existed; and in such case the Magistrate shall cancel his said order, and all further proceedings thereon shall be stayed, but, subject to such cancellation, the order of the Magistrate under sub-section (1) shall be final. Party in possession to retain possession until legally evicted
- If the Magistrate decides that one of the parties was or should under the first proviso to sub-section (4) be treated as being in such possession of the said subject, he shall issue an order declaring such party to be entitled to possession thereof until evicted therefore in due course of law, and forbidding all disturbance of such possession until such eviction and when he proceeds under the first proviso to sub-section (4), may restore to possession the party forcibly and wrongfully dispossessed.
- When any party to any such proceeding dies, the Magistrate may cause the legal representative of the deceased party to be made a party to the proceeding and shall thereupon continue the inquiry, and if any question arises as to who the legal representative of a deceased party for the purpose of such proceeding is, all persons claiming to be representatives of the deceased party shall be made parties thereto.
- If the Magistrate is of opinion that any crop or other produce of the property, the subject of dispute in a proceeding under this section pending before him, is subject to speedy and natural decay, he may make an order for the proper custody or sale of such property, and, upon the completion of the inquiry, shall make such order for the disposal of such property, or the sale-proceeds thereof, as he thinks fit.
- The Magistrate may, if he thinks fit, at any stage of the proceedings under this section, on the application of either party, issue a summons to any witness directing him to attend or to produce any document or thing.

Section-146: Power to Attach Subject of Dispute:

1. If the Magistrate decides that none of the parties was then in such possession, or is unable to satisfy himself as to which of them was then in such possession of the subject of dispute, he may attach it

until a competent Court has determined the rights of the parties thereto, or the person entitled to possession thereof: Provided that such Magistrate]may withdraw the attachment at any time if he is satisfied that there is no longer any likelihood of a breach of the peace in regard to the subject of dispute.

2. When the Magistrate attaches the subject of dispute, he may, if he thinks fit and if no receiver of the property, the subject of dispute, has been appointed by any Civil Court appoint a receiver thereof, who, subject to the control of the Magistrate, shall have all the powers of a receiver appointed under the Code of Civil Procedure, 1908]: Provided that, in the event of a receiver of the property, the subject of dispute, being subsequently appointed by any Civil Court, possession shall be made over to him by the receiver appointed by the Magistrate, who shall thereupon be discharged.

Summary Trial:(Section-260 to Section-265 of the CrPC)

Section-260 to section-265 of the code of criminal procedure, 1898 dealt with the procedure regarding summary trial by the magistrates' court and relevant procedure arise out of summary trial.

Section-260: Power to Try Summarily:

- Notwithstanding anything contained in this Code,-
- The Metropolitan Magistrate ,
- Any Magistrate of the first class and
- Any Bench of Magistrates invested with the powers of a Magistrate of the first class shall try in a summary way all or any of the following offences:- offences not punishable with death, transportation or imprisonment for a term exceeding two years;
- Offences relating to weights and measures under sections 264, 265 and 266 of the Penal Code;
- Hurt, under section 323 of the same Code;
- Theft, under section 379, 380 or 381 of the same Code, where the value of the property stolen does not exceed ten thousand taka];
- Dishonest misappropriation of property under section 403 of the same Code, where the value of the property misappropriated does not exceed ten thousand taka;
- Receiving or retaining stolen property under section 411 of the same Code, where the value of such property does not exceed ten thousand taka];
- Assisting in the concealment or disposal of stolen property, under section 414 of the same Code, where the value of such property does not exceed ten thousand taka;

- Mischief, under sections 426 and 427] of the same Code;
- Criminal trespass, under section 447, and] house trespass, under section 448, and offences under sections 451, 453, 454, 456 and 457 or the same Code;
- Insult with intent to provoke a breach of the peace, under section 504, and criminal intimidation, under section 506, and offences under sections 509 and 510] of the same Code;
- Offence of bribery and personating at an election under sections 171E and 171F of the same Code;]
- Abetment of any of the foregoing offences;
- An attempt to commit any of the foregoing offences, when such attempt is an offence;
- Offences under section 20 of the Cattle-trespass Act,1871: Provided that no case in which a Magistrate exercises the special powers conferred by section 33A] shall be tried in a summary way.
- [Omitted by section 22 of the Code of Criminal Procedure (Second Amendment) Ordinance, 1982 (Ordinance No. XXIV of 1982).

Section-262: Procedure for Summary Trials:

1. In trials under this Chapter, the procedure prescribed in Chapter XX] shall be followed except as hereinafter mentioned.

Limit of Imprisonment

(2) No sentence of imprisonment for a term exceeding two years shall be passed in the case of any conviction under this Chapter

Appeal:(Section-404 to Section-431 of the CrPC):

Section-404 to section-431 of the code of criminal procedure, 1898 laid down procedure regarding appeal. The provisions of appeal are clear and specific in this code. Section-417 deals with appeal in case of acquittal and section-417A deals with appeal against conviction.

Section-417: Appeal in Case of Acquittal:

1. Subject to the provisions of sub-section (4), the Government may, in any case, direct the Public Prosecutor to present an appeal-
   a. To the High Court Division from an original or appellate Order of acquittal passed by any Court of Session;
   b. To the Court of Session from an original or appellate Order of acquittal passed by any Magistrate.]
2. Notwithstanding anything contained in section 418, if such an order is passed in any case instituted upon complaint, and if the order involves an error of law occasioning failure of justice, the complainant may present an appeal-

   a. To the High Court Division from an original order of acquittal passed by any Court of Session;
   b. To the Court of Session from an original order of acquittal passed by any Magistrate.]
3. No appeal by the complaint from an order of acquittal shall be entertained by the High Court Division or a Court of Session] after the expiry of sixty days from the date of the order of acquittal.
4. If, in any case, the admission of an appeal from an order of acquittal is refused, no appeal from that order of acquittal shall lie under sub-section (1)

Section-417A: Appeal Against Inadequacy of Sentence:

- The Government may, in any case of conviction on a trial held by any court, direct the Public Prosecutor to present an appeal to the High Court Division against the sentence on the ground of its inadequacy.
- A complainant may, in any case of conviction on a trial held by any Court, present an appeal to the Appellate Court against the sentence on the ground of its inadequacy:
- Provided that no appeal under this sub-section shall be entertained by the Appellate Court after the expiry of sixty days from the date of conviction.
- When an appeal has been filed against the sentence on the ground of its inadequacy, the Appellate Court shall not enhance the sentence except after giving to the accused a reasonable opportunity of showing cause against such enhancement and while showing cause, the accused may plead for his acquittal or for the reduction of the sentence.

From the above sections it is clear that the procedure of appeal is much codified in the criminal procedure code, 1898. The code includes procedure regarding appeal against acquittal as well as appeal against conviction.

Bail and Bond Section-496 to Section-502 and Section-513 to Section-516 of CrPC):

The word Bail is derived from the old French verb bailleier meaning to five or deliver. Bail in English common law is the security or on surety being taken for his appearance on certain day and a place named. In other words, bail is the delivery of arrested person to his sureties upon their giving security for his appearance at a designated place and time, to the jurisdiction and judgment of the court.

Section 496 to section 502 of the Cr.PC deals with the procedure as to grant bail or bail and Section 513 to section 516 of the same Code deals with the Bond. Following are the mother of the provisions of appeal:

Section-496: In what Cases Bail to be Taken:

When any person other than a person accused of a non-bailable offence is arrested or detained without warrant by an officer in charge of a police-station, or appears or is brought before a Court, and is prepared at any time while in the custody of such officer or at any stage of the proceedings before such Court to give bail, such person shall be released on bail: Provided that such officer or Court, if he or it thinks fit, may, instead of taking bail from such person, discharge him on his executing a bond without sureties for his appearance as hereinafter provided:

Provided, further, that nothing in this section shall be deemed to affect the provisions of section 107, sub-section (4), or section 117, sub-section (3).

Section- 497: When Bail May be Taken in Case of Non-bailable Offence:

- When any person accused of any non-bailable offence is arrested or detained without warrant by an officer in charge of a police-station, or appears or is brought before a Court, he may be released on bail, but he shall not be so released if there appear reasonable grounds for believing that he has been guilty of an offence punishable with death or transportation for life:
- Provided that the Court may direct that any person under the age of sixteen years or any woman or any sick or infirm person accused of such an offence be released on bail.
- If it appears to such officer or Court at any stage of the investigation, inquiry or trial, as the case may be, that there are not reasonable grounds for believing that the accused has committed a non-bailable offence, but that there are sufficient grounds for further inquiry into his guilt, the accused shall, pending such inquiry, be released on bail, or, at the discretion of such officer or Court, on the execution by him of a bond without sureties for his appearance as hereinafter provided.
- An officer or a Court releasing any person on bail under sub-section (1) or sub-section (2) shall record in writing his or its reasons for so doing.
- If, at any time after the conclusion of the trial of a person accused of a non-bailable offence and before judgment is delivered, the Court is of opinion that there are reasonable grounds for believing that the accused is not guilty of any such offence, it shall release the accused, if he is in custody on the execution by him of a bond without sureties for his appearance to hear judgment delivered.
- The High Court Division or Court of Session and, in the case of a person released by itself, any other Court may cause any person who has been released under this section to be arrested and may commit him to custody.

The code of criminal procedure as well as clarified in section 500 release of the person from custody for whose release a bond has been founded in section-499 of the code.

PROCEDURE REGARDING TRANSFER OF CASES (SECTION-525A TO SECTION-528 OF CRPC)

The objects of transfer of criminal cases are to ensure justice.Transfer of criminal case may take following three forms:

a. Transfer for trial to an appropriate court after taking cognizance under section 191,192,205C or 205CC
b. Transfer for sentence to an appropriate court under sections 245 and 349
c. Transfer of a pending case by the appellate division, High Court Division or Sessions Court under chapter XLIV of the Cr.PC.

The provisions regarding transfer of cases in criminal justice system of the Country specified by section 525A to Section 528 of the code of criminal procedure, 1989

Section-525A: Power of Appellate Division to Transfer Cases and Appeals:

1. The Appellate Division may direct the transfer of any particular case or appeal from one permanent Bench of the High Court Division to another permanent Bench of the High Court Division, or from any Criminal Court within the jurisdiction of one permanent Bench of the High Court Division to any other Criminal Court of equal or superior jurisdiction within the jurisdiction of another permanent Bench of the High Court Division, whenever it appears to it that such transfer will promote the ends of justice, or tend to the general convenience of parties or witnesses.
2. The permanent Bench of the High Court Division or the Court, as the case may be, to which such case or appeal is transferred shall deal with the same as if it had been originally instituted in, or presented to, such Bench or Court, as the case may be.]

526B- Power of Sessions Judge to Transfer Cases:

1. Whenever it is made to appear to a Sessions Judge that an order under this section is expedient for the ends of justice, he may order that any particular case be transferred from one Criminal Court to another Criminal Court in his sessions division.
2. The Sessions Judge may act either on the report of the lower Court, or on the Application of a party interested, or on his own initiative.
3. The provisions of sub-sections (4) to (10) (both inclusive) of section 526 shall apply in relation to an application to the Sessions Judge for an order under sub-section (1) as they apply in relation to an

application to the High Court Division for an order sub-section (1) of section 526.]

Section-528: Sessions Judge may withdraw Cases from Assistant Sessions Judge:

1. Any Sessions Judge may withdraw any case from, or recall any case which he has made over to, any Joint] Sessions Judge subordinate to him.
   a. At any time before the trial of the case or the hearing of the appeal has commenced before the Additional Sessions Judge, any Sessions Judge may recall any case or appeal which he has made over to any Additional Sessions Judge.
   b. Where a Sessions Judge withdraws or recalls a case under sub-section (1) or recalls a case or appeal under sub-section (IA), he may either try the case in his own Court or hear the appeal himself, or make it over in accordance with the provisions of this Code to another Court for trial or hearing, as the case may be.

Chief Metropolitan Magistrate, Chief Judicial Magistrate or District Magistrate may Withdraw or Refer Cases:

2. [The Chief Metropolitan Magistrate or [Chief Judicial Magistrate or District Magistrate] may withdraw any case from, or recall any case which he has made over to, any Magistrate subordinate to him, and may inquire into or try such case himself, or refer it for inquiry or trial to any other such Magistrate competent to inquire into or try the same.

Power to Authorize Chief Metropolitan Magistrate or the Chief Judicial Magistrate to Withdraw Classes of Cases:

3. The Government with the approval of the High Court Division] may authorize the Chief Metropolitan Magistrate or the Chief Judicial Magistrate] to withdraw from any Magistrate subordinate to him either such classes of cases as he thinks proper, or particular classes of cases.
4. Any Magistrate may recall any case made over by him under section 192, sub-section (2), to any other Magistrate and may inquire into or try such case himself.
5. A Magistrate making an order under this section shall record in writing his reasons for making the same.

PENAL CODE, 1860:

A penal code is a portion of a state's laws defining crimes and specifying the punishment. Other parts of the laws of a given state can define crimes and punishments, such as a traffic code or a building safety code, or laws addressing environmental resources by regulating hunting, fishing, or forestry.

In many states, the body of criminal law is published in one or more printed books for convenient reference by lawyers, other professionals of the criminal justice system, and. in principle, ordinary citizens.

Nature and Categories of Offences Under Penal Code 1860:

The penal code 1860 the earliest and the main body of laws which deals with different kinds of offences and punishments. Offences under the code have been classified as those

- Against the state;
- Related to the Army, Navy and the Air force;
- Against the public tranquility;
- By or related to the public servants;
- Related to elections;
- For contempt of the lawful authority of public servants;
- Affecting public health, safety, convenience , decency and morals;
- Related to religion
- Affecting the human body which have further been sub-divided into offence affecting life, and causing miscarriage, kidnapping, rape, dacoity, or related to marriage, criminal breach of trust and so on

Offences Under Penal Code 1860:

The offences against the State mainly consist of waging or attempting to wage war or abetting waging of war against Bangladesh; conspiring to commit the said offences; collecting arms with the intention of waging war against Bangladesh; sedition; waging war against any neighboring power in alliance with Bangladesh; and assaulting the President of Bangladesh or government with intent to restrain or compel exercise of any lawful power. Offences relating to Army, Navy and Air Force mainly consist of abatement of mutiny; attempting to seduce a soldier, sailor or airman from his duty; abatement of assault by soldier, sailor or airman on his superior officer when in execution of his office; abatement of desertion of soldier, sailor or airman; harbouring deserter and wearing garb or carrying token used by soldier, sailor or airman.

Offences related to religion consist of injuring or defiling place of worship; deliberate and malicious acts intended to outrage religious feelings of any class by insulting its religion; disturbing religious assembly; trespassing in any place of worship or any burial place or cremation ground with intent to insult the religion of any person, and uttering words or sound with intent to wound religious feelings of another person.

Rape of a woman, kidnapping, theft, extortion, robbery, dacoity, dishonest misappropriation of property, criminal breach of trust etc are all punishable under Penal laws. At the same time offences related to culpable homicide amounting to murder, fraudulent execution of deed of transfer containing false statement, killing or maiming cattle, house-trespass are crimes which are also subject to punishment.

The gravity of an offence provides for imposing death penalty, imprisonment for life, forfeiture of property, fine and whipping as the case may be. Death sentence is the highest form of punishment under the Penal Code and may be imposed for treason, abatement of mutiny, perjury resulting in an innocent person being convicted and executed, murder, abatement of suicide of a minor or insane or intoxicated person, attempt to murder by a person under sentence of imprisonment for life, kidnapping or abducting a person under the age of ten and murder while committing dacoity. Imprisonment for life may be imposed for the above offences and some other grave offences.

Imprisonment for various terms may be imposed with fine or without fine for the remaining offences. In case of some heinous offences court may impose fine only instead of imposing sentence of imprisonment. For some heinous offences court may impose sentence of whipping with imprisonment. In some of the offences court may order for forfeiture of the property of the accused. The government may commute a sentence of death including an imprisonment for life to imprisonment of either description for a term not exceeding twenty years. The President may grant pardons, reprieve respites or remissions of sentence.

NARI O SHISHU NIRJATON DOMON AIN,2000 :

Nature of the Code:

The object behind enactment of Nari O Shishu Nirjaton Domon Ain, 2000 is to suppress wrongdoer or offence against the backward group of peoples of the country the woman and Children. In the constitution of Bangladesh Article-28(4) stated, "Nothing in this article shall prevent the state from making special provision in favour of women or children or for the advancement of any backward section of citizens"

Thus the State has chosen and adopted law for their most backward section of citizens by imposing more severe punishments for the offence committed against woman and children.

Following are some fundamentals feature of the Act:

The Nari O Shishu Nirjatan Domon Ain 2000 provides that whoever causes death of any woman or child by any poisonous, combustible or corrosive substance shall be punished with death. Offence of grievous hurt caused by using the above substance resulting in permanent privation of the sight, disfiguration of head or face, privation of the hearing, permanent destruction of any member or joint of the body of a woman or child has been made punishable with death, imprisonment for life, or imprisonment up to 14 years with a minimum of 7 years imprisonment. Rape of any woman or child has been made punishable with imprisonment for life. If any woman or child dies as a result of raping, the offender would be punished with death. Causing death of a woman or child by gang rape is also punishable with death or imprisonment for life. Attempt to cause death or injury by raping a woman or child is also punishable with death or imprisonment for life. Illegal trafficking of women for the purpose of prostitution, illegal cohabitation or engaging in illegal or immoral work has been made punishable with imprisonment for life.

Abduction or kidnapping of a woman for the purpose of engaging or using in prostitution, to compel her to marry against her will or to compel her to sexual intercourse by using force or coaxing or cajoling her is punishable with imprisonment for life or imprisonment for 10 years with a minimum of 7 years imprisonment. Causing death of a woman for dowry is punishable with death. Causing grievous hurt to a woman for dowry is punishable with imprisonment for life or 14 years, which shall not be less than 5 years. Attempt to cause death of a woman for dowry is punishable with imprisonment for life. Illegal trafficking in children, custody or possession of children is punishable with death or imprisonment for life. Abduction or illegal confinement of a child is punishable with death or imprisonment for life.

Special Powers Act, 1974:

The Special Powers Act 1947 makes hoarding or dealing in black market, counterfeiting currency-note and government stamps, smuggling, adulteration of or sale of adulterated food, drinks, drugs or cosmetics punishable offences. Attempt to commit those offences has also been made punishable offence. The Act also provides that a partner, director, manager, secretary or other officer or agent of a firm, company, or other body corporate shall be liable to be punished for committing the above offences by the firm, company or body corporate. The Act provides for punishment with death or with imprisonment for life, or with rigorous imprisonment for a term which may extend from 7 years to 14 years, with a minimum punishment ranging from one year to two years and also to pay fine.

THE ARMS ACT,1878:

Punishment Under Arms Act, 1878:

The Arms Act 1878 Under this Act, unlicensed manufacture, conversion and sale of arms, import and export of arms, transport of any unauthorized arms over Bangladesh and possession of unlicensed fire arms etc have been prohibited. Provisions have been made for granting license to use arms and ammunitions and granting license to deal in arms and ammunitions. In certain case, an arm is to be deposited at police stations or with licensed dealers. Further provisions have been made giving power to the government to make rules as to license, restriction on movements with arms, cancellation and suspension of license etc. Committing any breach of the above prohibitions would be an offence punishable with imprisonment of different terms, including imprisonment for life, not less than 7 or 10 years as the case may be. It is also punishable offence to knowingly purchase arms from unlicensed person or delivering arms to persons not authorized to possess them. Breach of rule under this Act is punishable with imprisonment for a term which may extend to six months, or with fine, or with both, as the case may be.

The Explosive Substances Act 1908:

The Explosive Substances Act 1908 Explosive substance deems to include any material for making an explosive substance and also the apparatus, machine or any part thereof which may be used for causing or aiding in causing any explosion. Causing explosion by any explosive substance likely to endanger life, injury to person or property or with intent to commit an offence or to enable any other person to commit an offence are punishable under this act with death, imprisonment for life or imprisonment of any other term with a minimum mandatory sentence of 2 to 5 years. Attempt to cause explosion or making or keeping of explosive substance is also an offence punishable with imprisonment of various terms. Even abatement of above offences is also punishable with the same sentence as provided for the offence concerned

The Evidence Act,1872:

The Evidence Act, originally passed by the British parliament in 1872, contains a set of rules and allied issues governing admissibility of any evidence in the courts of law. The enactment and adoption of the Evidence Act was a path-breaking judicial measure introduced in British India, which changed the entire system of concepts pertaining to admissibility of evidences in the courts of law. Up to that point of time, the rules of evidences were based on the traditional legal systems of different social groups and communities of British India and were different for different persons depending on his or her caste, religious faith and social position. The Evidence Act removed this anomaly and differentiation, and introduced a standard set of law applicable to all citizens.

Bangladesh has adopted this law for her administration of justice on 1st September 1872.

COMPARISON BETWEEN CRIMINAL JUSTICE SYSTEM OF U.K AND BANGLADESH

Where the question is to find out the irrelevancy or comparison between laws or in large, criminal justice system, of the United Kingdom and Bangladesh, it is too hard to find out because the maximum laws of the sub continent has its origin from the British kingdom as the continent has dominated by the British rules and laws near about 200 years. Following may be some major difference between the legal justice system or criminal laws of United Kingdom and Bangladesh:

Jury:

Jury is one of the basic features of the United Kingdoms criminal justice system. They have adopted The Juries Act, 1974 for determining their procedure. It is observed by the country that the most acceptable and correct decision is found by the sentence passed by the jury further it is observed that most of the cases fails to seek justice and are made to question where trial done without jury.

Whereas, the legal system of United Kingdom adopt the Juries Act, 1974 but the legal system of Bangladesh has no such provision as to jury but section-15 and 19 empowers magistrates to sit together as bench subject to direction of the Government. The High Court Division of the country also operates benches consisted of several justice but it has no original jurisdiction to take cognizance of criminal case.

Ensuring Rule of Law:

Rule of law has great importance in judicial system of United Kingdom and one of the very important features of the British constitution As there rule of law is ensured no one can escape and also no one is beyond the judicial capacity so possibility of ensuring criminal justice becomes light. On the other hand, Rule of law has not yet established though Article-27 of the constitution of the country (Bangladesh)states "all citizens are equal before law and are entitled to equal protection of law" I short "Equality before law".

Summary Trial:

The process of summary trial is successful in the criminal system of United Kingdom. It has chosen summary trial for seeking the quick and easiest justice in some criminal matter.

Its only followed the following process in it trial and appreciated in almost every country:

- The plea:
- Defense case
- Submission of no case
- Prosecution case:
- Verdict

On the other hand,

Section 26 to section 265 of the Cr.PC laid down provisions for summary trial for some offences which is not yet accepted by the experts and the proper and justifiable judgment or justice has not been ensured from its judgment.

Appeal:

The English man who enacts laws regarding every navel matters. It chosen criminal appeal Act, 1968 foritself to deal with the procedure regarding appeal. An application for appeal on this process must be made within 21 days after the commencement of a sentence.

On the other hand, The code of criminal procedure,1898 itself the law regarding appeal. Section 404 to 431 of the code deals with the matter. The code in general provides 60 days to appeal against any judgment of acquittal and conviction.

Sentencing

On passing sentence regarding any criminal case the criminal system of the United Kingdom proves it intelligence. They usually prefer pecuniary compensation rather custodial sentences. Criminal justice system of United Kingdom avoid death penalty and In passing sentence they are more aware so that no injustice would done or no one suffer injustice.

They laid down provision various provisions so that it can surpress injustice and ensure justice to the both plaintiff and defendant. For example, Under s.11 (3) of the Magistrates' Courts Act 1980, the magistrates may not pass a custodial sentence on an absent offender.

Courts are not allowed to disqualify the offender from driving unless he is present or the case was previously adjourned for him to attend On the other hand, Criminal justice system of Bangladesh yet not god rid from passing capital punishment or the death penalty though it is avoided in developed country and on passing of sentences it showed its biasness, pressure either political or any way.

Bail:

The Bail Act 1976 directs the procedure of bail and other correlated matters of the bail. It has preclude every small exception as it may be arise before setting a person free in Bail.

On the other hand,

Section-496 to Section-502 of the code of criminal procedure, 1898 operates bail.

BODY RELATED TO CRIMINAL JUSTICE SYSTEM IN BANGLADESH

The objective of the chapter is to determine and define the body or other institution which are working for the development of law, for ensuring justice and in any way related with the law of the country especially in the field to co-operate criminal justice system of Bangladesh.

Following body or organization are the main to entrust with criminal judicial system of Bangladesh:

Police:

The Bangladesh Police is the main law enforcement agency of Bangladesh to provide service to all citizens and make Bangladesh a better and safer place to live and work. It also upholds the rule of law, ensures safety and security of citizens, prevents and detects crime, brings offenders to justice and maintains peace and public order. It is administered by the central interior ministry of the Government of Bangladesh. Outside the Dhaka capital region and other major cities, police is organized at the district and thana levels. Raised in 1976, the Dhaka Metropolitan Police is charged with maintaining security and order in the national capital and largest city.

Twelve female police officials were recruited for the Bangladesh Police Special Branch (SB) in 1974 and inducted in the Dhaka Metropolitan Police in 1978. In 2004, Rapid Action Battalion (RAB) was raised comprising of personnel of the Military of Bangladesh, Border Guard Bangladesh (BGB) and the Bangladesh Ansar and VDP. The Bangladesh Police Special Branch was established to assist in maintaining national security and also performs the functions of intelligence-gathering and counterintelligence. In 2008, Bangladesh police established the Special Women Police Contingent (SWPC) to fight prostitution, drug smuggling and human trafficking. Composing entirely of female officers, the SWPC would be used to gather intelligence on criminal activities and specifically track down female criminals.

Judiciary:

Bangladesh judiciary is organized and governed according to the constitutional and legal provisions and from this section enumerate the system and about what 'judicial independence' really means. It also elaborates types of judge, including where they sit, the types of cases they hear and how they are appointed. It has been separated and recognized by the constitution as an organ of the state.

How the Judiciary is Governed:

The Chief Justice of Bangladesh decides where Justices sit, and the type of cases they hear, while the Ministry of Law (MOL) decides the judges, magistrates and tribunals affairs. The Chief Justice of Bangladesh in the Supreme Court decides where Justices shall sit, and the type of cases they hear. His lord ship normally constitutes Benches of the Appellate and the High Court Division. In the Appellate Division he normally constitutes the Bench with three Appellate Division Justices or with five Justices including himself.

In the High court Division the chief Justice constitutes Benches with one or two justices known as Single Bench and Division Bench respectively. In a special case the Chief Justice may constitute Special Bench with Three Justices, called Full Bench or Larger Bench with Five Justices to hear and dispose off a referred case by him. The Chief Justice may withdraw any case from the bench of any Justice without ant assigned reason and transfer it to any other Bench. The chief justice reshuffles the benches of the High Court Division regularly The Ministry of Law (MOL) decides the subordinate judges, magistrates and tribunals affairs after consultation with the Supreme Court in accordance with the provision of Article 116 of the constitution which runs as follows :

The control (including the power of posting, promotion and grant of leave) and discipline of persons employed in the judicial service and magistrates exercising judicial functions shall vest in the President and shall be exercised by him in consultation with the Supreme Court.

Followings are also governed by the judiciary in judicial system by the judiciary:

Courts holidays & Vacations: The legal year traditionally begins in October and courts sit for four terms during the year.

Judicial accountability and independence: The importance of judicial independence and the consequences of that independence on the notion of judicial accountability

Law professional bodies: There are various Advocates Associations and a Bar Council to control the law professionals.

Judicial Training authorities: Training of the subordinate judicial officers is imparted by authority run by the MOL.

BANGLADESH PUBLIC SERVICE COMMISSION (PSC):

Preamble:

The Bangladesh Public Service Commission (BPSC) is a quasi judicial body established in 1972 under the Constitution of the People's Republic of Bangladesh. It works under the provisions of the Article 137 – 141 of the Constitution of Bangladesh and certain other rules and regulations made by the government from time to time. The Chairman and such other members as shall be prescribed constitute the commission. There is also a full fledged Secretariat to assist the Commission. The Chief Justice of the country administers the oath for Chairman and the members of the commission. The tenure of the Chairman and members of the commission is 5 (five) years or 65 years of age whichever comes earlier. If the age permits the tenure can be renewed for one more term. The chairman and the members are appointed by the Hon'ble President of the Republic.

Objective:

To help Govt. to establish an appropriate civil service for the 21st century through selection of capable & efficient officials for the Republic who would be endowed with high level of integrity and dynamism.

Mission:

It would generate its resources and energy for (a) selecting suitable candidates for the services of the Republic (b) help the govt. in formulating a welfare oriented service condition for its employees, and (c) to help the govt. in maintaining discipline in the service.

Law Commission:

The Government felt it necessary to make the Commission a permanent one under a regular statute. Steps were taken and the Law Commission Bill of 1996 was passed by the Parliament. Upon receipt of assent of the Hon'ble President on September 9, 1996 it became an Act of Parliament (The Law Commission Act 1996 Act no. XIX of 1996).

Composition of the Law Commission:

As per section 5 of the Law Commission Act, 1996, the Commission consists of a Chairman and two Members. Under the law the Government has got the power to increase the number of its Members, if it deems necessary. The Chairman and Members of the Commission hold their respective offices for a term of three years from the date of their respective appointments. The Chairman or a Member may be re appointed by the Government for the prescribed term after the expiry of the said term.

From the very beginning the Chairman of the Commission has been appointed from amongst the retired Chief Justices of Bangladesh and Members have been appointed from retired judges of Supreme Court of Bangladesh except on one occasion on which a Member was appointed from amongst legal academics.

Very recently another Member from the legal academics is appointed in the Commission. The Commission is presently supported by two Senior Research Officers, one Senior Assistant Secretary and one Research Officer. There are also some Ministerial Staff to support administrative works of the Commission.

Functions of the Commission:

The functions of the Commission have been described in Section 6 of the Act. Under the Section the functions of the Commission will be as follows:

- To identify the causes of delay of civil and criminal cases in various courts and with a view to accelerate their disposal and ensure justice as quickly as possible:
- To recommend amendment of laws concerned or enactment of new laws in appropriate cases after examination;
- To recommend necessary reforms in order to modernize the judicial system;

- To recommend training and other measures for the improvement of the efficiency of the persons involved with the judicial system such as judicial officers, staff, law officers and lawyers;
- To recommend necessary measures for improvement of the entire judicial system and specially to prevent the abuse of the application of the laws concerned:
- To recommend modernization of different aspects of court management, such as, distribution of works among judges, supply of copies, transmission and preservation of records, service of notices and other relevant matters;
- To recommend, an acceptable measure regarding the feasibility of introducing a more efficient and accountable system in place of the present system for conducting the various government cases properly and establishing a separate investigating agency for the investigation of the criminal cases;
- Keeping in mind the attraction of domestic and foreign investment and necessity of free market economy-
- To recommend amendment of relevant laws including company law or legislation of new law in appropriate cases in order to create competitive atmosphere in the field of trade and industry and to avoid monopoly;
- To recommend, after examination, measures with regard to relevant laws especially copyright, trademarks, patents, arbitration, contract, registration and similar other matters;
- To recommend necessary measures for the establishment of separate courts for disposal of cases arising out of commercial and bank loan matters;
- To recommend necessary and timely amendments and reforms of the existing electoral laws administered by the Bangladesh Election Commission;
- To recommend, after examination, necessary reforms of the existing laws and women and children and prevent repression of women;
- To recommend reforms of existing laws, enactment of new laws in appropriate cases and taking of other acceptable measures for the proper implementation of legal- aid programs;
- To identify the various laws which conflict with each other on the same subject and in probable cases, to recommend codification and unification of various laws on the same subject;
- To recommend repeal of existing laws which are inconsistent with the fundamental rights and in appropriate cases making amendments with regard thereto;
- To recommend, after identification repeal of obsolete and unnecessary laws and in case of necessity, legislation of laws on any subject;

- To recommend acceptable measures for the upgrading of legal education, and
- To recommend with regard to other legal matters referred by the government from time to time.

Working Methodology of the Commission:

On the basis of Section 6A of the Law Commission Act 1996, the Commission prepares a work plan for each two-year on the conduct of its affairs in which laws are taken on priority basis for review. The said plan is sent to the Government. The Government sends its opinion/recommendations if any on the work plan. The Commission after considering the opinion/ recommendations made by the Government finalizes the work plan and informs the Government. The Commission in its meeting discusses the priorities of laws of the work plan and reference if any, made by the Government. In the Commission's meeting each member is assigned to prepare a working paper/ report with the assistance of a Research Officer. Then the Research team considering the nature and scope of the research of the law adopts different methodologies for collection of data and in appropriate cases studies foreign system of law to see how they meet similar problems. The team in the working paper delineates different deficiencies and drawbacks of the law and suggests provisional recommendations regarding removal thereof. The working paper prepared by the team is placed before the Commission for consideration and approval. After approval the paper is widely circulated among the different stakeholders for comments and suggestions. The team scrutinizes different views received from the stakeholders and thereafter the Commission prepares final report and draft bill if necessary, and sends them to the government for necessary action. In addition to the work plan the Commission also works and recommends on the matters referred by the government from time to time.

Provided that The Commission's recommendations for reform of law will bring the desired result only if they are made into Acts of Parliament. The Law Commission can make research and recommendations, but Parliament alone can change the law for the welfare of the people. As a result of the Commission's ongoing work, large areas of the law has been the subject of systematic research and improvement.

The Anti Corruption Commission:(DUDOK):

The Anti Corruption Commission (ACC) Bangladesh was created through an act promulgated on 23 February 2004 that into force on 09 May 2004. The first set of office bearers were appointed on 21 November 2004. The following day, it commenced its journey with a mission, a vow to make a difference to the Nation's anti corruption initiatives and a fresh mandate. "Anti Corruption Commission" (ACC) in the Bangla language "DUDOK.

Vision:

The Commission has formulated some forms of corruption in Bangladesh, for everyone to know, understand and prepare ourselves to completely erase corruption from our lives, if not reduce it.

- *Bribery:* It is the offering of money, services or other valuables to persuade someone to do something in return. Synonyms: kickbacks, baksheesh(tips), payola, hush money, sweetener, protection money, boodle, and gratuity.
- *Extortion:* Demanding or taking of money, property or other valuables through use of coercion and/or force. A typical example of extortion would be when armed police or military men exact money for passage through a roadblock. Synonyms include blackmail, bloodsucking and extraction.

Abuse of discretion: The abuse of office for private gain, but without external inducement or extortion. Patterns of such abuses are usually associated with bureaucracies in which broad individual discretion is created, few oversights or accountability structures are present, as well as those in which decision-making rules are so complex as to neutralise the effectiveness of such structures even if they exist.

Improper political contributions: Payments made in an attempt to unduly influence present or future activities by a party or its members when they are in office.

Mission:

It controls corruption by identifying hot spots and areas of vulnerabilities for targeted investigative and prosecution action, prevention and curative treatment beside preventive education and advocacy. It ultimately suppresses corruption through the effective and cumulative effects of its combating, controlling and prevention efforts enumerated above.

Functions of the commission

- To enquire into and conduct investigation of offences mentioned in the schedule
- To file cases on the basis of enquiry or investigation and conduct cases
- To hold enquiry into allegations of corruption on its own motion or on the application of aggrieved person or any person on his behalf
- To perform any function assigned to Commission by any Act in respect of corruption
- To review any recognized provisions of any law for prevention of corruption and submit recommendation to the President for their effective implementation
- To undertake research, prepare plan for prevention of corruption and submit to the President, recommendation for action based on the result of such research

- To raise awareness and create feeling of honesty and integrity among people with a view to preventing corruption
- To organize seminar, symposium, workshop etc. on the subjects falling within the functions and duties of the Commission
- To identify various causes of corruption in the context of socio-economic conditions of Bangladesh and make recommendation to the President for taking necessary steps
- To determine the procedure of enquiry, investigation, filing of cases and also the procedure of according sanction of the Commission for filing case against corruption and
- To perform any other duty as may be considered necessary for prevention of corruption.

Power to Make Rules

- The Commission for carrying out the purpose of Anti Corruption Act, 2004 has been vested with the power to make rules by notification published in the official Gazette with the prior approval of the President.

OBSERVATION THROUGH SOME CRIMINAL CASES IN BANGLADESH

This is a title attempt to find out some defects or problems visible or arise while adjudicating Criminal cases corresponding to Criminal Justice system of Bangladesh, going through some criminal cases. Thus the studies object to find out some problems which obstruct the fair and natural Justice. Here we are about to observe some criminal cases which have been either dismissed or failed to seek remedy to the victim in lieu of defects of laws or other technical problem.

OPINION AS TO FAULT OF CRIMINAL JUSTICE SYSTEM:

Opinion of Judges:

For the completion of the research and to gain some knowledge as to practical problems and as well as problems arise out of law I had communicate with two Magistrates of the country and with a former Additional Session judge.

They give their speech as following on the question how far Criminal justice ensured? Learned Magistrate Mr. Samsuddin Badal states, "Bangladesh had conferred or enacted the best laws except some but still it could not establish natural justice because of its enforcement, dishonesty of the peoples includes court staff, police etc. and political pressure also."

Former Additional session judge Mr. Hasnat Kobir stated much strictly in his answer, "Constitution of the country had ensured provision as to separation of judiciary but it is till now exist in the papers but the real situation is dangerous.

The laws enacted by the country is enough but their execution is in question. E.g. appointment of the judges, staffs of the court, executive body (police or others) and members of others organization have not been yet doing in fair way. Eventually appointments of unqualified person and disability as to ensure qualified training are also responsible to failure to the criminal justice system." Though they showed that the criminal justice system is yet not been ensured but they express that they are hopeful and believe the country will surely develop and will be able to ensure criminal justice

Opinion of the Lawyers:

The present condition of the judicial system of the country becomes much defected in the language of some lawyers. Almost every lawyer stated that the seeking justice becomes much harder. One of them stated, "The justice is going to hide from the country behind the money and political pressure."

Learned advocate Md. Junayedullha Shoeb that, "Justice is going far away from the reach of the poor people. The costs are unbearable for the person who is victimized by any act of other person. Usually poor people are suffering for commission of an offence but they can't claim justice only because of poverty though government in papers operate suit for the poor." Learned Advocate P.M.Mahady Hasan expresses himself, "Appointment of the corrupted judges, staffs, police, political unrest, dishonesty and disqualification of them and as well as some lawyers are liable for the failure to criminal justice system." Learned Advocate Md. Emdadul Hanif stated differently, "The dishonesty of the citizens, Institution of false cases, to gain political benefit filing cases against opposite party have made jam to the courts and judicial system is sinking to adjudicate them and so remedy to the real victim is denied or delayed. And the corruption, bribery etc are along with them."

Opinion of the Police:

S.I Golam Rabbani a member of the Bangladesh police serving for 16 years state, "Without giving money the appointment and promotion is not possible besides the facilities or remuneration given by the Govt. is not adequate for his family. So taking bribery is essential." Former warrant officer Jahangir Bhuiyan— "The police man of the country can work freely. Political pressure, scarcity of weapon, man power and less remuneration is liable for non performance of police."

Opinion of the Courts staff:

Monir Hossain Working in the courts for 3 months. He claimed, "5, 00000 taka had to give for the job. I borrowed it from his relatives and will have to pay them. I am only the boy of my family so i need some benefits out of the remuneration given by the Government"

Opinion or Suggestion as to Solution or Development:

They have suggested to the development of the following matters as following are the main problem of the criminal justice system besides ambiguity of laws:

- Disability of the Victim to seek remedy because of poverty as well as non performance of the organization whose duty is to assist poor people.
- Bribery or taking benefit of the post (judges, staffs, police)
- Appointment of unqualified peoples as judge, police or staff
- Appointment by taking money.
- Burden of cases
- Shorten of man power. (Police, court staff etc.)
- Political pressure over the judiciary
- Dishonesty of the peoples related with the justice system
- Certain limitation to train the judges and police

PROBLEMS OR OBSTACLE TO THE CRIMINAL JUSTICE SYSTEM OF BANGLADESH

Bangladesh is a unitary, independent, sovereign Republic to be known as the People's Republic of Bangladesh has enacted various criminal laws procedural and penal laws for administration of criminal justice. After the independence of the country it is hard working to reach to the top stage of success. It is bounded by Corruption, bribery, poverty etc. so that the country has not yet got reasonable development it should have. The main reason behind stepping back is the criminality of the citizens and non punishment for the commission offence. Whenever criminal justice system is secured and absolute the development become mandatory and it should be because criminal justice system enter fear in the mind that's why everyone participate equally on the development and no one can escape himself from harming the public property or tranquility.

But the dishonesty, corruption, bribery, omission from giving tax etc. are the main cause for the present situation of the country which are criminal in there nature. So if criminal administration of justice be ensured the development will come to the door definitely. But it is very matter of sad that we have the laws and all other body require for administration of justice but yet it has not reasonably face to light.Following are some practical issues behind non administration of criminal justice:

Laws:

Laws of the people's republic of Bangladesh especially Criminal laws are well but its enforcement cause the criminal system failure. The country yet enforces death penalty as capital punishment whilst other developed country keeps them away from such severer punishment. There exist some laws which should be reconsidered for the present time being. For example where any offence punishable with imprisonment or fine, if fine is awarded for that offence by the court the fine is so small in amount e.g. 500tk, 1000tk.

Lengthy Process of Trial:

The second main cause of failure to the administration of criminal justice in Bangladesh is its lengthy process of trial. Though the country itself full of crimes the adjudication should be hurry. In adjudicating a criminal case in the present time it takes almost 5 to 10 years, depended on nature of the case, which impliedly allow the criminal that he can find any way to get rid of the charges alleged against him.

Incapacity and Incapability of the Judges:

Incapacity or incapability of the judges here means limitation to the judges in functioning their work. They are subjected to certain limitation either imposed by law or by the local and political pressure.

Besides they are deprived of training on judicial system and deprived from using good conscience as they always kept in pressure. It is held in many case that the judges try themselves to use good conscience but failed to ensure justice. The root cause of this failure is lake of training as well as international training on judicial system.

Appointment of Judges:

Power of appointment of the judges is provided by the constitution of the country and the process of appointment is directed and selected by the examination hold by the Bangladesh Judicial Service Commission. The appointment and selection of judges must have to be fair. It is often claim appointment made out of money and political thinking which allow less qualified person to a judge where the more qualified person are deprived so the qualification of the brilliance become waste which may reasonably develop the criminal justice system and in large development of the country.

It is hard to believe "a judge appointed in a way other than the fair way can adjudicate fair."

Bribery or Biasness of the Judges:

Bribery and biasness of judges is also liable for the failure to administration of criminal justice. It's often claimed that the magistrates or judges of the judicial system are engaged in bribery. They take pecuniary benefit and give judgment towards them or by taking money for granting bail or not granting bail also.

Biasness in its sense may be economical, political or relational in its nature. Whatever, the judgment given by taking pecuniary benefits or biased in other way the ultimate cause is failure to criminal justice system.

Incapacity of the Lawyers:

Incapacity of lawyers means role of some unqualified lawyers. The enrolment process of the earlier time had allowed various numbers of incapable or unqualified people to be enrolled as an advocate. It is often told that whoever have unsuccessful professional carrier has just ensured a degree in law and in any way get enrolled it means they consider law profession as the last choice..

Enrolment as an Advocate:

It is also claim that enrolment can be got by political linking, giving money and many other way though the enrolment is followed by the procedure of Bar Council Order, 1972.

Dishonesty of the Lawyers:

Dishonesty of the lawyers is also a vital cause of failure of justice. In many case it is observed the lawyers are dealing dishonestly. In that case they are also violating Canons of Professional Conduct and Etiquette as enacted for fixing duty of the advocates by The Bangladesh Legal Practitioners and Bar Council Rules, 1972

Granting Bail in Non Bailable Offence:

Granting bail in case of non bailable offence is another root cause of failure to administration of criminal justice. The offender gets bail after commission of an offence from the court and habitually engaged themselves in other offence and as well as intimidation to the plaintiff who is seeking remedy. Bail in case of non bailable offence is the discretion of the court but in most of the cases it is seen that the judges took pecuniary benefit and apply their discretion in the wrong way or in considering the part of the accused in the offence consider wrong. Granting bail in case of non bailable offence using discretion power of the judges in corrupt manner is another vital cause for the failure to criminal justice.

Incapacity and Incapability of the Police:

Police is the most important part of criminal justice system. This is the main body which enforce the laws and as well as who brings the offender within judicial capacity. The police of Bangladesh are working hard on ensuring criminal justice but it is suffering from various incapacity and incapability. They are suffering from lake of weapons and high qualified training on crime.

Appointment of the Police:

Appointment of the police is largely connected with the administration of criminal justice. It is often seen that the appointment is made out of money or political thinking. In every term of the government it becomes visible that the persons of the government side is appointed and as well as promotion is also given by breaking all the rules. Thus it can not be desired that a police man appointed in a corrupt or illegal way can work legally.

Bribery and Biasness of the Police:

Taking bribery and working with biasness are the other obstruct to the prevention of crime and in large criminal justice system. Corruption of the police man, releasing accused on taking money, harassing common people for money, cruelty to the accused, rude behavior with the plaintiff or victim, torturing in remand for money etc are some function done by some corrupted police officer which are opposed to natural criminal justice. Though it is often claim lower standard of remuneration is the cause of corruption by the police.

Appointment of the Staffs of the Court:

Staffs of the court have unbeaten role in judicial system. There are empowered to deal with the judicial documents and so far s every dealings with this documents is over their hand. Any conspiracy or wrong to the documents may destroy a case infact judicial system. Appointment or the staffs are subjected to question form the earlier time. It is often claim that they are appointed on his post by providing brinbary or money. They have to count a big amount for the post which renders judicial system to fail. Relation to powerful man or political support is also allowed during appointment.

Bribery of the Court Staffs:

Bribery of the staff of the court may injure judicial system. Bribery of the staffs may give unlawful facilities to the offender which may cause failure to eh criminal justice system.

Shorten of Man Power:

The court is suffering from shorten from of man power. Where the courts of the country are about to sink on burden of cases but It is suffering from shorten of man power.

Efficient Working of the Body Related to Criminal Justice System e.g. Law Commission:

Efficient work of the body or organization related to criminal justice system for example Law Commission, Bangladesh Judicial Service Commission etc. is largely related to the justice system of Bangladesh. Whenever they are interfered or they are used for benefit of any group the justice system gets it leg to be cut off.

Poverty of the victim is also liable for seeking justice. This is in the way that whenever any criminal act is done against him he can not claim remedy only thinking that" the case or justice is only for the rich people". Low trust on the judicial system by the common people is another cause of failure to criminal justice system. People's in the mean time going to believe traditionally that nothing can be done to the offender.

Failure to give security to the Plaintiff and Witnesses are most important cause for failure to justice. Generally offender is more powerful than the victim or plaintiff. After filing a case it often found the plaintiff or witnesses of the case are threatened to participate in judicial proceeding but security of the plaintiff or victim or witnesses can not be guaranteed. Institution or filing of false and vogue case are also liable to failure to ensure criminal justice in the country. False and vogues cases are often filed whereas the trial of real offence are pending for long times.

Burden of cases in the criminal courts of the country is also liable to failure to administer criminal justice. Withdrawal of complaint in consideration of money or in force is made in many cases which refer no trust over the judicial system and impliedly give strength to the offender that money can withdrawn complain".

Unqualified laboratory and Forensic department or hospitals are specifically connected with the criminal judicial system. In criminal case by an authentic report of that institution may specify or give the nature of the offender. But unfortunately Bangladesh is not much advanced in this matter. Even for a simple DNA test the sample shall have to send to the foreign country which delay the judicial procedure and at large cause harm to the criminal judicial system.

Withdrawal of cases in political thinking is also a vital cause to the failure of ensuring criminal justice. The Constitution of Bangladesh has expressed no one is over the law. But in real the cases can be withdrawn by political thinking which dis encourages the natural criminal justice. The judiciary one of the fundamental organs of the state though in papers works independently but in real aspect the judicial proceedings are yet interfered by the political impact or pressure.

Forgiving the Convicted:

After completion of a case passing though a lengthy process a conviction is made but he get rid from the conviction by the president in political thinking which give strength to the habitual offender(political leader)

REMEDIAL MEASURES

Correction or Reconsideration of Laws:

The laws of the nation should be reconsidered as to their punishment or fine or for their enforcement. The law has given the procedure but it can not be enforced because of the poor process of its enforcement. Besides law, the procedure of the laws how can be followed or enforced more efficiently and quickly should be considered in considering the present condition of the country.

Trial Process Should be Completed as Early as Possible:

Trial process of the criminal cases are too lengthy and that why the criminal got opportunity to find way to rid him from the alleged charges.

The trial process should be ensured more quickly by enactment of laws or by inspecting on it. We are known to the well familiar principle that "delay deny justice"

Taking Steps to Remove Incapacity and Incapability of the Judges:

High qualified training and international training are required to be held because of gaining knowledge of judicial system of the other developed country to ensure development of the judicial system of our judicial system. Whenever the judges of the country can work without any pressure after having a good qualified national as well as international training the criminal judicial system of the country shall get its life.

Fair Appointment of Judges Must be Ensured:

Appointment of less qualified and also corrupted, biased man as a judges can totally break judicial system of the country as he will decide everything defectively for his disqualification and his decision shall not be pleasant because of his corruption or biasness. So fair appointment of the judges must have to ensure and qualification should be valued.

Strict Steps and Observation Against Bribery and Biasness of the Judges:

Strict observation and steps should have to take as the bribery and biasness of the judges may break down natural justice. Strict observation over the judges should keep always for preventing them from allowing bribery and from giving any judgment by biasness.

Taking Steps to Remove Incapacity of the Lawyers:

Necessary steps or training should be given to the advocates to build up them so that they can seek remedy to the victim. Specially international and national training should ensure for the government pleader as they are the pleaders who act on behalf of the plaintiff and in most cases plaintiffs are the sufferer. Steps should be taken to develop law profession so that the qualified people get interested in this profession.

Prevent Judges to use Discretionary Power in Corrupt Way:

Reasonable steps should be taken to prevent use of discretionary power of the judges in corrupt way. Also High qualified investigation should be done regarding the connection of the accused, when any person is brought before the court in charge of any non bailable offence so that the court in granting bail to non bailable offender can administer justice.

Ensuring Fair Enrolment Procedure for Being Advocate:

The process for enrolment as an advocate must be completed in fair way. No political linking or pressure, money and any other unfair process should not to be allowed.

Taking Steps to Reduce Incapacity and Incapability of the Police:

High qualified training and availability of necessary weapon should be produce as require for ensuring criminal administration justice system. Police the law enforcing body should keep out of any pressure e.g. political pressure and everyone of the country should assist them in functioning their work.

Strict Steps and Observation Against Bribery and Biasness of the Police:

Observation to the function of the corrupted police officer should be made and if found guilty for such kind of corruption strict steps should be taken for their punishment. Remuneration of the police should be fixed to a minimum standard, other facilities as required for living should ensure so that they can run their family normally and pleasant atmosphere should given for seeking their performance.

Fair Appointment of Police Should Ensure:

Fair appointment of the police must ensure for the development of criminal justice system. Police is the main executive body which enforce laws and takes preventive measures against commission of crime so if the appointment of the members of this very important body is not made in fair way then fair criminal justice is impossible

Fair Appointment of Staffs of the Court

As staffs of the court are hardly connected with judicial system the appointment of the staffs must to be done in fair way. No allowance or Biasness should be taken in case of appointment because a person come through legal process is bind by duty to work legally.

Strict Steps to Prevent Bribery of Court Staffs:

Reasonable measures should be taken to stop taking bribery by the court staffs. Observation over their work or conduct and punishment for such bribery should be ensured. Efficient working of the body related to criminal justice system e.g. Law Commission must be ensured.

Security to the Plaintiff and Witnesses must be ensured because the part of the plaintiff or witnesses is very much important for the natural criminal justice system. Necessary action should be taken against false and vogue case. In case of filing false case the punishment procedure should be followed and precedent to be made so that no case shall be filed only for harassing others.

Steps should be taken to reduce burden of cases. For example by appointing man power as much it needed, by responsible duty abeyance by the judges, police and lawyers etc. Qualified laboratory and Forensic department should be established or constructed. High qualified training for the doctor or other person who may hold the post on that kind of institution.

Political pressure over judicial system will have to remove. As the judiciary or judicial system is a separate organ of the state it should given to work on its own way. No interference should be done in respect of judicial service. Further and reconsidering the admissibility and acceptance in case where convicted prisoners are to be pardoned.

INDONESIA: CRIMINAL JUSTICE

Reforming the criminal justice system, and in particular providing a fairer, equitable and transparent justice system, is one of the Indonesian Government's top priority areas for development. Justice system reform is also at the heart of UNODC's mission. Through Sub-Programme 4, UNODC seeks to leverage its expertise and support the Government of Indonesia by focusing on (1) enhancing the capacity of justice sector actors to provide for fair and transparent access to justice and (2) improving the justice system's response to vulnerable groups, particularly children and women.

UNODC, along with UNDP, has already completed a study on the effectiveness of internal oversight mechanisms of the Indonesian National Police, Attorney General's Office and Supreme Court. A follow-up on the study, including strengthening of institutional oversight mechanisms, both internal and external, will be a priority activity. UNODC has been engaged with the Witness and Victim Protection Agency and it has proposed to continue with advice and capacity building programmes, such as socializing standard operating procedures and victim protection schemes as carried out in other countries.

Specific programmes will be undertaken with the Directorate General of Correctional Services to enhance prison management and prison leadership capabilities in line with international standards and norms. These programmes will include improved database management and will emphasize alternatives to imprisonment and restorative justice and social reintegration initiatives.

To enhance justice responses to vulnerable groups UNODC will work toward strengthening child justice systems. This will begin with an assessment of existing child justice mechanisms in Indonesia. With regard to measures to prevent violence against women, UNODC envisions activities to address the needs of domestically abused women and to facilitate their ability to pursue their grievances through the justice system. UNODC will also work with provincial actors in gender mainstreaming and promoting women's rights and freedom from domestic violence in line with the newly adopted updated Model Strategies and Practical Measures on the Elimination of Violence against

Women in the Field of Crime Prevention and Criminal Justice (GA Resolution 65/228). Work will also be prioritised in line with the 2011 UN Women report highlighting the problem of unequal access of women to justice systems.

The implementing partners of UNODC in Indonesia for Sub-Programme 4 are: the Supreme Court, Attorney General's Office, Director General for Corrections, the Police Commission, the Judicial Commission, the Prosecution Commission, Minister for Women Empowerment and Child Protection, Director General for Corrections, Coordinating Ministry of People's Welfare, Ministry of Social Affairs, Ministry of Law and Human Rights, Indonesian National Police, Witness and Victim Protection Agency, NGOs and CSOs.

JUDICIAL SYSTEM OF ISRAEL

The judicial system of Israel consists of secular courts and religious courts. The law courts constitute a separate and independent unit of Israel's Ministry of Justice. The system is headed by the President of the Supreme Court and the Minister of Justice.

SECULAR COURTS

Supreme Court

Located in Jerusalem, the Supreme Court acts as a further appellate court, hearing both criminal and civil cases. The Supreme Court re-evaluates decisions by the lower, district courts. Sitting as the High Court of Justice, it acts as a court of first instance, often in matters concerning the legality of decisions regarding state authorities. The High Court of Justice or otherwise the Israeli Supreme Court acts sometimes not as an appellate body to the district court but as on over-seer of justice against the lower courts.

District Courts

The District Courts constitute the middle level courts of the judicial system, and have jurisdiction in any matter not within the sole jurisdiction of another court. In criminal matters, the courts have jurisdiction over cases where the accused faces a penalty of at least seven years imprisonment. In civil cases, they have jurisdiction over cases in which more than two and a half million shekels are in dispute. District courts also hear appeals of judgments of the magistrate courts, as well as cases involving companies and partnership, arbitration, prisoners petitions, and appeals on tax matters. Sitting as courts for administrative matters, they can hear petitions against arms of the government. One also sits as the court of admiralty, hearing all cases involving shipping commerce, accidents on the sea and the like. Most cases are heard by a single judge, though the court president can choose to appoint a three-judge panel. Cases where the accused is charged with an offense punishable by at least ten years in prison and appeals from magistrate courts are heard by three-judge panels. There are six such courts, one in each district of Israel.

Magistrate Courts

The Magistrate courts serve as basic trial courts. In criminal matters, they hear cases where the accused faces up to seven years imprisonment, and in civil cases, have jurisdiction over matters up to two and a half million shekels. They also have jurisdiction over the use and possession of real property. The courts also act as traffic courts, municipal courts and family courts. Sitting as small-claims courts, they have jurisdiction over cases involving claims up to 30,000 shekels. Rather than following standard evidentiary rules, they require extensive pleadings and documentation upon filing of a formally written complaint. Verdicts are expected seven days from trial. Cases are heard by a single judge unless the court president decides to appoint a three-judge panel. There are 30 magistrate courts.

Labor Courts

There are five Regional Labor Courts in Israel as a tribunal of first instance, and one National labor court in Jerusalem hearing appeals and few cases of national importance, as first tier. They are vested with exclusive jurisdiction over cases involving employer-employee relationship, pre-employment, post-employment strikes and labor union disputes, as well as labor related complaints against the National Insurance Institute, and claims under the National Health Insurance Law.

The Labor Courts Law sets forth those matters within the jurisdiction of the Labor Court. Substantially all causes of action arising from the employer-employee relationship are within the court's jurisdiction. In civil matters, the Labor Courts are not bound by the rules of evidence. Most cases are heard by a panel of three, including a Judge, a representative on behalf of employees and a representative on behalf of employers.

Military Courts

The Military Court of Appeals is the highest judicial body in the Israel Defense Forces (IDF). The land, air and naval branches of the IDF, each of its military districts, the General Staff and the Home Front Command maintain their own special military courts. Military courts are used to try soldiers charged with military offenses, and deal with most criminal and security cases in the Israeli-occupied territories.

CRIMINAL PROCEDURE

Israel is unusual among Common-law derived systems due to the absence of juries in its legal system. Rather, all trials are conducted before either one judge or a three-judge panel.

A suspect arrested in Israel is typically interrogated by police. Though police are allowed to lie to a suspect during interrogation, anyone facing police interrogation has the right to consult a lawyer beforehand, and an interrogating officer must warn a suspect that he or she does not have to say anything self-incriminating, and that anything said might be used against them in court. Everyone accused of a criminal offense has the right to be represented by an attorney, and if the accused cannot afford a private attorney, one is assigned to them from the Public Defender's Office. Prosecutions are handled by the State Attorney's Office, which consists of a central bureau and eight regional offices.

Following a verdict, the defense or prosecution has the right to appeal to a higher court. Israeli law also provides for the possibility to ask the Supreme Court for a new trial, though it is very rare to be granted a retrial. Between 1948 and 2012, only 21 cases were granted a retrial, about half of which ended in reconfirmation of a defendant's guilt. Administrative detention and closed trials are allowed in cases involving security and illegal immigration. Anyone subjected to administrative detention and a possible closed trial has the right to be represented by an attorney, and may appeal their detention to the Supreme Court. The burden of proof rests on the prosecution to prove that closed proceedings are necessary.

The vast majority of criminal cases investigated by police and considered for indictment are closed due to lack of evidence or lack of public interest. Of those cases that do go to court, over 85% end with a plea bargain. Though accepting a plea bargain is considered a de facto guilty plea, it also leads to a lighter sentence. Of the cases that do go to trial, 71.5% end with a conviction on some of the charges and acquittal on others, 21.6% with a conviction on all charges, and 0.3% with a full acquittal. Another 2.1% of cases are dismissed after the defendant is found incompetent to stand trial, 1.2% are dismissed over technicalities, and in 0.9% of cases the charges are dropped.

JUDICIAL SELECTION

Judges who serve on the Supreme Court, as well as the district and magistrate courts, are appointed by the Judicial Selection Committee, which consists of nine members: the Minister of Justice and another cabinet member, two Knesset members, two members of the Israel Bar Association, and the President of the Supreme Court and two other Supreme Court justices. The committee is chaired by the Minister of Justice.

RELIGIOUS COURTS

Jewish Religious Courts

The Jewish religious courts, known as Rabbinic Courts, whose dayanim ("judges") are selected by a committee headed by the Minister of Justice, have jurisdiction regarding marital issues of Jews (especially divorce). Divorce of a

Jewish couple can only be obtained at the Rabbinical Batei Din. However, if a petition for ancillary matrimonial reliefs, such as custody, support or equitable distribution of property is filed with the Civil Courts before a case for divorce is opened at the Batei Din, then all other marital issues may also be taken by Magistrate Courts sitting as Family Courts.

Otherwise, if one spouse opens some sort of an action with the Batei Din, (including asking the couple for reconciliation), the Batei Din assume that all ancillary relief is aggregated into the main complaint, and the spouses may find themselves facing judicial determination pursuant toHalakha (Jewish religious law), and not pursuant to the secular law. Thus, spouses may lose the equal protection and anti gender discrimination protections of the secular civil law.

The Supreme Rabbinic Court acts as the court of last resort for cases brought before the rabbinic courts.

Non-Jewish Religious Courts

The Muslim, legally recognized Christian communities, and Druze have their own religious courts which have similar jurisdiction over their followers, although Muslim religious courts have more control over family affairs. They are supervised by their own official religious establishments (although the Muslim and Druze kaddis judges are also elected by the Knesset). This is the maintenance of an agreement reached with the British Mandatory Authorities before the State of Israel's establishment in 1948.

The ten recognized Christian communities are the Greek Orthodox, Latin Catholic, Armenian Orthodox, Armenian Catholic, Syriac Catholic, Chaldean Catholic, Melkite Greek Catholic, Maronite, Syrian Orthodox and Evangelical Episcopalian communities.

LEGAL PRACTICE

As of 2012, there are 52,142 active lawyers in Israel, making it the country with the highest number of active lawyers per capita in the world. Law schools produce new graduates at the rate of 2,000 new lawyers a year. This creates a tight and highly competitive market.

CRIMINAL JUSTICE SYSTEM IN PAKISTAN

Pakistan is an Islamic republic. Islam is the state religion, and the Constitution requires that laws be consistent with Islam. The country has an area of 310,527 square miles and a population of 170 million. The legal system of Pakistan is derived from English common law and is based on the much-amended 1973 constitution and Islamic law (sharia). The Supreme Court, provincial high courts, and other courts have jurisdiction over criminal and civil issues.

CRIMINAL JUSTICE SYSTEM:

"A generic term for the procedure by which criminal conduct is investigated, arrests made, evidence gathered, charges brought, defenses raised, trials conducted, sentences rendered, and punishment carried out" "Criminal Justice is the system of practices and institutions of governments directed at upholding social control, deterring and mitigating crime, or sanctioning those who violate laws with criminal penalties and rehabilitation efforts. Those accused of crime have protections against abuse of investigatory and prosecution powers"

Criminal Justice refers to the agencies of government charged with enforcing law, adjudicating crime, and correcting criminal conduct. The criminal justice system is essentially an instrument of social control: society considers some conducts so dangerous and destructive that it either strictly controls their occurrence or outlaws them outright. It is the job of the agencies of justice to prevent these behaviors by apprehending and punishing transgressors or deterring their future occurrence.

Although society maintains other forms of social control, such as the family, school, and church, they are designed to deal with moral, not legal, misbehavior. It is only the criminal justice system in a legal system which has the power to control crime and punish criminals.

The main objectives of the criminal justice system can be categorized as follows:

- Prevent the occurrence of crime.
- Punish the transgressors and the criminals.
- Rehabilitate the transgressors and the criminals.
- Compensate the victims as far as possible.
- Maintain law and order in the society.
- Deter the offenders from committing any criminal act in the future.

The United States Criminal Justice System

The United States Criminal Justice System is the structural basis used to maintain social control. It has many components that work together to provide justice for criminals and victims of crimes, enabling law violators to be prosecuted in a fair trial. One of the fundamental theories of the U.S. criminal justice system is that those on trial remain innocent until proven guilty. As a result, the rights to a fair and regular trial are upheld for criminals on trial in the US Criminal Justice System. The laws are in place to ensure that criminals are not abused or cruelly punished.

Components of the Criminal Justice System:

The U.S. Criminal Justice System operates through five major components. If a crime cannot be resolved through local law enforcement, it progresses to the next step. The five components are:

Local Law Enforcement: If a citizen observes a crime, he will point out the offender to local law enforcement. The police force is the main component that brings criminals to the Criminal Justice System. Some crimes (such as speeding or trespassing) can be resolved directly by the police with the issue of a ticket or fine. For more severe offenses that involve victims, the police turn to the court system for a fair trial.

Court Trial: Once the offender has entered into the legal system, a court trial is the next step for the criminal. The law enforcement officer or other witnesses present the facts and evidence of the case to the prosecutor. The prosecutor decides if charges should be filed for the violator. If there are charges filed, a court case will follow.

Court Case: The case is brought to a judge in a court of law. If the offenses are minor and the criminal is obviously guilty, the judge will often offer a sentence of punishment, and the court case will be over. However, if the offense is more involved or the criminal pleads "not guilty," an entire trial must follow.

Trial with Grand Jury: A grand jury is used in the court of law to hear both sides of the case and help determine guilt and punishment. Having a jury of peers oversee and rule on the court proceedings is important in the rights of the criminal because the jury is a third party uninvolved in law enforcement or in the lives of the victim or offender.

Decision and Punishment: Once the jury members have heard the case, they make a decision on whether the offender is guilty or innocent. If proven guilty, in most cases, the judge will deliver the sentence of punishment. In some instances, however, the jury will decide on the criminal's punishment.

The Criminal Justice System in UK

The criminal justice system in the UK is made up of a number of agencies each responsible to a government department. There are two main aims of the criminal justice system:

"To reduce crime and the fear of crime and their social and economic costs"
"To increase confidence in the system"

What is the Criminal Justice System?

The Criminal Justice System in England and Wales is made up of a number of agencies and departments.

The main agencies are:

- The Police Servicelegal aid image
- The Court Service
- The Prison Service
- The Probation Service

The government departments that oversee the Criminal Justice System are:

1. The Ministry of Justice (MOJ)
2. The Home Office

If someone is mentally ill and going through the criminal justice system, they may be 'diverted' to health and social care services. In the criminal justice system these are often referred to as Forensic Mental Health Services. These services include psychiatric hospitals and community mental health services.

How Does the System Work?

People come into contact with the Criminal Justice System because they are suspected of committing a criminal offence.

The usual process of going through the system is:

1. Being arrested having been suspected of committing an offence
2. Being taken to the police station where the person accused is interviewed
3. If the offence is relatively minor, the police may decide whether or not to charge the person with the offence
4. If the offence is more serious, the police may refer the case to the Crown Prosecution Service (CPS) who will decide whether or not wire rimmed glasses on top of a pile of papersto charge the person for the offence
5. If charged with an offence, the person (known as a defendant) will appear at a Magistrates' Court where the Magistrates may deal with the case themselves or send ('commit') the case to a Crown Court if the offence is particularly serious
6. There may be several court hearings during which the suspect will make a plea (say they are guilty or not guilty)
7. Sentencing which could include an array of ouctomes such as imprisonment, community order or fine
8. Being detained in a prison – either as a remanded prisoner (awaiting or going through a trial at court) or as a sentenced prisoner (convicted and found guilty of an offence)
9. Being supervised by the probation service either having been released from prison with conditions to meet in the community or if serving a community order

Mental health can be considered at any stage, which could result in the defendant being 'diverted' out of the criminal justice system and into health and social care services to get the help they need, which could be hospital.

EXECUTIVE SUMMARY AND RECOMMENDATIONS

The ineffectiveness of Pakistan's criminal justice system has serious repercussions for domestic, regional and international security. Given the gravity of internal security challenges, the Pakistan Peoples Party (PPP)-led government in Islamabad, and the four provincial governments should make the reform of an anarchic criminal justice sector a top domestic priority.

The low conviction rate, between 5 and 10 per cent at best, is unsurprising in a system where investigators are poorly trained and lack access to basic data and modern investigation tools. Prosecutors, also poorly trained, are not closely involved in investigations. Corruption, intimidation and external interference in trials, including by the military's intelligence agencies, compromise cases before they even come to court. Given the absence of scientific evidence collection methods and credible witness protection programs, police and prosecutors rely mostly on confessions by the accused, which are inadmissible in court. Militants and other major criminals are regularly released on bail, or their trials persist for years even as they plan operations from prison. Terrorism cases, too, produce few convictions.

The failure of prosecutors to achieve convictions in major cases, such as the June 2008 Danish embassy bombing, the September 2008 Marriott Hotel bombing in Islamabad, and the March 2009 attack on a police academy in Lahore, has weakened public confidence in the state's ability to respond to terrorism. Despite the increasing urgency of reform, Pakistan's police, and indeed the whole criminal justice system, still largely functions on the imperative of maintaining public order rather than tackling 21st century crime.

A military-led counter-terrorism effort, defined by haphazard and heavy-handed force against some militant networks, short-sighted peace deals with others, and continued support to India and Afghanistan-oriented jihadi groups, has yielded few successes. Instead, the extremist rot has spread to most of the country. The military's tactics of long-term detentions, enforced disappearances and extrajudicial killings provoke public resentment and greater instability, undermining the fight against violent extremism.

Wresting civilian control over counter-terrorism policy, a key challenge of the current democratic transition, will require massive investments in police and prosecutors, specifically to enhance investigative capacity and case building. Successes in combating serious crime, including kidnappings-for-ransom and sectarian terrorism, during the democratic transition of the 1990s demonstrate that civilian law enforcement agencies can be effective when properly authorised and equipped. With the scale of violence far greater today, the government needs all the more to utilise political and fiscal capital to modernise the criminal justice sector.

Criminal justice cannot, however, be isolated from the broader challenges of the democratic transition. The repeated suspension of the constitution by military regimes, followed by extensive reforms to centralise power and to strengthen their civilian allies, notably the religious right, have undermined constitutionalism and the rule of law. General Zia-ul-Haq's Islamisation of the constitution and laws during the 1980s altered the basic structure of parliamentary democracy, introduced religious, sectarian and gender biases into law and made the violation of fundamental rights not just common practice but a matter of state policy. As a result, Pakistan moved farther and farther away from international standards of justice. The current parliament has, through the eighteenth constitutional amendment, reversed many of these distortions and added new provisions that, if implemented, may indeed strengthen constitutionalism and political stability. More legal reforms are needed. Discriminatory religious laws remain in force, and the justice system is still predisposed towards miscarriage.

In May 2009, the National Judicial (Policy Making) Committee (NJPC), headed by the Supreme Court chief justice, produced the National Judicial Policy (NJP) 2009 to make the justice system more responsive to citizen needs. The policy applies enormous pressures on civil and criminal courts to resolve cases within a fixed timeframe. However, with a lopsided emphasis on speedier delivery, the NJP has failed to address critical weaknesses in the judiciary, including the criminal justice system. An already low conviction rate could decline even further. While slow delivery remains a critical problem, policymakers should avoid resorting to quick fixes and procedural short-cuts such as parallel court systems and informal dispute resolution mechanisms. Such measures, including anti-terrorism courts, have failed to produce the desired results, and have also undermined the quality of justice. An enhanced and reformed criminal justice sector remains the best and only sustainable option. International allies, particularly the U.S. and the EU, should allocate the necessary resources to make Pakistan a strong criminal justice partner. A lopsided partnership with Pakistan's military has yielded few sustainable counter-terrorism successes. Al-Qaeda affiliated jihadi groups continue to operate in the Pakistani heartland, undermining the country's security and the security of its neighbours and the international community more broadly. The international community must shift the focus of security assistance to the civilian law enforcement agencies, which would yield long-term counter-terrorism dividends.

To the Federal Government of Pakistan and Provincial Governments:

1. Repeal all laws that discriminate on the basis of religion, sect or gender, including the blasphemy laws, anti-Ahmadi laws and Hudood Ordinances.
2. Amend the 1997 Anti-Terrorism Act to refine its definition of terrorism to include only those acts that are large in scale and intend to create a sense of fear and insecurity among segments of the public; and disband anti-terrorism courts (ATCs) and try terrorism cases in regular courts.
3. Amend the Criminal Procedure Code to establish a robust witness protection program, and make the protection of witnesses, investigators, prosecutors and judges in major criminal cases, particularly terrorism cases, a priority.

4. Address over-crowding in prisons by:
   a. Enforcing existing bail laws;
   b. Holding to account any trial judge failing to set bail where required by law;
   c. Passing a new law requiring judges to allow bail unless there are reasonable grounds to believe the prisoner would abscond or commit further offences; and
   d. Reforming the sentencing structure for non-violent petty crimes to include alternatives to imprisonment such as fines, probation and treatment.
5. Guarantee the rights of all prisoners under remand by:
   a. Ensuring that prison facilities are fully resourced, including with enough vehicles to transport prisoners to court on the designated dates;
   b. Ensuring that they are taken to court on the dates of their hearings;
   c. Taking action against jail authorities who assign labour to remand prisoners, prohibited by law; and
   d. Providing free legal aid to remand prisoners who cannot afford counsel.
6. Initiate a broad dialogue with stakeholders, including serving and retired senior police officials, jurists, criminologists, NGOs and other civil society groups to assess the strengths and weaknesses of the original Police Order (2002), and produce fresh bills in each legislature to strengthen law enforcement that have public support and political sanction.
7. Develop mechanisms for individual police stations to articulate resource needs and for these to be reflected in provincial police budgeting processes.
8. Carry out a comprehensive assessment of the gaps in investigation and prosecution, based on analyses of crime patterns, with the goal of identifying personnel, training and resource needs at the national, provincial and district levels; invest in producing cadres of specialists within investigation branches and agencies, in such fields as kidnapping, homicide, counter-terrorism and cyber-crime.
9. Engage the public as an effective partner in policing by establishing and empowering neighbourhood committees, citizen-police liaison committees and public safety commissions at the national, provincial and district level to oversee critical aspects of policing and by ensuring that police have adequate resources and operational independence.
10. Strengthen the police's investigative capacity by:

a. Computerising and maintaining centralised, serviceable records of all FIRs;
b. Amending the Telegraph Act to establish clear protocols for investigators' access to mobile phone data, and ensuring that this access is not undermined by the military's intelligence etc etc

SAUDI ARABIA: CRIMINAL JUSTICE SYSTEM

The judicial system is founded upon the sharia, particularly the Hanbali school of Sunni Islam, in accordance with a ruling by King Abd al Aziz in 1926. The Hanbali system of jurisprudence, which rejected analogy as a source of law and gave prominence to the traditions and sayings of the Prophet Muhammad, was regarded as especially rigid by most Muslim jurists. If there is no guidance in Hanbali texts, however, Saudi jurists could refer to other schools or exercise their own reasoning.

Two categories of crime are delineated in the sharia: those that are carefully defined and those that are implicit in the requirements and prohibitions of the sharia. For the first category, there are specific penalties; for the second, punishment can be prescribed by a judge (qadi) of a sharia court. A third category of crime has developed through the years as a result of various governmental decrees that specified codes of behavior and regulations considered necessary to maintain public order and security. The first two categories are tried in sharia courts. The third, dealing with corporate law, taxation, oil and gas, and immigration, is handled administratively by government officials (see The Legal System , ch. 4). The sharia carefully defines crimes—such as homicide, personal injury, adultery, fornication, theft, and highway robbery—and prescribes a penalty (hadd) for each. Various degrees of culpability for homicide and bodily injury are recognized depending on intent, the kind of weapon used, and the circumstances under which the crime occurred.

Homicide is considered a crime against a person rather than a crime against society in which the state administers justice of its own volition. Under the sharia, the victim or the victim's family has the right to demand punishment, to grant clemency, or to demand blood money (diya)—a set payment as recompense for the crime.

An act of self-defense is recognized as a right nullifying criminality. Retaliation is permitted to the male next of kin of the victim by killing the criminal in the case of a homicide or exacting the same bodily injury that was inflicted on the victim. Acceptance of diya is, however, considered preferable under the sharia. In cases involving death or grievous injury, the accused is usually held incommunicado. Imprisonment before trial can last weeks or even several months. The right of bail or habeas corpus is not recognized, although persons accused of crimes are sometimes released on the recognizance of a patron or employer. The accused is normally held not more than three days before being formally charged, but it is common for detainees to be held for long periods if the investigation is incomplete.

At trials for minor offenses, qadis hear complaints and then cross-examine plaintiffs, defendants, and any witnesses. The judge assigns great significance to a defendant's sworn testimony, although the testimony of two women is required to equal that of one man. In the absence of two witnesses, oral confessions before a judge are almost always required for conviction. Trials are held without jurors and are generally closed. They are normally held without counsel, although lawyers can advise the accused before the trial. Attorneys may also be allowed to act at interpreters for those unfamiliar with Arabic. Consular access is not usually permitted during the trials of foreign nationals. After determining guilt or innocence, a sentence, if appropriate, is imposed by the judge. In certain criminal cases, punishment can be referred to a local governor or shaykh for sentencing upon the advice of a local Muslim jurist or the ulama. Appeals against judges' decisions are automatically reviewed by the Ministry of Justice or in more serious cases by a court of appeal. There were two sharia courts of appeal, one sitting in Riyadh and the other in Mecca. Appeals are heard by panels of three judges except for sentences of death or amputation, which can only be adjudicated by a panel of five judges. Decisions of the appellate courts are final except for sentences of death and amputation. Cases of capital punishment are automatically referred to the king for final review.

JUDICIAL SYSTEM OF VIETNAM

The judicial system of Vietnam is governed under the Constitution of Vietnam, the Law on the Organization of People's Courts (2014), and the Law on the Organization of People's Procuracies (2014). Since Vietnam is a one-party socialist republic, the judiciary falls under the leadership of the Communist Party of Vietnam, and judges and procurators are all members of the Party. The judiciary is nominally accountable to the National Assembly of Vietnam, which is the highest institution of government power in the country.

STRUCTURE

The judicial system of Vietnam comprises the "people's courts," military tribunals, and people's procuracies. The highest court in the country is the Supreme People's Court. Underneath the Supreme People's Court are three levels of courts: the superior people's courts (toà án nhân dân c-p cao), of which there are three; the provincial-level people's courts (toà án nhân dân c-p t-nh), of which there are 63; and district-level people's courts (toà án nhân dân c-p huy-n), which is the lowest level. The superior courts are appellate courts based in Hanoi, Danang, and Ho Chi Minh City, each responsible for the northern, central, and southern region of the country, respectively. Provincial and municipal courts are both trial courts and appellate courts, while district courts are trial courts. There are military tribunals established at various levels in the Vietnam People's Army, the highest one being the Central Military Tribunal, which is subordinate to the Supreme People's Court. The Supreme People's Court is headed by the Chief Justice of the Supreme People's Court (Chánh án Toà án nhân dân t-i cao), who is appointed by the National Assembly of Vietnam. The people's procuracies (also known as the people's office of inspection and supervision, vi-n ki-m sát nhân dân) serve as the prosecutorial authority in Vietnam. They also have the responsibility to supervise and inspect judicial compliance by government agencies and officials. There is a people's procuracy for every people's court, and the military has its own military procuracies. The highest procuracy is the Supreme People's Procuracy (Vi-n Ki-m sát nhân dân t-i cao), headed by the Chief Procurator of the Supreme People's Procuracy (Vi-n trý-ng Vi-n Ki-m sát nhân dân t-i cao), who is appointed by the National Assembly.

CRITICISMS

Although the constitution provides for independent judges and lay assessors (who lack administrative training), the U.S. Department of State maintains that Vietnam lacks an independent judiciary, in part because the Communist Party of Vietnam selects judges and vets them for political reliability. Moreover, the party seeks to influence the outcome of cases involving perceived threats to the state or the party's dominant position. In an effort to increase judicial independence, the government transferred local courts from the Ministry of Justice to the Supreme People's Court in September 2002. However, the Department of State saw no evidence that the move actually achieved the stated goal. Vietnam's judiciary also is hampered by a shortage of lawyers and rudimentary trial procedures.

DEATH PENALTY

The death penalty often is imposed in cases of corruption and drug trafficking. As of February 2014, the death penalty remains a punishment that can be applied to those who have been found guilty of criminal activity. In January 2014, a court in northern Vietnam sentenced 30 Vietnamese citizens to death after they were found guilty of heroin trafficking—the largest number of defendants sentenced to death in a single trial in the country's legal history. At the same time, there are around 700 people awaiting on death row in Vietnam. The January 2014 decision received condemnation from numerous international organizations, such as the World Coalition Against the Death Penalty.

5

Cyber Crime

DEFINITIONS OF CYBER CRIME

Most reports, guides or publications on cyber crime begin by defining the term "cyber crime". One common definition describes cyber crime as any activity in which computers or networks are a tool, a target or a place of criminal activity. One example for an international approach is Art. 1.1 of the Draft International Convention to Enhance Protection from Cyber Crime and Terrorism (CISAC) that points out that cyber crime refers to acts in respect to cyber systems. Some definitions try to take the objectives or intentions into account and define cyber crime more precisely, defining cyber crime as "computer-mediated activities which are either *illegal or considered illicit* by certain parties and which can be conducted *through global electronic networks*". These more refined descriptions exclude cases where physical hardware is used to commit regular crimes, but they risk excluding crimes that are considered as cyber crime in international agreements such as the "Convention on Cyber crime". For example, a person who produces USB -devices containing malicious software that destroy data on computers when the device is connected commits a crime as defined by Art. 4 Council of Europe Convention on Cyber crime. However, the act of deleting data using a physical device to copy malicious code has not been committed through global electronic networks and would not qualify as cyber crime under the narrow definition.

This act would only qualify as cyber crime under a definition based on a broader description, including acts such as illegal data interference. This demonstrates that there are considerable difficulties in defining the term "cyber crime". The term "cyber crime" is used to describe a range of offences including traditional computer crimes, as well as network crimes.

As these crimes differ in many ways, there is no single criterion that could include all acts mentioned in the Stanford Draft Convention and the Convention on Cyber crime, whilst excluding traditional crimes that are just committed using hardware. The fact that there is no single definition of "cyber crime" need not be important, as long as the term is not used as a legal term.

TYPOLOGY OF CYBER CRIME

The term "cyber crime" includes a wide variety of crime. Recognised crimes cover a broad range of offences, making it difficult to develop a typology or classification system for cyber crime. An interesting system can be found is found in the Council of Europe Convention on Cyber crime.

The Convention on Cyber crime distinguishes between four different types of offences:

1. Offences against the confidentiality, integrity and availability of computer data and systems;
2. Computer-related offences;
3. Content-related offences; and
4. Copyright-related offences.

This typology is not wholly consistent, as it is not based on a sole criterion to differentiate between categories. Three categories focus on the object of legal protection: "offences against the confidentiality, integrity and availability of computer data and systems"; content-related offences; and copyright-related offences. The fourth category of "computer-related offences" does not focus on the object of legal protection, but on the method. This inconsistency leads to some overlap between categories. In addition, some terms that are used to describe criminal acts (such as 'Cyber terrorism' or 'phishing') cover acts that fall within several categories. Nonetheless, the categories provided by the Convention on Cyber crime serve as a useful basis for discussing the phenomena of cyber crime.

STATISTICAL INDICATORS ON CYBER CRIME OFFENCES

It is difficult to quantify the impact of cyber crime on society. The financial losses caused by cyber crime, as well as the number of offences, are very difficult to estimate. Some sources estimate losses to businesses and institutions in the United States due to cyber crime to be as high as USD 67 billion; however, it is uncertain if the extrapolation of sample survey results is justifiable.

This methodological criticism applies not only to the losses, but also to the number of recognised offences. It is difficult to measure the number of cyber crimes. Since, targets may not always report these offences. Nevertheless, surveys can help in understanding the impact of cyber crime. More relevant than the precise number of cyber crimes in any single year is the trend, which can be found by comparing results over several years. One example is the United States CSI Computer Crime and Security Survey 2007 that analyses the number of computer-related offences committed, among other trends.

It is based on the responses of 494 computer security practitioners from U.S corporations, government agencies and financial institutions in the US. The survey documents the number of offences reported by respondents between 2000 and 2007. It shows that, Since, 2001, the proportion of respondents who experienced and acknowledged virus attacks or unauthorised access to information (or system penetration) decreased. The survey does not explain why this decrease has occurred.

However, this decline in the number of recognised offences in the mentioned categories is supported by surveys from other institutions (contrary to what reports in the media sometimes suggest). Similar developments are observed by analysing crime statistics – for example, the German crime statistics show that, after a peak in 2004, the number of computer-related offences has reduced to close to the level of 2002.

The statistics on cyber crime are unable to provide reliable information about the scale or extent of offences. The uncertainty about the extent to which offences are reported by targets, as well as the fact that no explanation for the reducing numbers of cyber crimes can be found, render these statistics open to interpretation. At present, there is insufficient evidence for predictions on future trends and developments.

ECONOMIC IMPACT OF CYBER CRIME

Without any doubt, the financial damage caused by computer and Internet crimes is significant. Various recent surveys have been published analysing the economic impact of cyber crime, highlighting its significant impact. The same general concerns about crime statistics also apply to estimates of financial damage – it is uncertain to what extent surveys provide accurate figures and statistics, as many victims may not report crimes.

RESULTS OF SELECTED SURVEYS

The Computer Security Institute (CSI) Computer Crime and Security Survey 2007 analysed the economic impact of cyber crime, based on the responses of 494 computer security practitioners in U.S corporations, government agencies and financial institutions. It is mainly relevant for the United States. Taking into account the economic cycle, the survey suggests that, after rising until 2002, the financial impact of cyber crime decreased over the following years.

The survey suggests that this finding is controversial, but it is unclear why the number of reported crimes and the average loss of the victims may have decreased. In 2006, the extent of losses climbed again. The survey does not explain the reduced losses in 2002 or the rise in 2006. From 21 categories identified by the survey, the highest dollar losses were associated with financial fraud, viruses, system penetration by outsiders and theft of confidential data. The total losses for 2006 of all respondents amounted to some USD 66.9 million. After a number of years of decreasing average losses per respondent, a turnaround is taking place. In 2006, the average loss was USD 345,000. In 2001, the average loss was nearly ten times higher (USD 3.1 million). The average loss per respondent depends strongly on the composition of respondents - if mainly small and medium sized enterprises (SMEs) respond one year and are replaced by larger companies the next year, the change in participants strongly affects the statistical results.

The FBI Computer Crime Survey 2005 follows an approach similar to the CSI Survey, but with a greater and more extensive coverage. The FBI survey estimates that the cost of security incidents from computer and Internet crimes amounted to USD 21.7 million. The most popular offences that detected by respondents organisations were virus attacks, spyware, port scans and sabotage of data or networks. The FBI Computer Crimes Survey 2005 includes an estimate of the total loss for the United States economy.

Based on average losses and the assumption that some 20 per cent of US organisations are affected by computer crime, a total loss of USD 67 billion was calculated. However, there are concerns as to how representative these estimates are, and the consistency of participants year on year. The 2007 Computer Economics Malware Report focuses on the impact of malware on the worldwide economy by summing up total estimated costs caused by attacks. One of its key findings is the fact that offenders designing malicious software are shifting from vandalism to a focus on financial profits.

The report finds that the financial losses caused by malware attacks peaked in 2000 (USD 17.1 billion) and 2004 (USD 17.5 billion), but have reduced Since, 2004 to USD 13.3 billion in 2006. However, similar to the survey results, there is uncertainty as to whether the statistics on the impact of malware are realistic.

There are large discrepancies between reported losses and proven damages – take the case of the Sasser Worm, for example. Millions of computer systems were reported to be infected. In the civil law suit against the software designer, very few companies and private individuals responded to the request to prove their losses and join the lawsuit. The case ended with a settlement that the designer of the virus should pay compensation of less than ten thousand US dollars.

DIFFICULTIES RELATED TO CYBER CRIME STATISTICS

It is unclear how representative the statistics on the economic impact of cyber crime are and whether they provide reliable information on the extent of losses. It is uncertain to what extent cyber crime is reported, not only in surveys, but also to law enforcement agencies. Authorities engaged in the fight against cyber crime encourage victims of cyber crime to report these crimes.

Access to more precise information about the true incidence of cyber crimes would enable law enforcement agencies to better prosecute offenders, deter potential attacks and enact more appropriate and effective legislation. Several public and private sector organizations have tried to quantify the direct and indirect costs of malware. While it is difficult to estimate the cost to businesses, it is even more difficult to assess the financial losses inflicted by malware and the like to individual consumers, although there is scattered evidence that damages can be very large. However, such costs have different components. They may result in direct damages to hardware and software as well as financial and other damages due to identity theft or other fraudulent schemes. The range of estimates differs, although the emerging overall picture is quite coherent. Businesses on the other hand may avoid reporting cyber crime offences for several reasons: Businesses may fear that negative publicity could damage their reputation.

If a company announces that hackers have accessed their server, customers may lose faith. The full costs and consequences could be greater than the losses caused by the hacking attack. However, if offenders are not reported and prosecuted, they may go on to reoffend. Targets may not believe that law enforcement agencies will be able to identify offenders. Comparing the large number of cyber crimes with the few successful investigations, targets may see little point in reporting offences. Automation also means that cybercriminals follow a strategy of reaping large profits from many attacks targeting small amounts (*e.g.*, as happens with advance fee fraud). For only small amounts, victims may prefer not to go through with time-consuming reporting procedures. Reported cases are often based on extremely high fees. By targeting only small amounts, offenders design scams that will often not be followed up.

CONVENTION ON CYBER CRIME

The Convention on Cyber crime includes a provision on illegal access protecting the integrity of the computer systems by criminalising the unauthorised access to a system. Noting inconsistent approaches at the national level, the Convention offers the possibility of limitations that – at least in most cases – enable countries without legislation to retain more liberal laws on illegal access.

THE PROVISION

- Article 2 – Illegal access: Each Party shall adopt such legislative and other measures as may be necessary to establish as criminal offences under its domestic law, when committed intentionally, the access to the whole or any part of a computer system without right. A Party may require that the offence be committed by infringing security measures, with the intent of obtaining computer data or other dishonest intent, or in relation to a computer system that is connected to another computer system.

The Covered Acts

The term "access" does not specify a certain means of communication, but is open-ended and open to further technical developments. It shall include all means of entering another computer system, including Internet attacks, as well as illegal access to wireless networks. Even unauthorised access to computers that are not connected to any network (*e.g.,* by circumventing a password protection) are covered by the provision. This broad approach means that illegal access not only covers future technical developments, but is also covers secret data accessed by insiders and employees. The second sentence of Article 2 offers the possibility of limiting the criminalisation of illegal access to access over a network. The illegal acts and protected systems are thus defined in a way that remains open to future developments. The Explanatory Report lists hardware, components, stored data, directories, traffic and content-related data as examples of the parts of computer systems that can be accessed.

Mental Element

Like all other offences defined by the Convention on Cyber crime Art. 2 requires that the offender is carrying out the offences intentionally. The Convention does not contain a definition of the term "internationally". In the Explanatory Report the drafters pointed out that the definition of "intentionally" should happen on a national level.

Without Right

Access to a Computer can only be prosecuted under Article 2 of the Convention, if it should happen "without right". Access to a system permitting free and open access by the public or access to a system with the authorisation of the owner or other rights-holder is not "without right".

In addition to the subject of free access, the legitimacy of security testing procedures is also addressed. Network administrators and security companies that test the protection of computer systems in order to identify potential gaps in the security measures were wary of the possibility of criminalisation under illegal access. Despite the fact that these professionals generally work with the permission of the owner and therefore act legally, the drafters of the Convention emphasised that "testing or protection of the security of a computer system authorised by the owner or operator, are with right". The fact, that the victim of the crime handed out a password or similar access code to the offender does not necessary mean that the offender then acted with right when he accessed the computer system of the victim.

If the offender persuaded the victim to disclose a password or access code due to a successful social engineering approach it is necessary to verify if the authorisation given by the victim does cover the act carried out by the offender. In general this is not the case and the offender therefore acts without right.

Restrictions and Reservations

As an alternative to the broad approach, the Convention offers the possibility of restricting criminalisation with additional elements, listed in the second sentence. The procedure of how to utilise this reservation is laid down in Article 42 of the Convention. Possible reservations relate to security measures, special intent to obtain computer data, other dishonest intent that justifies criminal culpability, or requirements that the offence be committed against a computer system through a network. A similar approach can be found in the EU Framework Decision on Attacks against Information Systems.

Commonwealth Computer and Computer Related Crimes Model Law

A similar approach can be found in Sec. 5 of the 2002 Commonwealth Model Law:

- Sec. 5.: A person who intentionally, without lawful excuse or justification, accesses the whole or any part of a computer system commits an offence punishable, on conviction, by imprisonment for a period not exceeding, or a fine not exceeding or both.

The main difference to the Convention on Cyber crime is the fact that Sec. 5 of the Commonwealth Model Law does, unlike Art. 2 Convention on Cyber crime, not contain options to make reservations.

Stanford Draft Convention

The informal 1999 Stanford Draft Convention recognises illegal access as one of those offences the signatory states should criminalise.

The Provision

- Art. 3 – Offences:
  - 1. Offenses under this Convention are committed if any person unlawfully and intentionally engages in any of the following conduct without legally recognised authority, permission, or consent:
  - (c) enters into a cyber system for which access is restricted in a conspicuous and unambiguous manner;

The Covered Acts

The draft provision shows a number of similarities to Art. 2 of the Convention on Cyber crime. Both require an intentional act that is committed without right/without authority. In this context requirement of the draft provision (*"without legally recognised authority, permission, or consent"*) is more precise than the term "without right" used Convention on Cyber crime and explicitly aims to incorporate the concept of selfdefence. The main difference to the Convention is the fact that the draft provision uses the term "cyber system".

The cyber system is defined in Art. 1, paragraph 3 of the Draft Convention. It covers any computer or network of computers used to relay, transmit, coordinate, or control communications of data or Programmes.

This definition shows many similarities to the definition of the term 'computer system" provided by Art. 1 a) Convention on Cyber crime. Although the Draft Convention refers to acts related to the exchange of data and does therefore primarily focus on network based computer systems both definitions include interconnected computer as well as stand alone machines.

DATA ESPIONAGE

The Convention on Cyber crime as well as the Commonwealth Model Law and the Stanford Draft Convention provide legal solutions for illegal interception only. It is questionable whether Article 3 of the Convention on Cyber crime applies to other cases than those where offences are carried out by intercepting data transfer processes. The question of whether illegal access to information stored on a hard disk is covered by the Convention was discussed with great interest. Since a transfer process is needed, it is likely that Art. 3 of the Convention on Cyber crime does not cover forms of data espionage other than the interception of transfer processes. One issue frequently discussed in this context is the question if the criminalisation of illegal accesses renders the criminalisation of data espionage unnecessary. In those cases where the offender has legitimate access to a computer system (e.g. because he is ordered to repair it) and on this occasion (in violation of the limited legitimating) copies files from the system, the act is in general not covered by the provisions criminalising illegal access. Given that much vital data is today stored in computer systems, it is essential to evaluate whether existing mechanisms to protect data are adequate or whether other criminal law provision are necessary to protect the user from data espionage. Today, computer users can use various hardware devices and software tools in order to protect secret information.

They can install firewalls, access control systems or encrypt stored information and by this decrease the risk of data espionage. Although user-friendly devices are available, requiring only limited knowledge by users, truly effective protection of data on a computer system often requires knowledge that few users have. Especially data stored on private computer systems is often not adequately protected against data espionage. Therefore criminal law provisions can offer an additional protection.

Examples

Some countries have decided to extend the protection that is available through technical measures by criminalising data espionage. There are two main approaches. Some countries follow a narrow approach and criminalise data espionage, only where specific secret information is obtained - an example is 18 U.S.C § 1831, that criminalises economic espionage. The provision does not only cover data espionage, but other ways of obtaining secret information as well.

Economic Espionage

(a) In General — Whoever, intending or knowing that the Offence will benefit any foreign government, foreign instrumentality, or foreign agent, knowingly—
   (1) Steals, or without authorization appropriates, takes, carries away, or conceals, or by fraud, artifice, or deception obtains a trade secret;
   (2) Without authorization copies, duplicates, sketches, draws, photographs, downloads, uploads, alters, destroys, photocopies, replicates, transmits, delivers, sends, mails, communicates, or conveys a trade secret;
   (3) Receives, buys, or possesses a trade secret, knowing the same to have been stolen or appropriated, obtained, or converted without authorization;
   (4) Attempts to commit any Offence described in any of paragraphs (1) through (3); or
   (5) Conspires with one or more other persons to commit any Offence described in any of paragraphs (1) through (3), and one or more of such persons do any act to effect the object of the conspiracy, shall, except as provided in subsection (b), be fined not more than $500,000 or imprisoned not more than 15 years, or both.

(b) Organizations — Any organization that commits any Offence described in subsection (a) shall be fined not more than $10,000,000.

Other countries have adopted a broader approach and criminalised the act of obtaining stored computer data, even if they do not contain economic secrets.

Section 202a. Data Espionage

(1) Any person who obtains without authorization, for himself or for another, data which are not meant for him and which are specially protected against unauthorised access, shall be liable to imprisonment for a term not exceeding three years or to a fine
(2) Data within the meaning of subsection 1 are only such as are stored or transmitted electronically or magnetically or in any form not directly visible.

This provision not only covers economic secrets, but stored computer data in general. In terms of its objects of protection, this approach is broader compared to § 1831 USC, but the application of the provision is limited as obtaining data is only criminalised where data are specially protected against unauthorised access.

The protection of stored computer data under German criminal law is thus limited to persons or businesses that have taken measures to avoid falling victim to such offences.

Relevance of Such Provision

The implementation of such provision is especially relevant with regard to cases, where the offender was authorised to access a computer system (e.g. because he was ordered to fix a computer problem) and then abused the authorisation to illegally obtain information stored on the computer system. With regard to the fact that the permission covers the access to the computer system it is in general not possible to cover with provisions criminalising the illegal access.

Without Right

The application of data espionage provisions in general requires that the data was obtained without the consent of the victim. The success of phishing attacks clearly demonstrates the success of scams based on the manipulation of users. Due to the consent of the victim offenders who succeed in manipulating of users to disclose secret information cannot be prosecuted on the basis of the above mentioned provisions.

ILLEGAL INTERCEPTION

The use of ICTs is accompanied by several risks related to the security of information transfer. Unlike classic mail order operations within a country, data transfer processes over the Internet involve numerous providers and different points where the data transfer process could be intercepted. The weakest point for intercept remains the user, especially users of private home computers, who are often inadequately protected against external attacks.

As offenders generally always aim for the weakest point, the risk of attacks against private users is great, all the more so given:

- The development of vulnerable technologies; and
- The rising relevance of personal information for offenders.

New network technologies (such as "wireless LAN") offer several advantages for Internet access. Setting up a wireless network in a private home, for example, allows families to connect to the Internet from anywhere inside a given radius, without the need for cable connections. But the popularity of this technology and resulting comfort is accompanied by serious risks to network security.

If an unprotected wireless network is available perpetrators can log on to this network and use it for criminal purposes without the need to get access to a building. They simply need to get inside the radius of the wireless network to launch an attack. Field tests suggest that in some areas as many as 50 per cent of private wireless networks are not protected against unauthorised interception or access. In most cases, lack of protection arises from a lack of knowledge as to how to configure protection measures. In the past, perpetrators concentrated mainly on business networks for illegal interceptions. Interception of corporate communications was more likely to yield useful information, than data transferred within private networks. The rising number of identity thefts of private personal data suggests that the focus of the perpetrators may have changed. Private data such as credit card numbers, social security numbers, passwords and bank account information are now of great interest to offenders.

The Convention on Cyber crime

The Convention on Cyber crime includes a provision protecting the integrity of non-public transmissions by criminalising their unauthorised interception. This provision aims to equate the protection of electronic transfers with the protection of voice conversations against illegal tapping and/or recording that currently already exists in most legal systems.

The Provision

- Article 3 – Illegal interception: Each Party shall adopt such legislative and other measures as may be necessary to establish as criminal offences under its domestic law, when committed intentionally, the interception without right, made by technical means, of non-public transmissions of computer data to, from or within a computer system, including electromagnetic emissions from a computer system carrying such computer data. A Party may require that the offence be committed with dishonest intent, or in relation to a computer system that is connected to another computer system.

The Covered Acts

The applicability of Article 3 is limited to the interception of transmissions realised by technical measures. Interceptions related to electronic data can be defined as any act of acquiring data during a transfer process. The question if illegal access to information stored on a hard disk is covered by the provision is controversially discussed. In general the provision only applies to the interception of transmissions - access to stored information is not considered as an interception of a transmission.

The fact that the application of the provision is discussed even in cases where the offender physically access a standalone computer system partly arises as a result of the fact, that the Convention on Cyber crime does not contain a provision related to data espionage and the Explanatory Report to the Convention contains two slightly imprecise explanations with regard to the application of Art. 3:

- The Explanatory Report first of all points out that the provision covers communication processes taking place within a computer system. However, this still leaves open the question of whether the provision should only apply in cases where victims send data that are then intercepted by offenders or whether it should apply also when the offender himself operates the computer.

- The guide points out that interception can be committed either indirectly through the use of tapping devices or "through access and use of the computer system". If offenders gain access to a computer system and use it to make unauthorised copies of stored data on an external disc drive, where the act leads to a data transfer (sending data from the internal to the external hard disc), this process is not *intercepted*, but rather *initiated*, by offenders. The missing element of technical interception is a strong argument against the application of the provision in cases of illegal access to stored information.

The term "transmission" covers all data transfers, whether by telephone, fax, e-mail or file transfer. The offence established under Article 3 applies only to non-public transmissions. A transmission is "non-public", if the transmission process is confidential.

The vital element to differentiate between public and non-public transmissions is not the nature of the data transmitted, but the nature of the transmission process itself. Even the transfer of publicly available information can be considered criminal, if the parties involved in the transfer intend to keep the content of their communications secret. Use of public networks does not exclude "nonpublic" communications.

Mental Element

Like all other offences defined by the Convention on Cyber crime, Article 3 requires that the offender is carrying out the offences intentionally. The Convention does not contain a definition of the term "internationally". In the Explanatory Report the drafters pointed out that the definition of "intentionally" should happen on a national level.

Without Right

The interception of communication can only be prosecuted under Article 3 of the Convention, if it should happen "without right".

The drafters of the Convention provided a set of examples for interceptions that are not carried out without right:

- Action on the basis instructions or by authorisation of the participants of the transmission;
- Authorised testing or protection activities agreed to by the participants;
- Lawful interception on the basis of criminal law provisions or in the interests of national security.

Another issue raised within the negotiation of the Convention was the question if the use of cookies would lead to criminal sanctions based on Art. 3. The drafters pointed out that common commercial practices (such as cookies) are not considered to be interceptions without right.

Restrictions and Reservations

Article 3 offers the option of restricting criminalisation by requiring additional elements listed in the second sentence, including a "dishonest intent" or relation to a computer system connected to another computer system.

Commonwealth Computer and Computer Related Crimes Model Law

A similar approach can be found in Sec. 8 of the 2002 Commonwealth Model Law.

- Sec. 8.: A person who, intentionally without lawful excuse or justification, intercepts by technical means:
  (a) Any non-public transmission to, from or within a computer system; or
  (b) Electromagnetic emissions from a computer system that are carrying computer data; commits an offence punishable, on conviction, by imprisonment for a period not exceeding, or a fine not exceeding, or both.

Stanford Draft Convention

The informal 1999 Stanford Draft Convention does not explicitly criminalise the interception of computer data.

DATA INTERFERENCE

The protection of tangible, or physical, objects against intentional damage is a classic element of national penal legislation. With continuing digitalisation, more critical business information is stored as data. Attacks or obtaining of this information can result in financial losses. Besides deletion, the alteration of such information could also have major consequences. Previous legislation has in some not completely brought the protection of data in line with the protection of tangible objects. This enabled offenders to design scams that do not lead to criminal sanctions.

Convention on Cyber crime

In Article 4, the Convention on Cyber crime includes a provision that protects the integrity of data against unauthorised interference. The aim of the provision is to fill existing gaps in some national penal laws and to provide computer data and computer programmes with protections similar to those enjoyed by tangible objects against the intentional infliction of damage.

The Provision

- Article 4 – Data interference:
  (1) Each Party shall adopt such legislative and other measures as may be necessary to establish as criminal offences under its

domestic law, when committed intentionally, the damaging, deletion, deterioration, alteration or suppression of computer data without right.

(2) A Party may reserve the right to require that the conduct described in paragraph 1 result in serious harm.

- The covered acts:
  - The terms "damaging" and "deterioration" mean any act related to the negative alteration of the integrity of information content of data and programmes;
  - "Deleting" covers acts where information is removed from storage media and is considered comparable to the destruction of a tangible object. While providing the definition the the drafters of the Convention did not differentiate between the various ways data can be deleted. Dropping a file to the virtual trash bin does not remove the file from the hard disk. Even "emptying" the trash bin does not necessary remove the file. It is therefore uncertain if the ability to recover a deleted file hinders the application of the provision.
  - "Suppression" of computer data denotes an action that affects the availability of data to the person with access to the medium, where the information is stored in a negative way. The application of the provision is especially discussed with regard to Denial-of-Service attacks. During the attack the data provided on the targeted computer system are not available anymore for potential user as well as the owner of the computer system.
  - The term "alteration" covers the modification of existing data, without necessarily lowering the serviceability of the data. This act is especially covering the installation of malicious software like spyware, viruses or adware on the victim's computer.

Mental Element

Like all other offences defined by the Convention on Cyber crime Article 4 requires that the offender is carrying out the offences intentionally. The Convention does not contain a definition of the term "internationally". In the Explanatory Report the drafters pointed out that the definition of "intentionally" should happen on a national level.

Without Right

The acts must be committed "without right". The right to alter data was discussed, especially in the context of "remailers". Remailers are used to modify certain data for the purpose of facilitating anonymous communications. The Explanatory Reports mention that, in principle, these acts are considered a legitimate protection of privacy and can thus be considered as being undertaken with authorisation.

Restrictions and Reservations

Article 4 offers the option of restricting criminalisation by limiting it to cases where serious harm arises, a similar approach to the EU Framework Decision on Attacks against Information Systems, which enables Member States to limit the applicability of the substantive criminal law provision to "cases which are not minor".

Commonwealth Computer and Computer Related Crimes Model Law

An approach in line with Art. 4 Convention on Cyber crime can be found in Sec. 8 of the 2002 Commonwealth Model Law.

Sec. 6

(1) A person who, intentionally or recklessly, without lawful excuse or justification, does any of the following acts:
  (a) Destroys or alters data; or
  (b) Renders data meaningless, useless or ineffective; or
  (c) Obstructs, interrupts or interferes with the lawful use of data; or
  (d) Obstructs, interrupts or interferes with any person in the lawful use of data; or
  (e) Denies access to data to any person entitled to it; commits an offence punishable, on conviction, by imprisonment for a period not exceeding or a fine not exceeding [amount], or both.

(2) Subsection (1) applies whether the person's act is of temporary or permanent effect.

Stanford Draft Convention

The informal 1999 Stanford Draft Convention contains two provisions that criminalise acts related to interference with computer data.

The Provision

Art. 3:

1. Offenses under this Convention are committed if any person unlawfully and intentionally engages in any of the following conduct without legally recognised authority, permission, or consent:
   (a) Creates, stores, alters, deletes, transmits, diverts, misroutes, manipulates, or interferes with data or Programmes in a cyber system with the purpose of causing, or knowing that such activities would cause, said cyber system or another cyber system

to cease functioning as intended, or to perform functions or activities not intended by its owner and considered illegal under this Convention;

(b) Creates, stores, alters, deletes, transmits, diverts, misroutes, manipulates, or interferes with data in a cyber system for the purpose and with the effect of providing false information in order to cause substantial damage to persons or property;

The Covered Acts

The main difference between the Convention on Cyber crime and the Commonwealth Model Law and the approach of the Draft Convention is the fact, that Draft Convention does only criminalise the interference with data if this interferes with the functioning of a computer system (Art. 3, paragraph 1a) or if the act is committed with the purpose of providing false information in order to causing damage to a person or property (Art. 3, paragraph 1b). Therefore the draft law does not criminalise the deletion of a regular text document of a data storage device as this does neither influence the functioning of a computer nor does it provide false information. The Convention on Cyber crime and the Commonwealth Model Law both follow a broader approach by protecting the integrity of computer data without the mandatory requirement of further effects.

SYSTEM INTERFERENCE

People or businesses offering services based on ICTs depend on the functioning of their computer systems. The lack of availability of webpages that are victim to Denial-of-Service (DOS) attacks demonstrates how serious the threat of attack is. Attacks like these can cause serious financial losses and affect even powerful systems. Businesses are not the only targets. Experts around the world are currently discussing possible scenarios of "cyber terrorism" that take into account attacks against critical infrastructures such as power supplies and telecommunication services.

Convention on Cyber crime

To protect access of operators and users to ICTs, the Convention on Cyber crime includes a provision in Article 5 criminalising the intentional hindering of lawful use of computer systems.

The Provision

Article 5 – System interference:

- Each Party shall adopt such legislative and other measures as may be necessary to establish as criminal offences under its domestic law, when committed intentionally, the serious hindering without right of the functioning of a computer system by inputting, transmitting, damaging, deleting, deteriorating, altering or suppressing computer data.

The Covered Acts

The application of the provision requires that the functioning of a computer system was hindered.

- "Hindering" means any act interfering with the proper functioning of the computer system. The application of the provision is limited to cases where hindering is carried out by one of the mentioned acts.

The list of acts by which the functioning of the computer system was influences in a negative way is conclusive.

- The term "inputting" is neither defined by the Convention itself, nor by the drafters of the Convention. With regard to the fact, the transmitting is mentioned as an additional act in Art. 5 the term "inputting" could be defined as any act related to use of physical input-interfaces to transfer information to a computer system whereas the term "transmitting" is covering acts that go along with the remote input of data.
- The terms "damaging" and "deteriorating" are overlapping and defined by the drafters of the Convention in the Explanatory Report with regard to Art. 4 as negative alteration of the integrity of information content of data and programmes.
- The term "deleting" was also defined by the drafters of the Convention and the Explanatory Report with regard to Article 4 covers acts where information is removed from storage media.
- The term "alteration" covers the modification of existing data, without necessarily lowering the serviceability of the data.
- "Suppression" of computer data denotes an action that affects the availability of data to the person with access to the medium, where the information is stored in a negative way.

In addition, the provision applies limited to cases where hindering is "serious". It is the parties' responsibility to determine the criteria to be fulfilled in order for the hindering to be considered as serious. Possible restrictions under national law could include a minimum amount of damage, as well as limitation of criminalisation to attacks against important computer systems.

Application of the Provision with Regard to Spam

It was discussed whether the problem of spam e-mail could be addressed under Article 5, since spam can overload computer systems. The drafters stated clearly that spam may not necessarily lead to "serious" hindering and that "conduct should only be criminalised where the communication is intentionally and seriously hindered". The drafters also noted that parties may have a different approach to hindrance under their own national legislation *e.g.,* by making acts of interference administrative offences or subject to sanction.

Mental Element

Like all other offences defined by the Convention on Cyber crime Art. 5 requires that the offender is carrying out the offences intentionally. This includes the intent to carry out one of listed acts as well as the intention to seriously hinder the functioning of a computer system. The Convention does not contain a definition of the term "internationally". In the Explanatory Report the drafters pointed out that the definition of "intentionally" should happen on a national level.

Without Right

The act needs to be carried out "without right". Network administrators and security companies testing the protection of computer systems were afraid of the possible criminalisation of their work. These professionals work with the permission of the owner and therefore act legally. In addition, the drafters of the Convention explicitly mentioned that testing the security of a computer system based on the authorisation of the owner is not without right.

Restrictions and Reservations

Unlike Articles 2 – 4, Article 5 does not contain an explicit possibility of restricting the application of the provision to implementation in the national law. Nevertheless, the responsibility of the parties to define the gravity of the offence gives them the possibility to restrict its application. A similar approach can be found in the European Union Framework Decision on Attacks against Information Systems.

Commonwealth Computer and Computer Related Crimes Model Law

An approach in line with Article 5 of the Convention on Cyber crime can be found in Sec. 7 of the 2002 Commonwealth Model Law.

Sec 7:

(1) A person who intentionally or recklessly, without lawful excuse or justification:

(a) Hinders or interferes with the functioning of a computer system; or

(b) Hinders or interferes with a person who is lawfully using or operating a computer system; commits an offence punishable, on conviction, by imprisonment for a period not exceeding [period], or a fine not exceeding [amount], or both.

In subsection (1) "hinder", in relation to a computer system, includes but is not limited to:

(a) Cutting the electricity supply to a computer system; and
(b) Causing electromagnetic interference to a computer system; and
(c) Corrupting a computer system by any means; and
(d) Inputting, deleting or altering computer data.

The main differences to the Convention is the fact, that based on Sec. 7 of the Commonwealth Model Law even reckless acts are criminalised. With this approach the Model Law even goes beyond the requirements of the Convention on Cyber crime. Another difference is the fact, that the definition of "hindering" in Sec. 7 of the Commonwealth Model Law lists more acts compared to Article 5 of the Convention on Cyber crime.

Stanford Draft Convention

The informal 1999 Stanford Draft Convention contains a provision that criminalises acts related to the interference with computer systems.

The Provision

Art. 3:

1. Offenses under this Convention are committed if any person unlawfully and intentionally engages in any of the following conduct without legally recognised authority, permission, or consent:
   (a) Creates, stores, alters, deletes, transmits, diverts, misroutes, manipulates, or interferes with data or Programmes in a cyber system with the purpose of causing, or knowing that such activities would cause, said cyber system or another cyber system to cease functioning as intended, or to perform functions or activities not intended by its owner and considered illegal under this Convention.

The Covered Acts

The main difference between the Convention on Cyber crime and the Commonwealth Model Law and the approach of the Draft Convention is the fact, that Draft Convention does cover any manipulation of computer systems while the Convention on Cyber crime and the Commonwealth Model Law limit the criminalisation to the hindering of the functioning of a computer system.

EROTIC OR PORNOGRAPHIC MATERIAL

The criminalisation and gravity of criminalisation of illegal content and sexually-explicit content varies between countries. The parties that negotiated the Convention on Cyber crime focused on the harmonisation of laws regarding child pornography and excluded the broader criminalisation of erotic and pornographic material. Some countries have addressed this problem by implementing provisions that criminalise the exchange of pornographic material through computer systems. However, the lack of standard definitions makes it difficult for law enforcement agencies to investigate those crimes, if offenders act from countries that have not criminalised the exchange of sexual content.

Examples

One example of the criminalisation of the exchange of pornographic material is Section 184 of the German Penal Code:

- Section 184 Dissemination of Pornographic Writings:

  (1) Whoever, in relation to pornographic writings (Section 11 subsection (3)):

  1. Offers, gives or makes them accessible to a person under eighteen years of age;
  2. Displays, posts, presents or otherwise makes them accessible at a place accessible to persons under eighteen years of age, or into which they can see;
  3. Offers or gives them to another in retail trade outside of the business premises, in kiosks or other sales areas which the customer usually does not enter, through a mail-order business or in commercial lending libraries or reading circles;

     3a. offers or gives them to another by means of commercial rental or comparable commercial furnishing for use, except for shops which are not accessible to persons under eighteen years of age and into which they cannot see;
  4. Undertakes to import them by means of a mail-order business;
  5. Publicly offers, announces, or commends them at a place accessible to persons under eighteen years of age or into which they can see, or through dissemination of writings outside of business transactions through normal trade outlets;
  6. Allows another to obtain them without having been requested to do by him;
  7. Shows them at a public film showing for compensation requested completely or predominantly for this showing;
  8. Produces, obtains, supplies, stocks, or undertakes to import them in order to use them or copies made from them within the meaning of numbers 1 through 7 or to make such use possible by another; or
  9. Undertakes to export them in order to disseminate them or copies made from them abroad in violation of the applicable penal provisions there or to make them publicly accessible or to make such use possible,shall be punished with imprisonment for not more than one year or a fine.

This provision is based on the concept that trade and other exchange of pornographic writings should not be criminalised, if minors are not involved.

On this basis, the law aims to protect the undisturbed development of minors. If access to pornography has a negative impact on the development of minors is controversially discussed. The exchange of pornographic writings among adults is not criminalised by Section 184. The term "writing" covers not only traditional writings, but also digital storage. Equally, making "them accessible" not only applies to acts beyond the Internet, but covers cases where offenders make pornographic content available on websites.

One example of an approach that goes beyond this and criminalises any sexual content is Section 4.C.1, Philippines draft House Law Bill No. 3777 of 2007.

- *Sec. 4.C1*: Offenses Related to Cybersex – Without prejudice to the prosecution under Republic Act No. 9208 and Republic Act No. 7610, any person who in any manner advertises, promotes, or facilitates the commission of cybersex through the use of information and communications technology such as but not limited to computers, computer networks, television, satellite, mobile telephone, [...]
- *Section 3i*: Cybersex or Virtual Sex – refers to any form of sexual activity or arousal with the aid of computers or communications network

This provision follows a very broad approach, as it criminalises any kind of sexual advertisement or facilitation of sexual activity carried out over the Internet. Due to the principle of dual criminality international investigations with regard to such broad approaches go along with difficulties.

CHILD PORNOGRAPHY

The Internet is becoming the main instrument for the trade and exchange of material containing child pornography. The major reasons for this development are the speed and efficiency of the Internet for file transfers, its low production and distribution costs and perceived anonymity. Pictures placed on a webpage can be accessed and downloaded by millions of users worldwide. One of the most important reasons for the "success" of web pages offering pornography or even child pornography is the fact that Internet users are feeling less observed while sitting in their home and downloading material from the Internet.

Unless the users made use of means of anonymous communication the impression of a missing traceability is wrong. Most Internet users are simply unaware of the electronic trail they leave while surfing.

Council of Europe Convention on Cyber crime

In order to improve and harmonise the protection of children against sexual exploitation, the Convention includes an Article addressing child pornography.

The Provision

- Article 9 – Offences related to child pornography:

(1) Each Party shall adopt such legislative and other measures as may be necessary to establish as criminal offences under its domestic law, when committed intentionally and without right, the following conduct:
   (a) Producing child pornography for the purpose of its distribution through a computer system;
   (b) Offering or making available child pornography through a computer system;
   (c) Distributing or transmitting child pornography through a computer system;
   (d) Procuring child pornography through a computer system for oneself or for another person;
   (e) Possessing child pornography in a computer system or on a computer-data storage medium.

(2) For the purpose of paragraph 1 above, the term "child pornography" shall include pornographic material that visually depicts:
   (a) a minor engaged in sexually explicit conduct;
   (b) a person appearing to be a minor engaged in sexually explicit conduct;
   (c) Realistic images representing a minor engaged in sexually explicit conduct.

(3) For the purpose of paragraph 2 above, the term "minor" shall include all persons under 18 years of age. A Party may, however, require a lower age-limit, which shall be not less than 16 years.

(4) Each Party may reserve the right not to apply, in whole or in part, paragraphs 1, subparagraphs d. and e, and 2, sub-paragraphs b. and c.

Most countries already criminalise the abuse of children, as well as the traditional methods of distribution of child pornography. The Convention is thus not limited to the closing of gaps in national criminal law - it also seeks to harmonise differing regulation.

Three controversial elements are covered by Article 9:

- The age of the person involved;
- The criminalisation of the possession of child pornography; and
- The creation or integration of fictional images.

Age Limit for Minors

One of the most important differences between national legislation is the age of the person involved. Some states define the term 'minor' in relation to child pornography in their national law in accordance with the definition of a 'child' in Article 1 of the UN Convention on the Rights of the Child as all persons less than 18 years old. Other countries define minors as a person under 14 years old. A similar approach is found in the 2003 EU Council Framework Decision on combating the sexual exploitation of children and child pornography and the 2007 Council of Europe Convention on the protection of children against sexual exploitation and sexual abuse. Emphasizing the importance of a uniform international standard regarding age, the Convention defines the term according to the UN Convention. However, in recognition of the huge differences in the existing national laws, the Convention permits parties to require a different age limit of not lower than 16 years.

Criminalisation of the Possession of Child Pornography

Criminalisation of possession of child pornography also differs between national legal systems. The demand for such material could result in their production on an ongoing basis. The possession of such material could encourage the sexual abuse of children, so drafters suggest that one effective way to curtail the production of child pornography is to make possession illegal.

However, the Conventions enable the parties in Paragraph 4 to exclude the criminalisation of mere possession, by restricting criminal liability to the production, offer and distribution of child pornography only.

The Creation or Integration of Fictional Images

Although the drafters sought to improve the protection of children against sexual exploitation, the legal interests covered by Paragraph 2 are broader. Paragraph 2(a) focuses directly on protection against child abuse. Paragraphs 2(b) and 2(c) cover images that were produced without violating children's rights – *e.g.,* images that have been created through the use of 3D modelling software. The reason for the criminalisation of fictive child pornography is that fact that these images can - without necessarily creating harm to a real 'child' - be used to seduce children into participating in such acts.

Mental Element

Like all other offences defined by the Convention on Cyber crime Article 9 requires that the offender is carrying out the offences intentionally. In the Explanatory Report the drafters explicitly pointed out that the interaction with child pornography without any intention is not covered by the Convention. A missing intention can especially be relevant if the offender accidentally opened a webpage with child pornography images and despite the fact that he immediately closed the Web site some images were stored in temp-folders or cache-files.

Without Right

The acts related to child pornography can only be prosecuted under Article 9 of the Convention, if it should happen "without right". The drafters of the

Convention did not further specify in which cases the user is acting with authorisation. In general the act is not carried out "without right" only if members of law enforcement agencies are acting within an investigation.

Council of Europe Convention on the Protection of Children

Another approach to criminalise acts related to Child Pornography is Art. 20 of the Council of Europe Convention on the Protection of Children against Sexual Exploitation and Sexual Abuse.

The Provision

Article 20 – Offences concerning child pornography:

(1) Each Party shall take the necessary legislative or other measures to ensure that the following intentional conduct, when committed without right, is criminalised:
   a) Producing child pornography;
   b) Offering or making available child pornography;
   c) Distributing or transmitting child pornography;
   d) Procuring child pornography for oneself or for another person;
   e) Possessing child pornography;
   f) Knowingly obtaining access, through information and communication technologies, to child pornography.

(2) For the purpose of the present article, the term "child pornography" shall mean any materialthat visually depicts a child engaged in real or simulated sexually explicit conduct or anydepiction of a child's sexual organs for primarily sexual purposes.

(3) Each Party may reserve the right not to apply, in whole or in part, paragraph 1.a and e to the production and possession of pornographic material:
   - Consisting exclusively of simulated representations or realistic images of a non-existent child;
   - Involving children who have reached the age set in application of Article 18, paragraph 2, where these images are produced and possessed by them with their consent and solely for their own private use.

(4) Each Party may reserve the right not to apply, in whole or in part, paragraph 1.f

The Covered Acts

The provision is based on Art. 9 Convention on Cyber crime and therefore up to a large degree comparable to this provision. The main difference is the fact, that the Convention on Cyber crime is focusing on the criminalisation of acts related to information and communication services ("producing child pornography for the purpose of its distribution through a computer system") while the Convention on the Protection of Children is mainly following a broader approach ("producing child pornography") and even covers acts that are not related to computer networks.

Despite the similarities with regard to the covered acts, Art. 20 of the Convention on the Protection of Children contains one act that is not covered by the Convention. Based on Art. 20, paragraph 1f of the Convention on the Protection of Children the act of obtaining access to child pornography through a computer is criminalised.

This enables law enforcement agencies to prosecute offenders in cases where they are able to prove that the offender opened websites with child pornography but they are unable to prove that the offender downloaded material. Such difficulties in collecting evidence do for example arise if the offender is using encryption technology to protected downloaded files on his storage media. The Explanatory Report to the Convention on the Protection of children points out that the provision should also be applicable in cases, where the offender does only watch child pornography pictures online without downloading them. In general opening a Web site does automatically initiate a download process– often without the knowledge of the user. The case mentioned in the Explanatory Report is therefore only relevant in those cases where a download in the background is not taking place.

Commonwealth Model Law

An approach in line with Art. 9 Convention on Cyber crime can be found in Sec. 10 of the 2002 Commonwealth Model Law.

Sec. 10:

(1) A person who, intentionally, does any of the following acts:
  (a) Publishes child pornography through a computer system; or
  (b) Produces child pornography for the purpose of its publication through a computer system; or
  (c) Possesses child pornography in a computer system or on a computer data storage medium; commits an offence punishable, on conviction, by imprisonment for a period not exceeding [period], or a fine not exceeding [amount], or both.

(2) It is a defence to a charge of an offence under paragraph (1) (a) or (1)(c) if the person establishes that the child pornography was a bona fide scientific, research, medical or law enforcement purpose.

(3) In this section: "child pornography" includes material that visually depicts:
  (a) a minor engaged in sexually explicit conduct; or
  (b) a person who appears to be a minor engaged in sexually explicit conduct; or

(c) Realistic images representing a minor engaged in sexually explicit conduct. "minor" means a person under the age of [x] years. "publish" includes:

(a) Distribute, transmit, disseminate, circulate, deliver, exhibit, lend for gain, exchange, barter, sell or offer for sale, let on hire or offer to let on hire, offer in any other way, or make available in any way; or

(b) Have in possession or custody, or under control, for the purpose of doing an act referred to in paragraph (a); or

(c) Print, photograph, copy or make in any other manner (whether of the same or of a different kind or nature) for the purpose of doing an act referred to in paragraph (a).

The main differences to the Convention on Cyber crime is the fact, that the Commonwealth Model Law does not provide a fixes definition of the term minor and leaves it to the Member States to define the age limit.

Stanford Draft Convention

The informal 1999 Stanford Draft Convention does not contain a provision criminalising the exchange of child pornography through computer systems. The drafters of the Convention pointed out, that in general no type of speech, or publication, is required to be treated as criminal under the Stanford Draft. Recognising different national approaches the drafters of the Convention left it to the states to decide about this aspect of criminalisation.

CYBER CRIME LAW IN INDIA

The general laws in India were drafted and enacted in the 19th century. Whilst each of the general laws have undergone modifications and amendments, the broad and underlying provisions have withstood the test of time, including unimaginable advancements in technology, which speaks to the dynamism of the General laws. The general laws referred to in this Article are the Indian Penal Code, 1860 ("IPC"), which is the general penal law of India and the Indian Evidence Act, 1872 ("Evidence Act"), the general law pertaining to admissibility of evidence in civil and criminal trials.

The manner in which trial of criminal cases are to be conducted is dealt with under the Criminal Procedure Code, 1973 ("Cr. P. C"). India got its first codified Act in the Information Technology Act, 2000 ("IT Act), which fell far short of the Industry's requirements to meet global standards. The focus if the IT Act was however recognition of electronic records and facilitation of e - commerce. Barely ten sections were incorporated in the IT Act to deal with Cyber Crime. At the time when the IT Act was passed several acts deemed to be illegal in most jurisdictions including virus attacks, data theft, illegal access to data/ accessing and removal of data without the consent of the owner, etc., were listed as civil penalties under the IT Act. The IT Industry continued to rely on self –regulation and contractual undertakings to appease its global clients, as it had done before the passing of the IT Act.

The primary offences under the IT Act were:

- Tampering with source code;
- Deleting, destroying or altering any data on any computer resource with mala fide intent to cause wrongful loss or to diminish its value;
- Publishing or transmitting pornographic material through a computer resource;
- Provisions pertaining to encryption technology, the right of the Government authorities to intercept and decrypt such data and to call upon any entity or individual to decrypt such data were also included in the IT Act. Certain acts affecting the integrity and sovereignty of the nation were classified as offences.

The saving grace of the IT Act were the amendments carried out to the IPC and Evidence Act, which to some extent provided for prosecution of rampant offences like the Nigerian Scams, Phishing and other Banking frauds may be prosecuted. Cyber Crime prosecution was however not resorted to in many instances due to lack of awareness (amongst both the victims and the enforcement authorities) about the applicability of such general Laws to cyber crimes (like Phishing).

To add to this, administrative delegation of powers treated offences under the IT Act differently to those falling under general laws! Further, crimes like data theft; illegally accessing/ removal of data; virus attacks etc., could not be prosecuted due to the lack of relevant penal provisions.

S.66 of the Act misleadingly titled "hacking" is one of the most misused and abused provisions in India. Recently *i.e.,* in September 2009, the Delhi High Court has quashed the criminal proceedings initiated in or about July 2005, under S.66 of the IT Act by M/s. Parsec Technologies Ltd., against some of its former employees, who left and started their own Company, holding that the continuation of the proceedings would amount to abuse of process of law.

Likewise the IT Act did not provide sufficient recourse for women and child victims of cyber crimes like Cyber Stalking and paedophilia. Controversy has dogged the IT Act from its inception. The Ministry of Information Technology prepared and posted proposed draft amendments to the IT Act in 2005. In 2006, the IT Bill with substantial changes brought about as a result of the objections to the proposed amendments of 2005 was tabled before the Parliament. In December 2008 as a knee–jerk reaction to the November 2008 terror attacks in Mumbai, India, the Information Technology (Amendments) Act, 2008 ("ITA, 2008") was hastily tabled before the Parliament and was passed hastily and without any debate whatsoever. Unlike the IT Act of 2000, the focus of the new ITA 2008 is clearly on Cyber Terrorism and to a significant extent, Cyber Crime. This paper deals with some important provisions of ITA, 2008 relating to data protection, privacy, encryption and cyber crime and to what extent it arms one against emerging trends in Cyber Crime.

DEFINITIONS

The replacement of the word "Digital" with the word "Electronic", which makes the IT Act more technology neutral and expands its applicability beyond just the digital medium.

- Inclusion of cell phones, personal digital assistants and other such devices in the definition of "Communication Devices" broadens the scope of the statute.
- The modified definition of "Intermediary" includes all service providers in respect of electronic records again broadens the applicability while inclusion of Cyber cafes in the definition of Intermediaries removes the need to interpret the statute.

The extensive definition of "cyber security" as including protection of both data and the equipment from unauthorised access, use, disclosure etc., is another vital inclusion that impacts the new Data Protection provisions included under the ITA, 2008. The relevance of these definitions, where applicable are set out below.

DATA PROTECTION

The IT industry has been lobbying for a law to protect Data and the new legislation has addressed the industry's demands to a certain extent particularly since Mphasis Limited, a Pune based Company suffered the notoriety of puncturing the Indian BPO fairy tale in April 2004, when some of its employees stole confidential credit card information of clients and used it to siphon substantial amounts. Apart from highlighting the security lapses within the Company, this case also brought to the limelight the lack of suitable Data Protection Laws in India. Several cases have now been reported where former employees are accused of data theft and misuse of Confidential and proprietary Information and data. In one instance, a BPO Company purportedly closed down due to rampant data theft.

The Indian Legislature's response to the hue and cry raised is the transposition of certain civil penalties into criminal offences and the addition of one section under civil penalties as set out hereunder:

- The only provision under the IT Act for data protection was S.43, which only imposed Civil Penalties in the event of the commission of certain acts without the permission of the owner or person in charge of the computer or computer systems such as:
  - Securing access (without permission);
  - Downloading or copying of data stored in a computer or computer system;

- Introducing computer viruses;
- Damaging computers and or data stored therein;
- Disrupting computers;
- Denial of access;
- Abetting such acts; or
- Illegal charging for services on another's account.

S.43A has now been added under the ITA 2008 to address the data protection requirements of the Industry. S.43A stipulates that any "Body Corporate" possessing, dealing with or handling any "sensitive personal data or information" in a computer resource it owns, controls or operates, is liable for negligence, if it fails to maintain "reasonable security practices and procedures" and thereby causes wrongful loss or wrongful gain to any person. What amounts to reasonable security practices and procedures remains to be finalised by the Central Government.

Apart from the above addition under Civil Penalties, the Civil wrongs set out under S.43 of the IT Act have now been qualified as criminal offences under the ITA 2008 under S. 66. A reverse transposition has further been carried out under the ITA 2008 of two criminal provisions from the IT Act (S.66 and S.65) as civil penalties under S.43 (i) & S.43 (j), respectively. Any act set out under S.43, if committed "dishonestly or fraudulently", would amount to a criminal offence, punishable with punishment of up to three years or fine of a maximum of Rupees Five Lakhs or both, under the ITA 2008.

Though S.66 of the IT Act has purportedly been deleted, the addition of S.43 (i) under the ITA 2008 has in effect resulted in the retention of the contentious S.66 of the IT Act. However retention of S.65 of the IT Act without any modification despite its transposition into S.43 appears to be a tautology, which could be due to oversight. S.66B inserted by the ITA, 2008 is on the lines of similar provisions in the Indian Penal Code ("IPC"), which provides for punishment of the receiver of stolen property. S.66B makes the receipt or retention of a stolen computer resource or communication device punishable with imprisonment up to three years or with fine up to Rupees One Lakh or both. Whilst S.66B may seem to also apply to hardware, which is also covered under the IPC, the term "computer resource" is defined under the IT Act as a "Computer, computer system, computer network, data, computer database or software." The extension of the above provision to the receiver of stolen data, software etc., may prove to be substantially useful when faced with issues of Corporate Espionage.

FURTHER ANALYSIS OF THE DATA PROTECTION LEGISLATION

Although the data protection provisions introduced by the ITA, 2008 may not comprehensively address the industry specific requirements applicable to data providers and handlers; nevertheless this is an important head start towards introduction of specific data protection legislation in India, which is absolutely essential in today's business environment. One of the important outcomes of the ITA, 2008 amendments is the clarity on whether Data theft is considered a criminal offence. Commission of acts provided in S.43 to 66 dishonestly or fraudulently, clearly implies "Data Theft" as an offence in such instances.

However these acts would amount to a punishable offence only if such data is "downloaded, copied or extracted" from a computer resource. Therefore it may be argued that the provisions of S.43 (b) are not inclusive, as they do not provide for removal of data through uploading. Criminal provisions give rise to liability only in cases of unambiguity.

If a provision has to be applied through interpretation, then such interpretation, which favours the Accused, would have to be applied. With the addition of S.43A by the ITA, 2008, the onus of implementing "Reasonable Security Practices" is on the business entity. Whilst this may be a known liability that parties agree upon, unsuspecting companies or firms may get mulcted with liability if duties and obligations are not specified, as the Central Government guidelines will then become applicable. As of now, violations under S.43 A are however not criminal offences.

Confidentiality and Privacy

India was shocked out of its complacent conservatism due to the widespread circulation of a MMS clip shot by a Delhi schoolboy. This case took an unexpected twist when this clip was circulated on Bazee.com and its Chief Executive Officer of American origin was arrested. S.66E has now been introduced under the ITA, 2008 for the protection of physical or personal privacy of an individual.

This section makes intentional capturing of the images of a person's private parts without his or her consent in any medium and publishing or transmitting such images through electronic medium, a violation of such person's privacy punishable with imprisonment of up to three years or with fine up to Rupees Two Lakhs, or both. A case of posting of the personal information and obscene material on a Yahoo! Site was touted as the fastest trial and conviction of a cyber crime case in Chennai. It appears that this conviction has recently been reversed.

S.72 A of the ITA, 2008 now explicitly provides recourse against dissemination of personal information obtained without the individual's consent through an intermediary or under a services contract, with intent to cause wrongful loss or wrongful gain. The maximum punishment prescribed for this offence is three years imprisonment, or fine up to Rupees Five Lakhs or both. Service providers on the Internet, social networking sites, Companies, firms, individuals and other intermediaries ought to now be careful in the collection, retention and dissemination of personal data. Interactive websites and P2P site operators also have to be extremely careful to ensure that the provisions of S.66E and S.72 A are not violated.

Other Cyber Crimes Including Cyber Terrorism

Provisions to combat cyber frauds have now been introduced under the ITA 2008. However certain issues relating to protection against banking frauds such as Phishing, money transfers through online hacking, e-mail frauds and cyber squatting (including through wilfully misleading domain names) to name a few have not been addressed separately in the ITA, 2008, even though these are significantly increasing problems. S.66C inserted by the ITA, 2008 makes dishonest or fraudulent use of a person's electronic signature or identity, password or any other unique identification feature punishable as theft with imprisonment of up to three years and fine up to Rupees One Lakh.

S.66D inserted by the ITA, 2008 makes cheating by personating through a computer resource punishable with imprisonment of up to three years and fine up to One Lakh Rupees. It may be noted that S.419 of IPC already provides for punishment for cheating by personating but does not provide for the maximum fine imposable. In addition to S.67 of the IT Act, S.67A and S.67B have been included by the ITA, 2008 *inter alia* to combat child pornography. S.67A makes transmission of a sexually explicit act or conduct punishable and S.67B makes publishing and transmission of child pornography an offence, punishments for which range from five to seven years and fine.

Several exceptions have also been set out to S.67 and S.67A, including for depictions in any book, pamphlet, paper, writing, drawing, painting representation or figure in electronic form. Further, S.67C introduced by the ITA, 2008 imposes liability on Intermediaries for retention and production of information. However the duration, manner and formats of retention of such information are still subject to prescription by the Central Government. This section appears to be directed mainly against Cyber Cafes and has already been subject to dissension. Failure to comply with such requirements is punishable with imprisonment up to three years and also fine.

Observations on the Cyber Crime Provisions under the ITA, 2008

- S.43 was included in the IT Act, 2000 to address certain kinds of illegal acts. However, the Legislature has not looked beyond S.43 to address recent trends in Cyber Crimes and for dealing with such issues.
- S.66 of the IT Act, under the heading "Hacking" which was misleading was criticised for its ambiguity and for the possibility of abuse. However, whilst the proposed amendments sought for its deletion, this section has been transposed to not only being applicable as a civil penalty but is also retained as a criminal offence. With the retention of S.66 of the IT Act, one of the main issues that need to

be addressed is the criminality of actions resulting in "diminishing of value" of any information residing in a computer resource. Even if the law – makers thought fit to retain this provision, its use and abuse Since, 2000 ought to have been evaluated when re-defining this provision.

- S.66C only addresses some kinds of cyber frauds and not all such frauds committed without using digital or electronic signatures. Further S.66D may be considered redundant in the light of the amendments made to the IPC after the enactment of the IT Act in 2000, save and except for the maximum fine imposable under the ITA, 2008.
- S.67A is a much – needed introduction to the IT Act and would help in combating the pernicious offences of child pornography as observed in some recent shocking incidents involving school children. Several new provisions have been introduced under the ITA 2008 to combat Cyber Terrorism. These provisions appear to be a necessary and welcome addition though there are apprehensions about their abuse and whether the Government authorities are well equipped to handle and protect the information, acquired by it in compliance with such provisions.
- S.66A inserted by the ITA, 2008 is an essential provision from the perspective of combating Cyber Terrorism and to address several instances of cyber stalking, cyber harassment, etc. However this provision can also be easily abused. S.66A provides for punishment of three years and fine against any person found guilty of: (i) sending information through a computer resource or devise, which is grossly offensive or of menacing character; (ii) false information intended to annoy, inconvenience, deceive or mislead the addressee or recipient about the origin of such message; or (iii) endanger, obstruct, insult, injure, intimidate or to cause enmity, hatred or ill will.
- This would not only help the police against anonymous and false messages etc., and harassed individuals, but also corporate bodies, which could rework their internal policies in consonance with this provision.
- S.66F directly addresses the issue of cyber terrorism. Acts intended to: (i) threaten the unity, integrity, security or sovereignty of India; (ii) to strike terror in the people or any section of the people by denial of access, hacking and virus attacks; and (iii) by such means does or may cause death or injuries to persons or damage to property or disrupts supplies or services essential to the life of the community; or (iv) adversely affects the critical information infrastructure; is the commission of Cyber Terrorism, the punishment for which ranges

from imprisonment from three years to life and fine depending upon the seriousness of the crime.

Encryption and Data Privacy

Mid 2008, customers in India thought twice about buying Blackberry phones – no reflection on the performance of the phones but due to a sudden conflict between the Department of Telecommunications of the Indian Government ("DoT") and Research in Motion ("RIM") Blackberry Services.

DoT requested RIM to share its encryption codes with the department, stating security concerns over data transmitted through e-mail services on Blackberry phones or to set up servers in India and permit DoT to monitor such transmissions. After several rounds of talks the Government of India dropped its request reversing its stand on the issue of a security threat. The Indian Telegraph Act, 1885 vests extensive and absolute power on the DoT *inter alia* to deal with, monitor and regulate transmission of messages within India. These provisions therefore stand automatically extended to transmission of encrypted Data also.

The Guidelines issued by the DoT for transmission of encrypted data and the ISP license requirements permits transmission of encrypted data of 40 bit key length in RSA algorithms or its equivalent in other algorithms without having to obtain permission from the Telecom Authority. However, if encryption equipments higher than this limit are to be deployed (which would be the case for most encrypted data), individuals/groups/organizations require prior written permission of the DoT and may be further called upon to deposit the decryption key, split into two parts, with the DoT. These provisions appear to have prompted the Blackberry case. Now in addition to the above powers vested in the Telecom Authority of India, certain provisions have been added under the ITA 2008 (as set out hereunder), which further strengthens the hands of the Telecom Authority in India.

S.69 of the IT Act, which dealt with encrypted data has been replaced with a new S.69, which empowers the Central Government or a State Government through their authorised officers to intercept, monitor or decrypt any information generated, transmitted, received or stored in any computer resource. These powers may be exercised for reasons set out in S.69 including in the interest of the sovereignty or integrity of India, defence, security of the State, or even for preventing commission of any cognizable offence or for investigation of any offence.

The only restraint in exercising such powers is the necessity of maintaining written records of such actions. The additions to S.69 and inclusion of new provisions under S.69A to S.69C under the ITA 2008 may be subject to criticism and concern. S.69A empowers the Central Government or any of its authorised officers to block or cause to be blocked access by public of any information generated, transmitted, received, stored or hosted in any computer resource. Under S.69B, the Central Government may, through its authorised agency, monitor and collect traffic data or information generated, transmitted, received or stored in any computer resource for enhancing cyber security and for identification, analysis and prevention of intrusion or spread of virus in the country. Intermediaries have to provide such data and assistance as sought by the authorised agency and failure to extend such assistance is punishable with imprisonment up to three years and fine.

S.70A and S.70B provides for notification of any Government organization as the national nodal agency for Critical Information Infrastructure Protection and notification of any Government organization as the Indian Computer Emergency Response Team, respectively. S.84A gives extensive powers to the Central Government to prescribe encryption methods to ensure secure use of the electronic medium and for promotion of e-governance and e-commerce.

Other Relevant Provisions

S.77A of the ITA, 2008 provides for compounding of offences under this Act, other than:

- Offences punishable with life or imprisonment for a term exceeding three years;
- In cases of enhanced punishment;
- Those affecting the socio economic conditions of the country; or
- Offences against a child below the age of 18 years or a woman.

Whilst some of these exceptions appear to be precise and appropriate, certain others appear ambiguous *i.e.,* exception on the grounds of socio economic conditions.

S.77B makes all offences punishable with three years and above imprisonment cognizable and bailable, notwithstanding the provisions of the Indian Code of Criminal Procedure, 1973. With the increase in cyber crimes amounting to offences under the ITA, 2008, the power to investigate offences under this Act has been vested with an Inspector instead of the Deputy Superintendent of Police. This may reduce the confusion relating to jurisdiction for registering of offences. Further this would entail commencement of extensive and immediate cyber law awareness measures by the investigation agencies throughout India. There is however anxiety in the minds of the industry about the ability of the police official of such rank being able to handle such additional responsibility.

S.79 has been modified by the ITA, 2008 to restrict the liability of an Intermediary under this section to specific instances, *i.e.,* if he provides access to communication systems for transmission or temporary storage of third party information, data or communication links made available or hosted by him. The

Intermediary should however observe due diligence and comply with the prescribed guidelines, while discharging his duties.

S.85 of the IT Act, which imputes vicarious liability in case of offences by companies, has been retained in its original form despite criticism by different industry sectors. As most of the offences under the IT Act have been made cognizable, and with the increase in the number of offences added under the ITA, 2008, this provision may be cause for concern.

CONCLUSION

Though the ITA 2008 has been passed by the parliament, the Amended Act is still not the law of the land. The ITA 2008 will come into effect only from the date notified by the Government of India, which still remains pending as on the date of publication of this paper.

Introduction of several provisions in the IT Act by the ITA, 2008, relating to data protection, are extremely essential in today's business environment as several Indian companies providing services to or in conjunction with foreign entities handle large amounts of data that are accessed and/or processed by their employees. Such cross border exchange/ transmission of Data further mandates compliance with the provisions of foreign enactments on Data Protection. The increased accountability of data handlers and data aggregators and the enhanced punitive measures, therefore meets such requirements to some extent. The existing provisions along with the additional/ revised provisions under the ITA, 2008 provide for criminal prosecution and stringent monetary penalties that are likely to act as effective deterrents. Whilst some inclusions in the ITA 2008 have been subject to criticism, the amendments and additions made to the IT Act are expedient and much awaited additions. Absence of effective provisions to combat offences like Cyber Stalking and cyber squatting are avoidable loopholes, which one hopes will soon be rectified. One could safely conclude that whilst the ITA 2008 is still work in progress, it is definitely headed in the right direction.

6

Criminal Justice System in Stopping Violence Against Women

Comprehensive, effective, and nondiscriminatory implementation of criminal justice system powers is essential to ending violence against women, both for freeing individual women and for ending the world wide epidemic of violence against women. No doubt, all segments of society must make profound changes before violence against women will be eliminated. But once there is violence or threat of violence, the criminal justice system is the only sector of society that has the power and authority to step in and stop the violence. The criminal justice system alone is invested with the power and authority to enforce the laws against violence, to carry out a criminal investigation, to arrest and detain a perpetrator, and to provide justice for criminal offences. If the criminal justice system doesn't fully do its part to put the perpetrator under control, you can social work these cases endlessly. In all likelihood the perpetrator will just turn around and easily undo any peace and equilibrium you and the victim have been able to establish in her life.

The pivotal importance of the criminal justice system in stopping violence against women can be illustrated in both the positive and the negative. On the positive side, a handful of diverse jurisdictions around the country that have implemented a consistent, aggressive, and modern criminal justice response to domestic violence have been able to reduce their domestic violence homicide rates by over 60% in just a matter of years. If domestic violence were a disease, this kind of dramatic reduction in deaths would be heralded a miracle cure.

You may recall a series of studies from the late 1980's which found that arresting perpetrators resulted in only minimal reduction of future violence in the relationship. These studies are still used to argue against the necessity of a strong criminal justice system response, so it's important to be aware of a core flaw, not in the studies themselves, but in the conditions at the time. The system in place at the time consisted principally of arrests by themselves, without the crucial follow-up investigations and prosecutions in place. It was like trying to make the airplane fly with only one wing. It's easy to see that if perpetrators are merely arrested and detained for a couple days and then let go without follow-through, they are likely to be even more dangerous to victims.

It wasn't until the early 1990's when a few jurisdictions, most notably San Diego, CA and Quincy, Massachusetts, began to pioneer the more modern, comprehensive law enforcement approach to domestic violence. In addition to pro-arrest policies, the new approach included a complete police investigation with an eye to prosecution, prosecutorial follow-up, no diversion/no-drop policies, victim support, and intensified probation monitoring and/or correctional follow through. It was only when this full spectrum criminal justice response was applied to domestic violence that the immediate and dramatic reductions in domestic violence homicides took place in those pioneering cities. These positive and striking results have now been successfully reproduced in a number of other jurisdictions throughout the country. No other approach to domestic violence-not educational, therapy based, and not diversion programmes-has shown anywhere near the effectiveness and impact obtained by the implementation of a comprehensive criminal justice response. If anything, studies of non-criminal justice remedies to domestic violence repeatedly demonstrate their ineffectiveness in bringing about any significant reduction in the levels of violence. Given the proven and unequivocal benefits of a full criminal justice response, it's sad that still today, the pivotal importance of good criminal justice system response is still more often manifested in the negative.

On the negative side, the consequences of law enforcement failures to implement their powers on behalf of women are all too evident by tracing law enforcement histories leading up to domestic violence homicides. What's found in case after case where women have been murdered by their partners is a history of gross failures of law enforcement to respond properly to the victims' previous requests for help. Half-baked investigations, officer bias against women, contempt of victims, inadequate prosecution, slap-on-the-wrist sentencing, careless follow-up, and overall system disregard paves the road to one domestic violence homicide after another. Sloppy law enforcement response emboldens the perpetrators, throws the women into despair, and leads to an incalculable number of severe injuries and deaths to women.

A year 2002, Domestic Violence Fatality Review from Washington State aptly names this all too common inadequate law enforcement response to domestic violence "the meaningless processing of cases". All too often, instead of implementing their powers on the victim's behalf, criminal justice officials were found to be carelessly handing the cases off from one to the next. Perpetrators were never really held accountable despite multiple rounds through the system, and ultimately the women were murdered.

When the criminal justice system withholds its powers from victims of rape and domestic violence, it bolsters the perpetrators, and, in fact, increases the danger to the victim. The perpetrators are emboldened by the immense authority behind the system's could-care-less attitude. The perpetrators feel they've been given the ultimate green light to carry on with the violence or to escalate. In fact, once law enforcement responds carelessly, it's not uncommon for perpetrators to invoke law enforcement authority in taunting the victim. "Go ahead, call the Sheriff," Avelino Macias would taunt his estranged wife Teresa, "The Sheriff protects me more than they protect you."

The victim, on the other hand, is dangerously weakened and driven into despair by the system's denial of help. Right at the moment she takes the great risk of exposing her intent to confront the perpetrator by bringing in law enforcement, she is betrayed by inadequate law enforcement response in front of the perpetrator. "Instead of helping me," Teresa had told her mother regarding authorities' responses to her calls for help, "they sunk me even more." Like many victims of domestic violence homicide, Teresa had been driven into such deep despair by the Sheriff's repeated disregard of her more than 25 calls for help, she had given up on calling the Sheriff for help in the weeks before Avelino lay in wait and executed her. Nor do you have to limit your observations to domestic violence homicides to see the harm of law enforcement disregard for violence against women. The same can be seen in the law enforcement histories of so many cases where there are serious injuries. Or in cases of serial rapists or serial child molesters. If you dig out the law enforcement histories in these felony cases, here again you'll most always find a trail of law enforcement disregard of the perpetrator's prior lower level violence against women and children.

Given the increased danger to women created by official's denial of protection and justice, it should be clear that any police officer or prosecutor who routinely mishandles violence against women, over the course of his or her career, or even over the course of a year, is more dangerous to women than a hundred batterers and rapists. What's more, if you look at the law enforcement history in cases of serial killers and mass murderers, you'll also frequently find a trail of inadequate law enforcement response to the perpetrator's earlier violence against women. A current case in the news is that of John Muhammad whose sniper killing spree in the fall of 2002 held the entire populace of Washington DC under siege for weeks and resulted in the killing of 13 people and the wounding of 5.

In the two years prior to that killing spree at least three police agencies, the Tacoma PD, the Bellingham PD, and the area Sheriff's Department had failed to respond properly to Muhammad's domestic violence related crimes against his wife and children and against the mother of Jahn Malvo, Muhammad's juvenile accomplice in the killing spree. These law enforcement agencies never once arrested Muhammad, nor obtained an arrest warrant for these crimes, despite the fact that Muhammad had abducted and concealed his children from his wife for over a year, despite the fact that he had made threats to kill that were heard by credible witnesses, and despite the fact that law enforcement was in touch with Muhammad and had ample evidence to prove those crimes.

As a point of insight into Tacoma Police mentality it's worth noting that in that same time period Tacoma PD had obtained an arrest warrant for Muhammad-But that arrest warrant had nothing to do with domestic violence. Tacoma PD obtained the arrest warrant because Muhammad had shoplifted $27 worth of meat from a Tacoma store. The Tacoma PD took stronger action on behalf of the store owner's loss of $27 worth of meat than on behalf of Muhammad's wife, including when Muhammad abducted and concealed their three children for over a year.

It's also worth noting that in April, 2003, Tacoma Police Chief Brame shot and killed his own wife in front of their two children. The Fallacy of Avoiding the Criminal Justice System. If you are a victim advocate reading this, it may seem silly to belabor the point that effective criminal justice system response is essential to stopping violence against women. But there are many women in the violence against women movement who are so disgusted by the sexism, the racism, and all the other abuses of power in the criminal justice system, that they are desperately looking for ways to circumvent the system altogether. They point not only to the system's mishandling of violence against women, but also to the system's persistent discriminatory violations of defendant's rights as well, especially abuses against defendants of color. And the point is undeniably true.

The criminal justice system, probably more than any other public entity, abuses its powers in a highly discriminatory manner, and, in fact, frequently actively uses its immense powers to enforce existing inequalities and injustices in the social order.

But it would be as foolhardy to divert women's energies away from the criminal justice system as it would be to advise a minority community not to call the fire department because their current fire department responds in such racist ways. What alternate solution could we possibly create that could respond at one in the morning when a woman has a knife to her neck? Who's going to investigate when the perpetrator says she started it and he was acting in self defence? Who's going to invest in the necessary equipment, training, and salaries to respond to millions of these cases? And when the perpetrator promises to stay away from the house, by what authority are we going to stop him when he breaks the promise?

And if, for the sake of argument, we were to create such a system, is there any question that the current law enforcement system would not sit idly by? They would, of course, immediately begin to arrest the members of our alternative system the moment we moved to restrict a perpetrator's freedom. So doesn't that bring us inevitably right back to the confrontation with the current justice system that we wanted to avoid in the first place?

What then? Are we going to make the millions of women who now call the police to secure their safety give up their housing and go into shelters? The kids too? And for how long? And let the violent perpetrators run free? To find more victims? And what about justice? Do we say, oh well, she may have been beaten to a pulp, but as long as she's safe, she doesn't need justice? Do we say that first we must stop all justice system abuses of male defendant's before we demand justice for women? Or do we create an alternate justice system as well as an alternate system of first response?

Or are we going to prevent this violence from happening in the first place? With education? And how many women are we willing to let die before the prevention education sinks in? And since most young boys turn to violence after growing up in violent homes, isn't stopping the current violence against women the first priority of any successful prevention programme? And doesn't that bring us right back to the original dilemma? Who's going to step in and stop the current violence that's ravaging millions of women's lives today? What good does it do to tell kids not to play with matches if there's a wildfire raging all around them and the firemen won't budge?

It doesn't take but a few minutes thought to see that when it comes to intervening in the rampant existing violence against women, the criminal justice system as exclusively authorized and empowered by the state is as pivotal and irreplaceable as the fire department is to fighting fires. But it's worth doing the mental exercise if only to beat down once and for all the temptation to give up on dealing with the criminal justice system. It's true the criminal justice system is permeated with abuses. And it's true these abuses can easily endanger and re-victimize victims, as well as victimize defendants. But this is all the more reason we need to confront this system head on, and to remake the current justice system into a system that responds adequately, equitably, and even handedly.

CRIMINAL JUSTICE SYSTEM STILL SKEWED AGAINST WOMEN

We keep being told that feminism has had its day. Women have pulled down all the barriers to their aspirations, have renegotiated their relationships with men and are now scaling the heights that were formerly beyond their reach. The f-word cannot be mentioned without a boo from the sidelines. Girls are doing better than boys in education; they are filling the universities; they are becoming priests. Childcare is being shared, new men are staying at home while their women bring home the bacon. If we are to believe certain newspapers our preoccupations now are simply to ensure our pay is high and our weight is low. A few more legislative changes and all will be well with the world. In many respects it is true that the battle for formal equality has been won. For the most part, old-fashioned rank prejudice has gone since the laws which underpin formal equality were introduced in 1976. Examples of crude, in-your-face prejudice are much more rare. The case which now has to be made is for substantive equality-treatment as equals, taking account of the real experiences of women and the context of their lives. There has to be greater understanding of the differential effects of policies which, on the face of it, are neutral. It is also important to acknowledge that women are not just one homogenous group. Discrimination now is much more subtle and nuanced and often operates most fiercely at that junction where different forms of prejudice intersect.

When race and class overlap with the social vector of gender, we see in sharp focus the disadvantages still suffered by so many women. Being poor and female makes for a very different experience from that of the middle-class professional. Add the brickbats of racism, and the burden of multiple discrimination can be unbearable. The backlash against feminism takes many forms. Men are the ones we are now to be concerned about. They are being battered; they are having false claims made against them of child abuse because of false memory syndrome; they are being refused access to their children; they are falling prey to shameless hussies who try to get money out of tabloids for their stories.

All of it does happen. Men can be used and abused too. Their pain at false accusation is no less. Their loss of their children is just as raw a wound. But the smoke and mirrors used to enlarge these claims are the products of fear that the old arrangements between the sexes might be reconfigured in ways that may be less to the satisfaction of some men. After September 11, American evangelical preachers even claimed that the events were a punishment for the behaviour of feminists and other deviants.

The creation of pilot programmes, where special domestic violence courts will operate a speedy, multi-agency response to abuse is a major development. The many projects within the police, prosecution and penal service to address women's concerns are to be welcomed.

There is a desperate need for special units to deal with rape cases and the Crown Prosecution Service is putting them in place. A lot has improved within the courts and legal system. We have more women on the bench and practising in the courts. There is no doubt that the government has taken on many women's issues and taken women's experience of victimisation to the heart of criminal law policy.

However, there has been a rolling of women's concerns into a generalised rhetoric about victims. All victims are bundled up together, when policy-makers should be brave enough to say that cases involving abuse of intimacy and the historic discrimination against women deserve special treatment. However, many ministers live in fear of being ridiculed as being in the thrall of "feminists"; they recoil from the reality that the most ill-treated victims within our system are women and children, and that this is still a reflection of some very disconcerting facts about male violence. What is the gender of most children abused over a long period and eventually killed by parents? From Jasmine Beckford to Victoria Climbie, go through the files of the NSPCC and you will find that they are almost invariably girls. Of course, boy children are also killed in outbursts of rage or to wreak revenge but the slow torture of children is most often directed at girls.

What is the gender of the partner most often beaten in a relationship? What is the gender of those most often sexually violated? When we hear a body has been found, someone killed in a park by a stranger, what sex is the victim? When we hear of honour killings who is found dead? The gendered nature of certain crimes and their victims and the gendered nature of so much law, because it is largely created and administered by men, is still insufficiently recognised or discussed.

Instead of debating all these questions boldly, politicians hide behind the much more acceptable cloak of a generalised heading, marked "victims". Often with victims as their alibi, huge inroads are made into civil liberties. The most troubling and pressing questions are never asked. What is it about men that they are so much more disposed to criminality as a sex? Is masculine violence a feature of a patriarchal culture and why is so much of it directed at women? If so what are we doing about it within the education system? What are we doing to divert men from abuse? Discussions about violence never get to the heart of these issues because they are so disconcerting for us, reaching into dark places where primordial power-play simmers.

If we consider just how our law has historically criminalised aggression-how certain types of antisocial behaviour have been targeted, while others have been either formally or practically left unregulated-then it seems that such law is about male patterns of behaviour and about male standards of acceptable conduct. The law on rape and the minimising of domestic violence are the paradigm examples of this perspective; the law is gendered, especially in relation to violence, and the new gender-neutral language of legislation does not fully disguise this fact.

It is why we had to go through such contortions to get the defence of provocation to work for women in domestic killings. Women rarely killed in a sudden blind rage; as the law required, more usually their loss of control arose from despair, like the final surrender of frayed elastic. Only now are the courts shifting to accommodate this different reality. Despite the fact that we know that men and women behave differently and seem to act for different reasons, we still watch governments provide universal theories of crime and formulate general criminal laws that are meant to work in a gender neutral manner. We are just not prepared to face the facts of crime. Sex is the most salient variable when it comes to offending.

Until women and children get justice in the system, certain special processes are justified, including anonymity for complainants in sexual offence cases and anonymity for children at all times. However, at regular intervals, we have to rehearse the arguments about why accused men should not be given the cover of anonymity in some spurious call for equality. Open justice means anonymity should be used sparingly. The coverage of a rape case at times leads to the discovery that the male accused is a multiple offender, because other women are given the confidence to come forward.

Redressing the profound historic failures in relation to women means having to take special steps and the government should be upfront about this. "Gender bias" does include bias against men, and there are cases, particularly those involving child custody, where this certainly applies. The difference is that the majority of men in court are stereotypically viewed as powerful, credible and independent. The men who do invoke negative stereotypical assumptions-homosexual, black, Irish, Arab, vagrant, Gypsy, unemployed-can suffer just as women do.

The law is also disfigured by pernicious stereotypes of women. The punitive pursuit of Maxine Carr, Ian Huntley's former girlfriend, who was acquitted of any involvement in the Soham murders, reveals a continuing belief that women have a special, nurturing responsibility towards children. Women who don't fulfil our expectiations of good womanhood are judged by double standards.

Increasingly, the arena of political change has moved to the courts, where individual cases become a way of raising wider political issues. As Rahila Gupta of Southall Black Sisters says, "It is as though individual pain is the only point of entry into an understanding of a systemic disorder." Law has become a political space for women that is capable of being used as an engine of change. Some of the most high-profile and important cases heard in the courts in recent years have involved women asserting their rights and testing the boundaries of the law: the case of Diane Pretty, who suffered from motor neurone disease, over the right to die; Diane Blood over the right to conceive using the sperm of her dead husband; the women in the military who were dismissed once they became pregnant. And then we have had the terrible appeals involving sudden infant deaths, such as those of Angela Cannings and Sally Clark, where women have been victims of miscarriages of justice, their mothering called into question.

The law is changing but the process is slow and sometimes cosmetic. The old myths and stereotypes of women are still alive, well and being enriched with new cliches; we now have women painted as "ladettes" and binge drinkers to show they were asking for it. What has changed during my professional life is women's expectations. Women are very clear that they will not settle for a system that does not listen to them or take account of their lives; the legal system is becoming wise to that fact. Women have gone through the stage where they did the adjusting; now they expect the institutions to change. The symbol of justice may be a woman but none of us will settle for symbols.

DEFINITIONS OF GENDER JUSTICE

The literature on gender justice as understood in law reflects several different understandings of the concept in the South Asian context. There are at least three distinct perspectives that are discernible in the literature, which in turn affect understandings of law and development, citizenship and entitlement. (Kapur and Cossman 1996) These three approaches are: protectionism, equality and patriarchy. Each is described in the following section, and I offer examples highlighting how the literature on gender justice fits into each category. These categories are flexible, and clearly not all writings on gender justice in the arena of law fit neatly and unequivocally into a single category.

PROTECTIONISM

Perhaps the most problematic articulation of gender justice in law is the one that posits the relationship between women and law as one of protection. Scholars who endorse this approach have reinforced an essentialist understanding of gender difference, assuming that women are naturally weaker than men. This position of helplessness is so much visible among women in general that it has ceased to be any longer of much significance even to themselves.

The protectionist approach accepts the traditional and patriarchal discourses that construct women as weak, biologically inferior, modest and incapable of decision-making. Such so-called feminine characteristics are perceived as natural, immutable and thus, as the appropriate starting place for legal regulation. Writers within this approach often extol the role of women within the family—roles which are assumed to be natural, selfless and sacred. Atray writes: A woman's position as a wife has been given the highest place over all other roles which she is required to play because it is here that she is required to perform the most arduous of duties and the most difficult of responsibilities... As a wife, she is beyond everything else and sits on a pedestal as high and as glorious as the imagination can reach.

Women's roles as mothers are similarly celebrated, and naturalized as an inevitable consequence of the biological differences between women and men. In this literature, the role of law is unproblematically asserted as protecting women. Laws that continue to treat women differently than men are accepted as a necessary part of this protection. This protectionist approach is often reflected in judicial approaches to the question of the relevance of gender difference. Since women are seen as weak and subordinate—and thereby in need of protection—they must be treated differently in law. Any differential treatment of women is deemed to be intended for women's protection and, therefore, for their benefit. Some recent examples of law enacted ostensibly for women's benefit include the imposition of minimum age limits on female workers going abroad for employment by Bangladesh, India and Nepal. In 1998, Bangladesh banned women from going abroad as domestic workers. In 2002, the government of Bangladesh announced it was considering removing the ban. However, the ban appears to have remained in effect. In the same vein, although not entirely prohibiting migration by women, the Nepal Foreign Employment Act, 2042 (1985) prohibits issuance to women of employment licences to work overseas without the consent of the woman's husband or male guardian. Women's ostensibly natural differences are deployed to justify any differential treatment in law, and in effect, operate to preclude any entitlement to equality. This approach is firmly located within patriarchal discourses. It does not problematize the way in which law treats women, nor does it consider women's subordinate status.

Gender justice is located exclusively within a protectionist framework, whereby laws are enacted in order to protect women as they are unable to decide and act for themselves. The effect is to infantilize women and pursue an agenda that merely reinforces this infantilization as it is contingent on male or state protection. While it is concerned with women as subjects of law, and even as subjects of rights, this literature is not within a feminist theoretical tradition. It is an approach that tends to essentialize the difference—that is—to take the existence of gender difference as natural and inevitable. It is an approach that affirms the legal relevance of gender difference and thus risks reinscribing this difference along with the underlying social relations that produced it. The legal recognition of this difference—within a protectionist approach—tends to both reflect and reinforce the common-sense understanding of this discrepancy as natural and inevitable.

This conception of gender justice is reproduced in the discourse of progressive groups, such as women's groups as well as the discourse of the religious and conservative groups as I will illustrate later. It is a conception that is highlighted as it continues to be relevant in the contemporary moment and because it has had a significant effect on how gender justice has come to be understood in law.

Bibliography

R. Thilagaraj, Jianhong Liu and S. Latha: *Crime and Criminal Justice in Asia*, Mittal Publications, 2011.

N.K. Chakrabarti: *Administration of Criminal Justice : The Correctional Services (5 Vols-Set* , Deep, 1997.

Robert Cryer, Elizabeth Wilmshurst, Hakan Friman and Darryl Robinson: *An Introduction to International Criminal Law and Procedure*, Cambridge University Press, 2012.

G Ramachandhra Reddy: *Archaic Criminal Laws, Enforcement and Interpretation*, APH, 2007.

Bellary Uma Devi: *Arrest Detention and Criminal Justice System: A Study in the Context of the Constitution of India*, Oxford University Press, 2012.

Sohoni, Revised by Justice M L Singhal: *Code of Criminal Procedure, Vol. 1 (Sections 1 to 128)*, LexisNexis, 2014.

Sohoni, Revised by Justice M L Singhal: *Code of Criminal Procedure, Vol. 2 (Sections 129 to 189)* , LexisNexis, 2014.

Sohoni Revised by Justice M L Singhal: *Code of Criminal Procedure, Vol. 3 (Sections 190 to 271)*, LexisNexis, 2014.

Sohoni Revised by Justice M L Singhal: *Code of Criminal Procedure, Vol. 4 (Sections 272 to 394)*, LexisNexis, 2014.

Sohoni Revised by Justice M L Singhal: *Code of Criminal Procedure, Vol. 5 (Sections 395 to 484 and Schedules)*, LexisNexis, 2014.

Sukhdev Singh: *Cognizance of Offences by Criminal Courts Practice and Procedure*, Universal Law, 2011.

DV Guruprasad: *Common Man's Guide to Police and Criminal Laws*, Manas Publications, 2011.

Warr: *Companions in Crime: The Social Aspects of Criminal Conduct*, Cambridge Univ Press, 2003.

Sumeet Malik: *Concise Law Dictionary : Pocket: Criminal Manual*, Eastern Book Company, 2015.

R. Thilagaraj, Jianhong Liu and S. Latha: *Crime and Criminal Justice in Asia* : , Mittal Publications, 2011.

R.C. Mishra: *Crime Trends and Criminal Justice* : , Authors Press, 2001.

H.R. Bhardwaj: *Crime, Criminal Justice and Human Rights*, Konark, 2001.

B.R. Sarangi: *Criminal Administration in India*, Sarup, 2012.

Monica Chawla: *Criminal Attempt and Punishment*, Deep and Deep, 2006.

Nina Verma: *Criminal Computer Behaviour*, Global Vision Pub, 2011.

Alf Hiltebeitel: *Criminal Gods and Demon Devotees: Essays on the Guardians of Popular Hinduism*, Manohar, 1989.

Shiv Kumar Dogra: *Criminal Justice Administration in India*, Deep and Deep Pub, 2009.

Scott M Mire and Robert D Hanser: *Criminal Justice and Beyond : An International Perspective*, Serials Pub, 2004.

Scott Mire, Robert D. Hanser and Salih Hakan Can: *Criminal Justice in Action: Essential Readings for the Practitioner* , Serials, 2010.

Haripada Chakraborti: *Criminal Justice in Ancient India*, Sharada, 1996.

Gurkirat Kaur: *Criminal Justice System*, Shree, 2006.

G.S. Bajpai: *Criminal Justice System Reconsidered : Victim and Witness Perspectives*, Serials Publications, 2012.

K D Gaur: *Criminal Law : Cases and Materials*, LexisNexis, 2015.

K.D. Gaur: *Criminal Law and Criminology*, Deep and Deep, 2002.

John N. Ferdico: *Criminal Law and Justice Dictionary*, Taxmann, 2000.

Anwarullah: *Criminal Law Of Islam*, Adam Publishers, 2010.

Subhash Chandra Singh: *Criminal Laws and Social Justice*, Serials Publications , 2012.

Lakshmanan Dr. Justice A.R.:*Criminal Major Acts (with Exhaustive Case Law)*, Universal Law Pub, 2012.

K.N. Chandrasekharan Pillai: *Criminal Procedure : R.V. Kelkar's Criminal Procedure*, Eastern Book Company, 2014.

R Mishra: *Criminal Psychology* , Sumit Enterprises, 2006.

Ray Bull, Claire Cooke, Ruth Hatcher and Jessica Woo: *Criminal Psychology*, Viva Books, 2010.

Index

I

J

L

M

O

P

Q

R

T

U

V

Y